TRAVELLING COMMUNIQUÉ

Studying practises of anticolonial thinking through the Presidential photo archive of Josip Broz Tito, at the Museum of Yugoslav History, Belgrade

Edited by the Travelling Communiqué project group (Kodwo Eshun, Armin Linke, Doreen Mende and Milica Tomić) with Sarah Poppel and Vanessa Vasić-Janeković

AF623019

TABLE OF CONTENTS

INTRODUCTION

What does it mean to learn about anticolonial thinking through a presidential photo archive? How do we examine the "question concerning poetics at the heart of insovereignty" (Fred Moten, p. 313) within an archive built with and out of statecraft? A notion of insovereignty stalks any state archive—any institution, any image, for that matter—it forms as the most internal point of any congregation of power or authority.

By inviting artists in 2010 to work with the presidential photo archive of Josip Broz Tito,[1] Katarina Živanović, then Director of the Museum of Yugoslav History (MYH) in Belgrade, had unfolded this point of insovereignty into a collaborative space[2] of research and exhibiting within which the Travelling Communiqué (TC) group formed itself. The TC group decided to focus on the records of Non-Aligned Movement's (NAM) trajectories of anticolonialism. By reorienting the gaze from the East-West axis of Cold War politics to a "South-North" discourse (Olga Manojlović Pintar, p. 38), the NAM demanded an end to colonialism through "peaceful economic and social development" (*Declaration*, p. 86).

The coherence and consistency of this epistemic shift are most clearly articulated in the NAM's "basic concept": "to include and organize the excluded" (Milica Tomić, p. 39). The "problematic of historical rhyming" (Moten, p. 313) is thus contained in a notion of universality implied by Françoise Vergès's account

1. Covering the period from 1948 to Tito's death in 1980.
2. Open also to other artists and researchers...

of our temporality as "the new era of land grabs, of vast spoliation of resources, of new forms of dispossession ... when the Wretched of the Earth are now found in the North, South, East and West" (p. 35). "Can we today even think politics of universalism" (Tomić, p. 39) and approach the task of "reclaiming [an active] neutrality as a politics of de-colonization?" How do we find support for "agonistic possibilities of production in contexts of re-colonization by multinational corporations" (Jelena Vesić and Rachel O'Reilly, p. 297)?

Such demands make "us all" into "students of Non-Alignment," for the "normalised discontinuities between post-, ex-, and former communisms, capitalisms, fascisms and nationalisms create historical voids and political silences" (Kodwo Eshun, Doreen Mende, p. 58). Glossed into a hidden sequence of Cold War modernity, the NAM is at once a "voided history" and a constellation thereof: an exercise in sovereignty of scale. At the 1961 Belgrade Conference[3] delegates "denounced the neo-colonial regimes" but simultaneously "overlooked the imperialist domination practiced" by Non-Aligned "member states over neighboring peoples and territories" (Eshun, Mende, p. 68).

To work with this Yugoslavian archive of statecraft as a student of the NAM therefore means to open oneself to tensions between state sovereignty as "the false universality" laced with all the pitfalls of post-colonial involutions described by Frantz Fanon,[4]

3. The first conference of the Non-Aligned Movement.
4. "Pitfalls of National Consciousness," in Fanon, Frantz, *Wretched of the Earth*, (London: Penguin, 2001) p. 119.

and the "actual universality" nestled in the "insovereign sociality of … flesh"[5] as "something more than a construction of sovereign power" (Moten, p. 318). It means exposure to psychic residues of another "hidden sequence," the "best that the Yugoslav Communists had produced," the antifascist, anticolonial WWII Partisan movement, which "never had a state as its final aim or its limit, but rather the absolute change, the creation of a new society" (Branimir Stojanović, p. 47). The "obligations of state creations" (*Ibid.*), evident in Yugoslav canons of image making (Radovan Cukić, p. 180, and Ivan Manojlović, p. 171), had, however, imparted a deep "internal split" within the presidential figure of Tito: into the leader of a movement and into the statesman, revealing the trauma of "radical desubjectivation" (Stojanović, p. 133) as underlying any grasp on universalism.

The movement of the epistemic shift continues therein, forcing a different framework of "interrogation" of the "assumptions, implications and heuristics of the archive … necessary for decoding its limits, structures of exclusion and the totality of temporal experience" (Elizabeth Giorgis, p. 105). Archives resist full understanding, full socio-economic contextualisation—their (and our) "right to not be understood"[6] emerges most fully through "images on which many differences are staged" (Heike Behrend, p. 196)—they teach us that tradition is not inflexible:

5. In parallel with Catherine Malabou's demand for "a new materialism asserting the coincidence of the symbolic and the biological." See http://criticalinquiry.uchicago.edu/one_life_only/. Accessed October 17, 2015.
6. See the Colophon, p. 323.

its continuous reinvention renders looking at archive images "dangerous" (Armin Linke, p. 207). The heterogeneity of the NAM, as a gathering of "very differently defined political subjects" (Manojlović Pintar, p. 46) has compelled a democratic manoeuvre of extending conversations within world politics.

By opening to artists, the MYH has, "especially in the frame of the *Travelling Communiqué* exhibition/ project"[7] assumed a "strange, yet liberating position" in giving up its authority as the "sole interpreter ... of the archive," (Manojlović, p. 159) and sharing its "sovereignty" with an expanded network of contributors and students, "practitioners from the fields of art, cinema, architecture, typography, theory and education" (Eshun, Mende, p. 53). Their joint research processes were translated into the space of exhibiting: projects, proposals and films appeared as fragile vocabularies of learning, of outlining group constellations and means of articulation still to arrive.

This book hopes to extend that collaborative pull by inviting readers to become students of Non-Alignment, especially within the "contemporary ... neoliberal (neocolonial) administration of the aesthetic" (Vesić, O'Reilly, p. 305). The pages that follow attempt to unfold contemporary trajectories for the study of the "question concerning poetics at the heart" of anticolonial thought.

Sarah POPPEL and
Vanessa VASIĆ-JANEKOVIĆ

7. From June to August 2014, at the Museum of Yugoslav History, Belgrade.

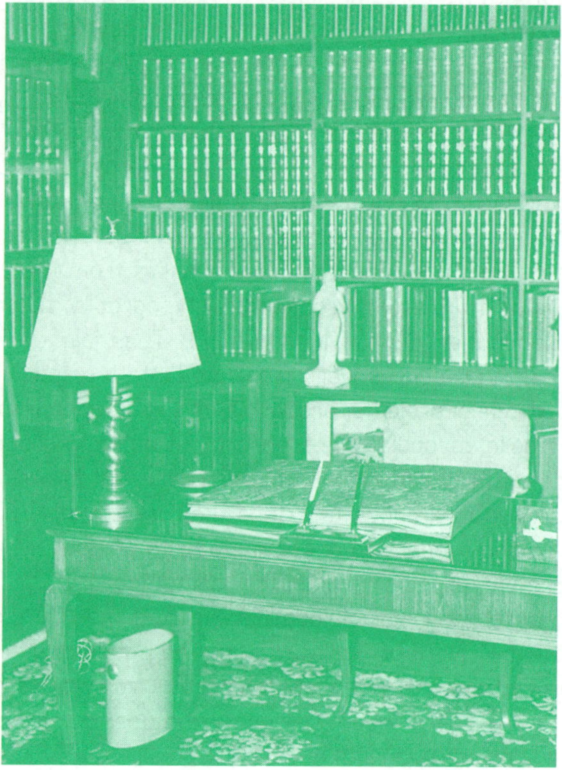

Photograph from the documentation of the Museum of Yugoslav History, depicting the original Fototeka, a room in the presidential residence of Josip Broz Tito. The photograph was taken after Tito's death.

Armin Linke (AL) and Fabian Bechtle (FB)

NOTES TOWARDS A PHOTO ESSAY (PART 1)

Armin Linke (AL) and Fabian Bechtle (FB) selected a number of images from the MYH archive with the attempt to construct a network of fragmented readings by Heike Behrend (HB), Radovan Cukić (RC), Sarah Poppel (SP), Dubravka Sekulić (DS), Philip Ursprung (PU), and Vanessa Vasić-Janeković (VVJ).

Each image is accompanied by its archival metadata: the archival number, the caption and the indexing information that enables cross-referenced searches on the MYH online database (http://www.foto.mij.rs/site/galleries). This data sets up the basic contextual frame.

Attempts to explore relations between these images, their broader contexts or historical knowledge they may point to, have opened gaps that signify limitations in understanding. Perhaps these gaps may be bridged by extended conversations, by inviting additional readers to engage in the process.

This approach reflects an idea of working with archives informed not solely by visual contents. Rather, it relies on a dialogue between an image and an individual, producing instant readings. Its nature can therefore only be speculative.

1948_001_001

The Brdo Castle near Kranj. State: Yugoslavia (Slovenia); Location: Brdo; Keywords: Exterior, Brdo Castle; Date: July 4, 1948; Comment: The first photograph, it all began from there...

FB & AL — This photo has the look of a pinhole photograph: reminiscent of beginning or end of a movie. The lens opens only slightly—this has often been used as a crossfade effect. Conceptually and aesthetically, this photo opens the body of the archive.

RC — It would appear that the archive began with Tito's activities in Slovenia and his stay in the Brdo Castle near Kranj.

1948_001_001

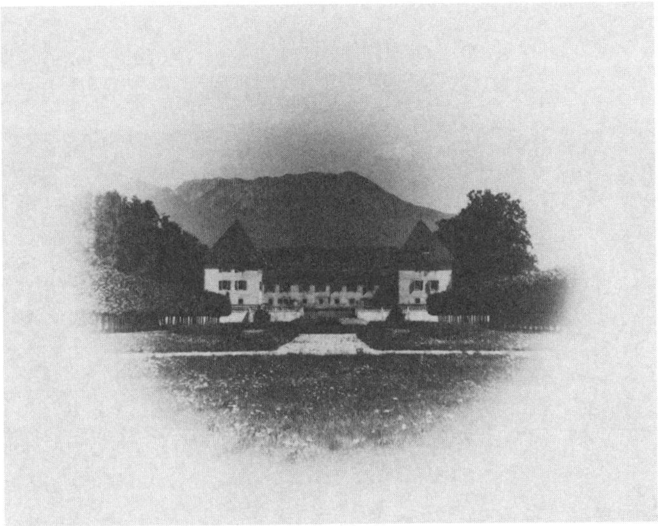

1957_074_203

1957_074_203

Bound sets of photographs given to President Tito. State: Yugoslavia; Location: Belgrade; Keywords: Receiving gifts, Youth Day, Republic; Date: May 26, 1957

RC — These sets probably contain a selection of images of the previous year, given to President Tito by the head of the Press Service. The sets were kept in a room called Fototeka, next to the library in Tito's residence.

1960_130_0213

With Hartini Soekarno in Croatia, in the Banski dvori presidential residence, before her departure for Vienna. State: Yugoslavia (Croatia); Location: Zagreb; Personalities: Hartini Soekarno, Marija Šoljan-Bakarić, R.A. Asmaun; Keywords: Automobile, Farewell, Gift-giving, First Lady, Banski dvori; Bilateral Relations: Indonesia; Date: April 9, 1960

FB — The four or five employees working in the Photo Service team were a "closed system," covering the entire production process: photographing, developing, selecting, printing and preparing albums for the diplomatic guest. Photographs of visits were produced immediately, almost in real time, and compiled into boxes to become a diplomatic tool of exchange. Each photograph could become part of different selections. Photographers must have been aware of the different kinds of outputs and occasions these images would enter.

1960_130_0213

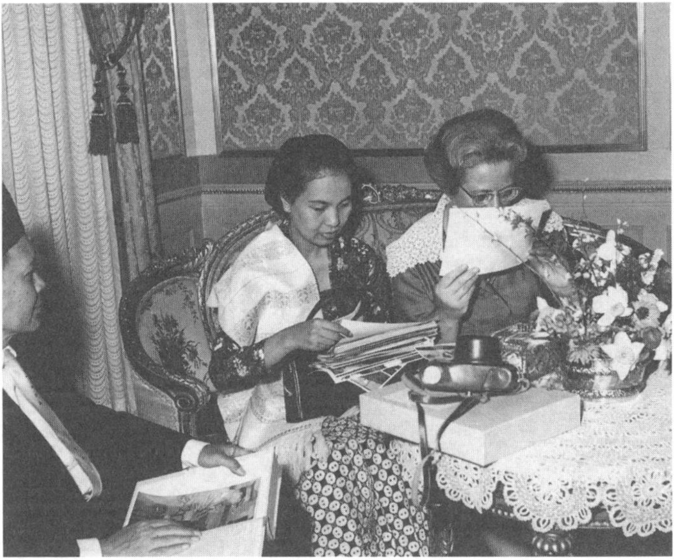

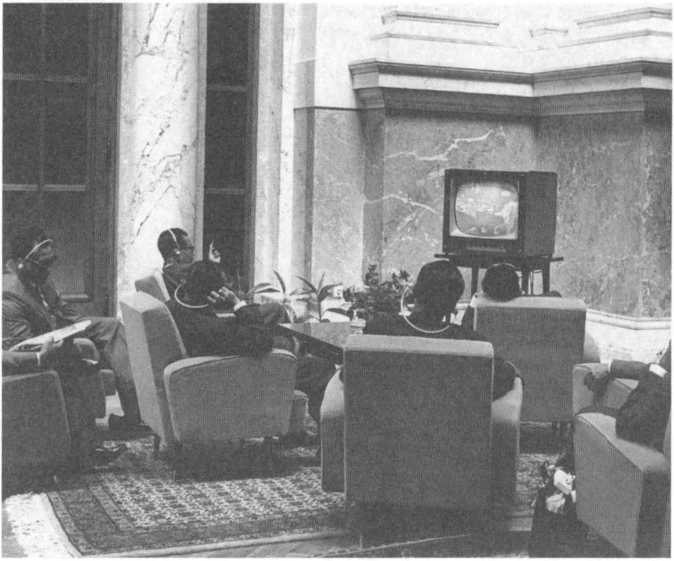

1961_177_0125

Belgrade Conference: during the speech by Louis Lansana Beavogui, the Minister of External Affairs of Guinea. State: Yugoslavia (Serbia); Location: Belgrade; Personalities: Louis Lansana Beavogui; Keywords: Non-Aligned Movement, Session, Minister of External Affairs, Conference, People's Parliament, Speech; Bilateral Relations: Guinea; Date: September 4, 1961

FB — The diplomatic space of the conference was enlarged through mediatic transmissions, extending access to the proceedings. However, photography was only one of the mediums that captured the narrative script of the conference.

1971_473_064

The "Sloboda 71" manoeuvres: demonstrating the readiness of military forces. State: Yugoslavia (Croatia); Location: Karlovac; Personalities: Viktor Bubanj; Keywords: Yugoslav People's Army, Manoeuvres; Date: October 4, 1971

FB & AL — Media and transmission technology was inscribed into the systems of Cold War and used as a tactical tool.

This is how the US based RAND corporation, which specializes in strategic system analysis, reported on the manoeuvres:

"The [...] manoeuvres [...] simulated a thrust from the northeast by a powerful, highly mobile enemy into the hilly region southwest of Zagreb. [...] The political authorities operated in simulated wartime conditions, directing local resistance from clandestine locations. The mass media also simulated wartime operations."

RAND, 1971.

1971_473_064

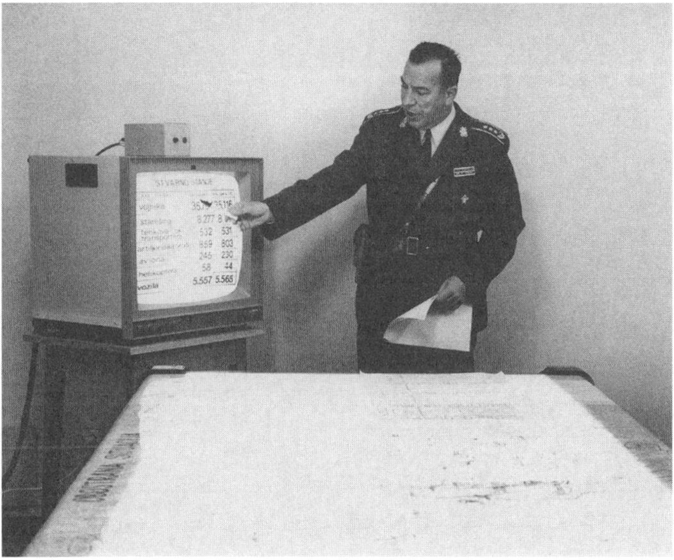

1971_465_096

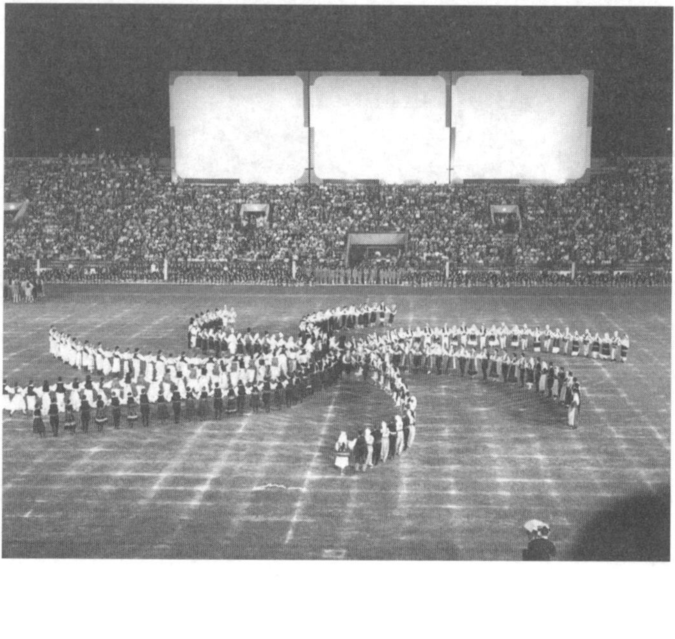

1971_465_096

Celebration of the Youth Day 1971, at the Yugoslav People's Army stadium: a mass games performance. State: Yugoslavia (Serbia); Location: Belgrade; Keywords: Mass games, Youth Day, Stadium, League of Youth of Yugoslavia; Bilateral Relations: Spain; Date: May 25, 1971

Welcome in Kiev, army parade, speech to the citizens of Kiev in front of the station, passing through the city on the way to the residence. Destination: USSR (Ukraine); Place: Kiev; Keywords: Welcome, Automobile, Parade, Train, Panorama, Gathering, Republic authorities, Train station; Bilateral Relations: USSR; Date: June 21, 1956

1956_62_007

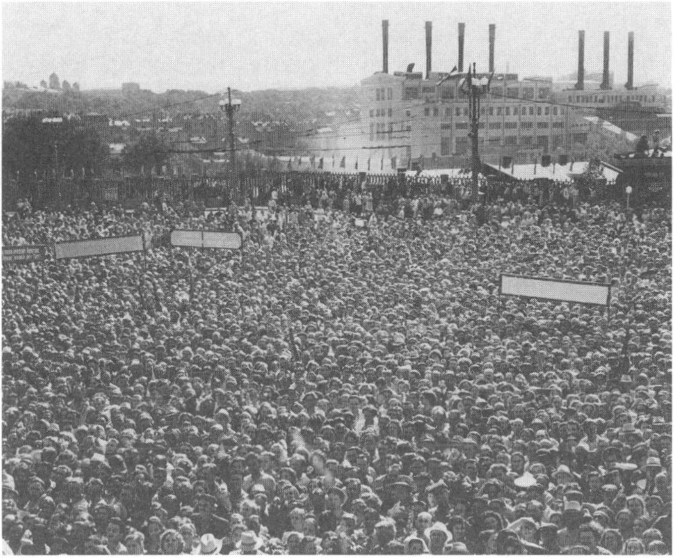

Armin Linke (AL) and Fabian Bechtle (FB)

NOTES TOWARDS A PHOTO ESSAY

PART 2 continues on page 89...

Françoise Vergès

I
MARTINSKA/MARTINIQUE. AIMÉ CÉSAIRE *RETURN TO MY NATIVE LAND*

In the summer of 1935, a young black man from Martinique, Aimé Césaire, traveled to Yugoslavia at the invitation of his dear and close friend Petar Guberina. It was his first travel outside France since his arrival in Paris in 1931, to study at the prestigious Lycée Saint-Louis. Césaire, then only twenty-two, found there the source of inspiration for the first opus, *Return to My Native Land*, of his oeuvre as a great anticolonial poet, writer, and political leader.

It was during that summer that he started to write his magnificent poem *Return to My Native Land*. It was in the city of Šibenik that this descendant of African slaves, this colonized of the French colonial empire, found his inspiration.

Sitting on his first day in Šibenik in front of a window facing the sea, he reflected, writing in a student notebook, on his native island, slavery, the fact of being Black, colonialism and anti-Black racism.

However, the genesis and the itinerary of the writing of *Return to My Native Land*—from Yugoslavia to Martinique, Martinique to France—has for a long time been barely acknowledged and never fully analyzed. Césaire's friendship with Guberina is often told in passing. Much more is made of his friendship with the Senegalese poet and political leader Léopold Sedar Senghor, even though Césaire and Guberina remained in contact until Césaire's death. Many critics look at *Return to My Native land* in relation to the binary space France/Martinique: distance from Martinique had engendered nostalgia and fostered a notion of authenticity. But the ways in which Césaire retold the starting point of his writing is not so much a tale of nostalgia and authenticity, but rather of the creative tension triggered by randomness, by the unexpected. His memories of the summer of 1935 are joyous, a respite from Paris where he had discovered freedom but not the capacity to be at ease with himself, to drop the guarded posture of a young black colonized man thrown into the capital of the empire.

> At the end of daybreak burgeoning
> with frail coves,
> the hungry Antilles, the Antilles pitted
> with smallpox,
> the Antilles dynamited by alcohol,
> stranded in the mud of this bay,
> in the dust of this town sinisterly stranded.

Friendship and Creativity

Césaire's meeting with Petar Guberina was pure serendipity. At the beginning of the summer of 1935, Césaire went to the Comédie Française. After the show, with no money in his pocket, he chose to walk home. Arriving at Porte d'Orléans, quite a walk from the Place du Palais Royal where the Comédie Française stands, he met some young men he knew. Among them, he noticed a "very good-looking guy, almost black, a guy who looked black, with very dark hair." His name was Petar Guberina and he was from

Yugoslavia. It was friendship "at first sight," Césaire remembered later. Petar became Pierrot, the affectionate form of Pierre (Petar) in French. They had long conversations during which they shared the history of their respective countries. Though neither Césaire nor Guberina recounted their conversations in detail, it is logical to presume that Césaire talked about slavery and colonialism and that the deep friendship that resulted was partly built on a shared understanding of oppression and emancipation.

When the summer vacation arrived, Guberina went back to his hometown, Šibenik, from which he wrote to Césaire telling him to join him right away. He knew Césaire was lonely in Paris, with no friends and no money. Traveling by train to Šibenik, Césaire was carried away by the beauty of the Dalmatian coast, which reminded him of a place in Martinique, Carbet. Taken to his room was on the first floor of the Guberina family home, he opened the window and asked Petar:

"What a magnificent scenery! Pierrot, what is the name of the small island that we see?"

"Martinska," Guberina answered.

"Martiniska!" Césaire cried.

"Translated into French, it means the island of Saint-Martin, but it is Martinique!" He said later

"I went to Yugoslavia. What did I find? Martinique, where I had not been in five years. I had no money to go to Martinique, but I had some to arrive in Martiniska! That night, I sat in front of the window and started to write *Return to My Native Land*." It seems though that there is not even an island with that name around Šibenik, but a bay on a peninsula, (http://www.worldcam.pl/mapa/8645/fr), which underlines the power of the imagination. Césaire went to Yugoslavia and found Martinique. That was enough.

Césaire felt safe in Guberina's home. In the fall of 1936 Césaire went back to Martinique and back to Paris where he finished his long poem. *Return to My Native Land* was first published in 1939 in the communist journal *Volontés*.

Serendipity, Detour and Anticolonialism

If meeting Petar Guberina was an act of serendipity, writing his opus in Šibenik was another act of serendipity. The term was coined in 1754 by Horace Walpole, after hearing the Persian story of *The Three Princes of Serendip* (from Persian Sarandip—or Sri Lanka—from Arabic Sarandib) which told the story of three princes sent by their father to a prolonged journey so that they can acquire empirical knowledge. The princes proved their sagacity along their journey. Walpole transformed this sagacity into the capacity for discovering, inventing, creating or imagining something new without having looked for it. It is the capacity to seize the fleeting moment of the unexpected. Thus, discovering is also about programming chance, happenstance, and randomness. In other words, you do not reach a goal by plotting a course for it. You have to set out in good faith for elsewhere and lose your bearings by happenstance. Reality is not law-governed.

Césaire went to Yugoslavia without a plan, except to spend the summer with a close friend and escape his solitude in Paris. He "found" Martinique, but without expecting to, by the sheer power of his memory triggered by the scenery of the Dalmatian coast, by the light and smell of summer. Writing was made possible after five years in Paris, far from his native land, thanks to the safety of friendship and the warm welcome to a young black man by a Yugoslav family. Even the terror of an old peasant woman surprised by the sudden appearance of a young black man on a path did not strike Césaire as being hostile, unlike the racist remarks directed at him in Paris. He understood that she could have been dumbfounded by his apparition and that her terror was caused not by hostility but by sheer surprise.

It is also possible that starting to write *Return to My Native Land* in Šibenik was also the result of what Edouard Glissant has called the detour. Shifting focus away from "origins" (or the loss thereof), Glissant points to the painful but necessary reconstruction of memory. Césaire's travel in the summer of 1935 took him to a country whose language, culture, and history he did not know, but which might have allowed him to lift the weight imposed by the confrontational relation with France. Away from the colonial power, away from Martinique, the native land could be remembered. With no French present, either in front of him or as a ghostly warden, Césaire could write about Martinique's ugly side, about its assimilated petty bourgeoisie for which he would later declare his full contempt, about the destructive aspect of slavery. He could write about his love for the "Nègres," for his people. He could recall the blood and the deaths, "So much blood in my memory! In my memory are lagoons

/ They are covered with death's-heads / They are not covered with water lilies/ In my memory are lagoons." And he could chant a possible future, of solidarity among the oppressed.

> As there are hyena-men and panther-men,
> I would be a jew-man
> a Kaffir-man
> a Hindu-man-from-Calcutta
> a Harlem-man-who-doesn't-vote
> the famine-man, the insult-man,
> the torture man you can grab anytime,
> beat up, kill—
> no joke, kill—without having to account
> to anyone,
> without having to make excuses to anyone
> a jew-man
> a pogrom-man
> a puppy
> a beggar ....

Return to My Native Land speaks for transnational link. The summer scenery and smell of a city in Yugoslavia, the history and scenery of a French colony where Césaire's ancestors had been enslaved... It brings forth a multifarious and diverse vision of colonial creativity that impels us to revise conceptual systems based on the notions of roots, fixity and linearity.

Return to My Native Land was conceived in a "periphery" of Europe, Yugoslavia, about a "periphery" of the French colonial empire. It is a text palimpsest. Anticolonial texts are palimpsests, they show successive episodes of deposition, layers of activity, that remain superimposed one upon the other without loss of evidence.

Return to My Native Land is a cry against slavery "We the vomit of slave ships / We the venery of the Calabars," against colonialism, its destructive impulse, and about the transnational routes of solidarity.

During the summer of 1935, Peter Guberina offered a refuge to his black friend. A gesture of friendship that led to the writing of one of the greatest texts against colonialism. Césaire experienced a moment of freedom from the French gaze, from the injunction of becoming what he did not want to become, a man who had rejected his past. James Baldwin wrote "One cannot claim the birthright without accepting the inheritance". Césaire's birthright was vast, connecting him to African women and men who had been enslaved, to all the oppressed peoples, to an old peasant woman near Šibenik, and to his friend, Petar, from Yugoslavia.

II
EMBEDDED MEMORIES
POSTCOLONIAL HISTORY IS GLOBAL HISTORY

I grew up in a communist, anticolonialist, and feminist family in Reunion Island, a French colony in the Indian Ocean, which became a French department in 1946. My father was among the founders of the Communist Party of Reunion Island in 1959. My paternal grandfather, who had lived for 32 years in Asia where he worked as an engineer, a doctor and a diplomat, was the founder of Reunion Communist Federation and of the Workers' Federation. My mother, who was French, was an active feminist and journalist in the communist newspaper.

Early on, I observed the legacies of colonial slavery and anti-Black racism, the power of repressive State policies to to instill fear and consent to one's own dependency, the price one pays if one resists, the conditions asked for being protected as a woman or a poor person (in other words, living by the rules enacted by those who declare to be your protectors), and quite early, I lost the illusion that the oppressed share a spontaneous solidarity. I experienced what [Antonio] Gramsci called the fragmentation of the subalterns. I had to understand why people did not fight back, and I could not explain everything with false consciousness or alienation.

As a child, I witnessed the searches by the police at six in the morning, when sleep is still there. We were taught to be on guard, we had been warned that they could plant something to accuse my parents of subversion against the State. My father had been accused of "offense to national security." I witnessed people being beaten, the determination of the post-colonial French power to crush any resistance to a program of assimilation to Frenchness.

There was only one connection that made sense, the connection to France, the connection with the "country of origins" of one's ancestors was accepted as long as it was within the frame of religion or "culture."

The Cold War was present in the local repressive policies against communists, the injunction to express loudly one's loyalty to France and the "free world," the association of anyone fighting against totalitarian and imperialist regimes (Apartheid, Mozambique, Angola, Vietnam…) with "Moscow," the censorship, the rivalry between Moscow and Washington to install military bases in the Indian Ocean, to protect the routes of oil, to contain people's aspirations. Tito was a familiar name at home, along with Nehru, Dos Santos, Che Guevara…

I was taught another cartography, the cartography of struggles, of time and space that were not those of the North/South axis, of European imperialisms, but of South/South exchanges, of the encounters of the "wretched of the earth" fighting for more justice.

Alternative cartographies of connections, exchanges and encounters that question the borders of the Nation-State and suggest routes and trajectories of people, ideas, music, ideals.

III
CONFLICTING LEGACIES OF THE NON-ALIGNED MOVEMENT

The first Conference of Non-Aligned Heads of State, at which twenty-five countries were represented, was convened in Belgrade, in September 1961, largely through the initiative of Yugoslav President Tito. He had expressed concern that an accelerating arms race might result in a war between the Soviet Union and the U.S. In May, negotiations had started between the French government and the Algerian nationalists who had been supported by many countries that would be present at the September meeting, among them Yugoslavia.

The conference was preceded by the conference held in Bandung on April 18–24, 1955, which gathered twenty-nine Heads of States belonging to the first post-colonial generation of leaders. The Non-Aligned Movement sought to build a multipolar world based on respect, equity and justice.

The writer Richard Wright recalled the headline on Bandung from the newspaper he had been sifting through in Paris in 1955: "Twenty-nine free and independent nations of Asia and Africa are meeting in Bandung, Indonesia, to discuss 'racialism and colonialism'." He decided to go. In his report, *The Color Curtain* (1956), he wrote: "The despised, the insulted, the hurt, the dispossessed—in short, the underdogs of the human race were meeting. Here were class and racial and religious consciousness on a global scale. Who had thought of organizing such a meeting? And what had these nations in common? Nothing, it seemed to me, but what their past relationship to the Western world had made them feel. This meeting of the rejected was in itself a kind of judgment upon that Western world! .... They were getting a new sense of themselves, getting used to new roles and new identities. Imperialism was dead here, and as long as they could maintain their unity, organize and conduct international conferences, there would be no return of imperialism."

The most important objectives of the 1961 meeting of the Non-Aligned Countries in Belgrade included ending of imperialism and colonialism, promotion of international peace and security and disarmament, creation of a New International Economic Order, ending racism and racial discrimination, and ending information imperialism. In the new era of land grabs, of vast spoliation of resources, of new forms of dispossession, forms of bondage, global traffic in domestic labor, of denial of rights, when the Wretched of the Earth are now found in the North, South, East and West, these ideals still resonate. But the new politics of colonization also require new politics of decolonization.

The model of the eighteenth/nineteenth-century European colonization has become hegemonic. It is still there in new forms, in new configurations but with the same Promethean ideology of mastering all living things, of indexing the entire world, animals, plants, humans... ; the belief in infinite progress, and the refusal to consider the world as a living entity.

IV
DECOLONIZING EUROPE

Among the legacies of imperialism is the mutilated and mutilating cartography of Europe. Mutilated because it excludes from its space entire groups and territories that have contributed to its making. Mutilating because it ignores the memories and histories of its "Others."

What kind of cartography appears when we try to establish connectivity, intersections between events? Certainly not a linear story, but the history of State experimentation with targeting groups (Rroms, Muslims...) for discrimination and racialization.

Let us think about the daily politics of humiliation these groups experience and what they produce: hatred, anger, loss of self-esteem, frustration. The myriad ways in which a woman, a man is humiliated daily. Broken lives, broken bones, broken hearts, women's and men's capacities totally negated, their opinions matter not.

Let us think about the benefits of hate: "I imagine one of the reasons people cling to their hates so stubbornly is because they sense, once hate is gone, they will be forced to deal with pain," James Baldwin wrote. He said, "We must not allow their fear to control us, and, indeed, we must not allow it to control them. Rather, we should attempt to release them from their panic and their unadmitted sorrow."[1] If we look at current politics of fear ravaging Europe today—fear of immigrants, of Islam, of "Roma," of LGBT—what could we do to release Europeans from their panic and *unadmitted sorrow?* The fear of imagined suffering controlling one's life echoes what [Sigmund] Freud said about pain: "The process of bringing this unconscious material to light is associated with pain, and because of this pain the patient again and again rejects it." In other words, xenophobic attitudes represent an unconscious tradeoff in exchange for the sufferer being spared other, experientially worse, displeasures.

To create new politics of decolonization, a struggle against power and its formidable machine of consent is necessary.

1. *The Cross of Redemption* (New York: Vintage, 2011), p. 272.

"WHITE SCREEN, BLACK LETTERS AND THE SOUND" SUBSEQUENTLY ON NON-ALIGNED MOVEMENT (2013, video, 23:30 min, acousmatic voice, white screen, text and sound)

Milica Tomić: The Non-Aligned Movement (NAM) is today analyzed primarily within the context of the Cold War divide into blocs. Some interpretations perceive the NAM as having legitimized, even stabilized this bipolar condition. Do you see the NAM as merely reactive, or could it be seen as urging affirmation of the revolutionary paradigm?

Olga Manojlović Pintar: In the context of the world after 1945, which today we perceive primarily as a bipolar world, that of the East and of the West, every political action could be perceived as legitimizing the divide. Anticolonial movements, all the newly established independent states who became members of the United Nations, could be perceived as part of the way of keeping frozen the state of world politics created after 1945. This very simplified analysis does not take into consideration the real meaning of the NAM, which could perhaps be perceived as a sort of a Foucauldian heterotopia, for that other world did actually exist in that period, not as a mere reflection of the two blocs, of two political powers, but rather as the introduction of a real, active element in world politics, changing the dichotomies established between the East and the West, between socialism and capitalism.

Foucault considered heterotopias to be "places outside of all places ... absolutely different from all the sites they reflect or speak about." The role of the heterotopic site is "to create a space that is other, another real space, as perfect, as meticulous, as well arranged as ours is messy, ill constructed, and jumbled." His spatial analysis introduces the possibility of re-thinking political and social concepts. The NAM is that radically different concept. From one point of view, it represented, but also, crucially, "contested and inverted" dominant global political paradigms. Not only did it bring into consideration the South-North relationship, but also the problem of the so-called "newcomers," "new nations," as the new states were pejoratively perceived. The totalizing concept that now prevails in considerations and elaborations of the period after 1945 and until, let's say the fall of the Berlin Wall in 1989, is misleading without an analysis of the NAM. In my opinion, that first meeting of Josip Broz Tito, Jawaharlal Nehru, and Gamal Abdel Nasser at Brioni in 1956, then the First Conference in Belgrade in 1961, and finally the Havana Conference in 1979, present a paradigmatic example of the attempt to introduce the idea of a new world politics. The first global politics was, in fact, established in that period.

MT: Peace as an urgent demand was inherent to the idea of the NAM. What did the concept of "peace" mean at the time of the Cold War and nuclear threat? How do we ponder the notion of "peace" today, beyond the dominant political and ideological concepts?

OMP: The idea of peace changed radically after August 1945, with the introduction of the atomic bomb. The nuclear threat transformed the fundamental categories of war and peace, and inevitably also the idea of active struggle for peace. The existence of the NAM epitomizes that change: the idea that the heterotopia of the NAM could be somehow the world's answer to nuclear threat. Today, the idea of peace is a neo-colonial concept of the Western world, primarily concerning the Western citizen living in Europe and North America, who has been, over the period of deconstruction of the idea of class-consciousness, completely identified with the idea of the human as an individual. The idea of peace is thus individualized.

> MT: If the basic concept of the NAM was to include and organize the excluded, can we today even think politics of universalism, when the dominant policy is that of exclusion, dictated by the globalization that also promotes a new form of unifying legitimized by the state of permanent war? Can we even talk about peace today, when the concept of peace has been irreversibly transformed?

Branimir Stojanović: Interestingly, the theme of war has been rather absent from dominant theoretical and philosophical thinking of the past forty to fifty years. Even less thematized has been the topic of peace; it no longer exists as a category. At the peak of the Cold War in the fifties and sixties, when it threatened destruction, it was very clear what peace meant: nuclear disarmament as the requirement established by the Non-Aligned. Put simply, the great powers would remove the threat of world destruction through a pact about not using nuclear weapons. Today, however, at the time of permanent war, as you said, the open question is: where did peace disappear?

Clausewitz's classical definition of war as a continuation of politics by other means is no longer current, for the permanent war is, in fact, waged in the name of the policy of reconciliation, which is not a politics of peace, but of freezing conflicts at a certain level. Warring parties are left in a situation of mutual monitoring, and are monitored by an administration establishing the ideology of reconciliation. The world does not know peace any longer, because peace, in the classical sense, meant the end of war or was a political condition for war. War had an internal structure and a goal: the realization of political aims was the moment of establishing peace. Today, in the epoch without politics, the category of peace is lost.

OMP: The difference between "appeasement" (reconciliation) and "peace" is very significant. The category of "peace" has become a soft currency in the policies of the Cold War in order to keep the frontiers manifest; as much as "solidarity with people in struggle" has become a bureaucratic act through its institutionalization by the state structures by the NAM countries.

MT: Partisans, the participants of the People's Liberation Struggle (PLS) in Yugoslavia during the Second World War, defined their struggle as war against war, a war for peace. Is there a continuity in this understanding of the war-peace relationship between the PLS and the NAM?

BS: The PLS is a hidden sequence of European political history of the twentieth century; a very limited political sequence tied to the territory of today's Bosnia and Herzegovina, very localized and temporally clearly defined: from December 22, 1941 to the spring of 1943. It is hidden also within the history of Yugoslavia and Yugoslav Socialism. The PLS is a political sequence of a new form of war in Europe of that epoch: a revolutionary war as anti-imperial and anticolonial, invented through the politics of the PLS, the struggle of Yugoslav Partisans on European soil.

Whilst all the other participants in the struggle against German National Socialism were states, like the Soviet Union, the United Kingdom, and the U.S., in Yugoslavia the Partisans waged a political project of including those excluded from dominant ideologies: the peasants as a leftover of non-participation in the dominant modernist ideologies of the epoch. The PLS is a significant sequence [in the context of the NAM] because Tito and Yugoslav political leadership saw similarities between anti-colonial struggles [beginning in the fifties] in the former colonies all over the world and the model of revolutionary war waged by the Partisans from 1941 to 1943. Yugoslavia actively and openly supported those movements with significant economic, military and cultural aid. Following its participation in the war in Algeria, one of the key anti-colonial wars of the time, Yugoslavia continued to very overtly participate in various liberation movements of the sixties. This new revolutionary sequence continued into the early seventies, with the model of revolutionary war as that of anti-colonial liberation movements in countries that had for centuries been colonially enslaved by Europe.

MT: Why do you consider the first NAM conference in Belgrade, in 1961, an early example of globalization?

BS: Because the very inclusion of all into the *world* is the first act of globalization. Behind this act is the idea that we are all in one world and no one is excluded from it any longer. The early political gesture of the Non-Aligned was to include all those whom the dominant West had been excluding from the world history for 1,500 years. All the "non-historical peoples" have become part of the world through this political articulation by the Non-Aligned.

MT: Who is today, in the era of globalization and permanent war, the addressee of the communiqué written during the first day of the NAM Conference in Belgrade in 1961? You proposed this question as the general concept of the "Travelling Communiqué": Who is the addressee of the communiqué today? How do you understand, in this light, the idea of European citizen and the kind of ideology it produces, in which form is it present and how does it define and draw Europe today?

BS: There is an internal rift in Europe today, a rift that has, for the past two hundred years, been aligned with the production of the ideology of European citizen. The political figure of European citizen, launched in the past decade, is meant as a form of universalism: we are all meant to be citizens of Europe. But we are refusing to acknowledge its internal split: the production of a new ideology of citizenry is utterly excluding, as it creates the split into citizens and non-citizens. This internal problem lies within the very concept of the citizen as bearer of private property and legitimate member of the community.

Those without private property and those who are not legitimate members are excluded from this concept: immigrants, workers, people with no property or citizenship status that can only be obtained through a very complicated procedure. This is now the relation of the world and the non-world. Europe is hermetically closed, but persecutes its non-citizens from within. The only possibility for the survival of Europe, as [Gilles] Deleuze and [Félix] Guattari state in *What is Philosophy?*, is for Europe to open its borders completely, for the most recent political subjectivation of European citizenry ended up in the *disaster* of national socialism. Although national socialism is usually identified with German National Socialism, it was the normal European condition—we merely need to invoke the level of collaboration and participation in this condition by the European countries just before the war. The first attempt at constituting a European citizen politics was the politics of national socialism prior to the Second World War. We have yet to fully examine the political project of national socialism, usually spoken of in theological categories. In today's utterly normalized and standardized political life we dare not admit that the politics of European citizenry was behind national socialism, that the modernist epoch of European citizenry is national socialism.

This is the key to the whole misunderstanding. I do not see any other potential as carried by today's call for constituting European citizenry: no horizon on which European citizens would be willing to give up their two key attributes of legitimate members of the community and bearers of private property. Private property is, in fact, the last taboo, the unquestionable, the fundamental limit. I think we will be repeating history until we seriously engage in a discussion over whether private property is the ultimate form of human relations.

> MT: The PLS had a complex structure; a revolutionary war, it was primarily a political sequence of internal emancipation from the ruling ideologies of that moment in Europe. Does this mean that political sequences of anti-colonial war are historically over? Why?

BS: To refer to Sylvain Lazarus's political axiom: politics is rare. It is an event strictly confined by time and place, absolutely local. A very simple axiom. The PLS represents the very rarity of politics as event. It produced the situation crucial for the constitution of a political subject, that is, it produced its entire politics from within absolute subjectivity, rather than out of conducting an empirical or phenomenological analysis of the outside world. Although National Socialism was a powerful and dominant ideology that had enslaved all of Europe, there were people who, at one point, due to the situation in which they found themselves and the decisions they made, constituted a subject that has, despite facing this absolute military and political dominance, found the space to produce an affirmative politics from within absolute subjectivity. This is the definition of the subject and of its absolute rarity and sequentiality. It is non-historical in a sense; a sequence, a rarity, the absolute singularity.

> MT: How would you describe the continuities and discontinuities of anticolonial struggles fundamental to the PLS and of the political act of creating the Non-Aligned Movement?

BS: The politics of the Non-Aligned has a very important internal gesture against the denial of the existence of the world as a whole. This was also one of the axioms of the PLS: no one may be excluded from the society we are producing, later transferred to the context of state politics as a motto according to which a non-world, that without equals, can no longer exist; no one may be excluded from the definition of humanity. One of the key achievements of the PLS was to gather this refuse of humanity and introduce them into the world through political subjectivation from within.

MT: Spanish Civil War and the PLS were historically linked through struggle against fascist occupation and imperialist war. Do you see a continuity of this struggle in the NAM?

OMP: The important element connecting the Spanish Civil War, the PLS in Yugoslavia and finally the establishment of the NAM is the active position of recognizing the need to fight against war. Spanish Civil War was defined as a war to stop war, the only way to stop fascism in Spain. The antifascist struggle in Yugoslavia represented the only possible active standpoint against Nazism and fascism. In that respect there is no logical continuation, as peaceful coexistence was one of the main positions of the NAM. This is in contradiction with the strong pro-militant proclamations of antifascist movement. After 1945, with the fear of global war as nuclear catastrophe, the framework changed and the same goals were aimed at in a different way. The organization of anticolonial movements and newly established states claimed more or less the same principles, but perceived the broader situation as very different. This is why the NAM functioned through huge round table discussions and dialogues between, ideologically and politically, very differently defined political subjects.

MT: Branimir, you mentioned that the PLS, just like the NAM, was absolutely affirmative. Josip Broz Tito, even as one of the conceivers and founders of the NAM, was from the very beginnings of this movement in the mid-fifties and all the way to the seventies, against the term "Non-Aligned." He tried to avoid uttering the term Non-Aligned in his speeches, letters, messages, etc. What can you tell us about that?

BS: Interestingly, Tito had an internal split, as did Socialist Yugoslavia, into the forgotten political sequence of the PLS [and the new state of Yugoslavia]. The context of this conversation does not lend itself to discussing the reasons for it being forgotten. Nevertheless, this hidden sequence is significant for us within the context of Non-Alignment, as the cause of Tito's split. Tito knew that this sequence of the PLS was the best that the Yugoslav Communists had produced. The obligations of creating the Yugoslav state, however, gradually removed this sequence, which never had a state as its final aim or its limit, but rather the absolute change, the creation of a new society. After this sequence of the PLS, Yugoslav Communists entered the production of a state, the complete opposite of the PLS as people's politics, popular politics. Tito was thus always split into the leader of the PLS and the statesman.

It was clear to Tito, however, that a new, global revolutionary sequence of anti-colonial liberation was opening in the sixties. He thus disliked the term Non-Alignment as too passive: to be non-aligned is to be in negation; he saw the concept of Non-Alignment as negation without affirmation. For the PLS defeated fascism and colonialism through its internal logic of affirmative politics, not through superior military might. We would be exhausting its meaning if we were to consider it merely within antifascism and anticolonialism; it must be considered as production of new society, as affirmative. Tito saw in this new revolutionary sequence the possibility for Yugoslavia to participate in anticolonial struggle, hence the 1961 Belgrade Conference and his active engagement throughout the sixties. He did not use the term Non-Alignment during this revolutionary sequence as too narrow a term for Yugoslavia's ambition to be actively involved in anti-colonial struggles.

In the seventies, he saw that the revolutionary sequence was over and started using the term Non-Aligned. Tito then became the statesman again, an authority within the politics of equidistance between two blocs, capable of preventing the attempts at usurpation by the Soviet Union under the formula "Non-Aligned naturally belong to the Socialist bloc," as well as the attempts by the Western bloc to hegemonize the Non-Aligned within itself. The two blocs constantly fought over which will include the Non-Aligned, as a lack of affirmative politics, as neutral, into their politics. The authority of Tito the statesman stemmed from his not falling for either the Western or the Eastern imperial offer. He managed this until the end of his life. In a polemic with Castro, at the last Non-Aligned Conference he took part in, in Cuba in 1979, Tito said, "The Non-Aligned do not belong to Soviet Socialist bloc, for Soviet Socialist policy is in its ultimate instance also imperialist policy."

MT: If we consider that the protagonists of Yugoslavia's revolutionary and anticolonial struggle in the the Second World War did not consider fascism an excess, can we think about the NAM as an emancipatory political sequence with a clear continuum of anticolonial struggle carried out after the Second World War?

OMP: Fascism is the capitalist world's answer to crisis: when in crisis, capitalism produces fascism, in different ways, by different means. Even when there is officially no crisis, there persist points that could produce new fascism. Umberto Eco's concept of Ur-Fascism is probably the best answer to how fascism can be born, raised in every society from a little "innocent" point and completely prevail. It is important to say that although the whole idea of NAM is in itself negation of fascism as the final step of capitalist development, the movement was so heterogeneous in approaches to crisis within world politics that, in the end, the principles on which it was established were not realised as expected.

Although there are very specific ideological and political developments in the way the main, let's say actors, from India, Yugoslavia, Ghana, Egypt and other states perceived international and global politics, they tried to find a way of overcoming those differences and, at the moment of global threat to peace, change their domestic politics through that dialogue. Although the main idea of the NAM was not to interfere in internal affairs of the states, such dialogues were meant to introduce changes into those very different societies.

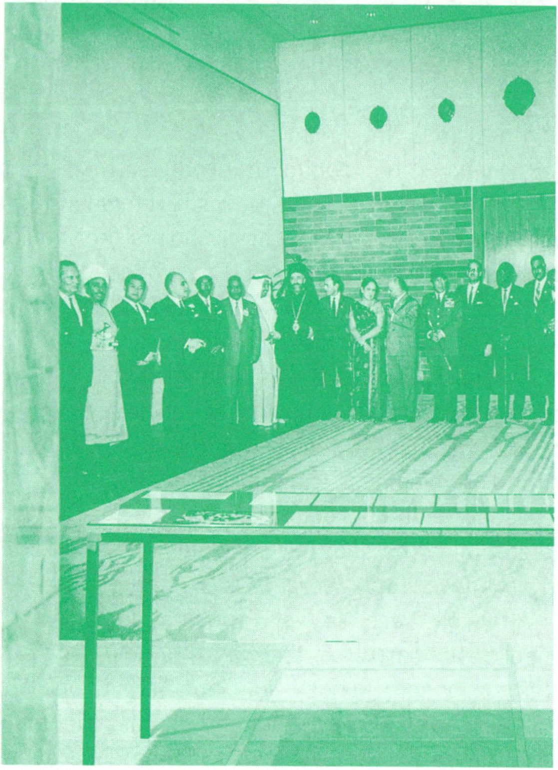

Authors of Travelling Communiqué, *Vitrine 7: Travelling Communiqué Berlin, September 2013*, installation view, Museum of Yugoslav History, Belgrade, 2014

Kodwo Eshun and Doreen Mende

PROLONGING 1961: A COMMUNIQUÉ SENT INTO THE FUTURE

In 2011, Katarina Živanović, then Director of the Museum of Yugoslav History in Belgrade, initiated the process of digitizing approximately 300,000 photographs and negatives of the Presidential Photo Service archived at the Museum. This unedited archive depicted the life and work of Josip Broz Tito from 1943 to 1980.[1] As well as providing an optic through which to observe the political iconography of Titoist statecraft, the archive offered insights into a specific photographic public sphere of Global Cold War visuality.[2]

The *Travelling Communiqué* project concentrated on photographs taken during the six days in 1961 when delegates from twenty-five countries gathered at the Federal Assembly Building in Belgrade for the first Conference of the Heads of State or Government of Non-Aligned Countries.[3]

1. Tito was the leader of the Partisan movement and of the People's Liberation Struggle in Yugoslavia, 1941–45, President of the Federal People's Republic of Yugoslavia, 1945–63, and of the Socialist Federal Republic of Yugoslavia, 1963–80.
2. See Jorge Ribalta, "Introduction," in *Public Photographic Spaces: Propaganda Exhibitions from Pressa to the Family of Man 1928-1955* (Barcelona: MACBA, 2009), p. 11. See also Odd Arne Westad, *The Global Cold War: Third World Interventions and the making of our Times* (Cambridge: Cambridge University Press, 2006).
3. See pp. 74-76.

From September 1 to 6, 1961, the photographers of the Presidential Photo Service took 1,200 medium format photographs and negatives that constituted a new mode of photographic internationalism. To focus upon the unedited internationalism of the Conference of 1961 is to ask the question:

Why gather around images of Non-Alignment?

Why do these images matter, to us, now?

What does it mean to engage with the images of the Non-Aligned Movement, more than 50 years after its inauguration?

And what significance does the Conference of 1961 hold today, in August 2015, when the European Central Bank, the International Monetary Fund and the European Union are enforcing financial sovereignty over the Coalition of the Radical Left known as Syriza, the Hellenic Parliament, and the electorate of Greece? When the Islamic Republic of Iran agrees with the U.S., UK, France, Germany, Russia and China to halt its nuclear weapons program in exchange for economic sanctions relief?

To engage with Yugoslavian state photographs of the Conference today requires a reckoning with the implications of the digital transformation of the means of production of the archive at the Museum of Yugoslav History. It is the digitization of photographs initiated by the Museum that provided the opportunity for *Travelling Communiqué* to work with historical documents formatted into JPEGs and TIFFs, email attachments and YouSendIt file transfers, thumbnails and printouts.

The process of digitization provided the conditions for the *Travelling Communiqué* project to invite practitioners from the fields of art, cinema, architecture, typography, theory, and education to copy and print files, transport them in suitcases and bags, on long distance flights, study them in working groups, discuss them by Skype and reimagine them through durational processes of exhibition-making.

Historically speaking, the Non-Aligned Movement preceded the Conference of 1961; it is surprising to realize that the Movement continues today, convening conferences in different cities attended by its 120 member states.[4] Its documents, dispersed across state and private collections, far exceed the photographs digitized by the Museum.[5] From its inception, its aims, intentions, and implications were to

4. Tito, Nehru and Nasser met at Brijuni in July 1956 to formulate the agenda for "peaceful co-existence" that was central to Non-Aligned diplomatic discourse. As a prelude to the Conference, Tito travelled to Liberia, Ghana, Togo, Mali and Guinea, from February to April 1961, on a so-called "Journey of Peace."

The Preparatory Meeting for the Conference of Uncommitted Countries, as it was initially titled, was held in Cairo from June 5 to 12, 1961. Subsequent Heads of State Conferences were held in Cairo in 1964, Lusaka in 1970, Algiers in 1973, Colombo in 1976, Havana in 1979, New Delhi in 1983, Harare in 1986, Belgrade in 1989, Jakarta in 1992, Cartagena de Indias in 1995, Durban in 1998, Kuala Lumpur in 2003 and Tehran in 2012.

Today, the Non-Aligned Movement has 120 member states. See http://namiran.org/wp-content/uploads/2014/07/Note-442-Circulation-of-Note-by-Peru-1-July.pdf. Accessed September 23, 2015.

See Vijay Prashad, T*he Darker Nations: A People's History of the Third World* (New York: The New Press, 2007), pp. 95–114, 305–310.

5. *Travelling Communiqué* accessed the key textual documents of the Conference such as the collectively signed letter addressed to Kennedy and Khrushchev and

disaggregate and disarm the bipolar discourse of foreign policy that dominated so-called "international relations" during the Cold War.[6] On December 23, 1954, after Tito's journey to India, Nehru and Tito issued a joint statement that sought to define the policy of Non-Alignment "adopted and pursued" by their respective countries. "Non-Alignment," the two statesmen declared," is not "neutrality" or "neutralism" and therefore passivity, but a positive, active and constructive policy seeking to lead to a collective peace on which collective security can alone truly rest... The President and the Prime Minister therefore repudiate the erroneous conception which has become prevalent in some quarters of a "third bloc" or a "third force" of Non-Aligned Countries. This is a contradiction in terms because such a bloc would involve them in the very system of alignments which they regard as undesirable."[7] From the perspective of a binary world order determined to divide the earth

the *Declaration of Heads of State or Government of Non-Aligned Countries* from the John F. Kennedy Presidential Library and Museum in Boston and the Archive of Yugoslavia in Belgrade.

Visual archives also exist at Telegrafska agencija nove Jugoslavije or TANJUG, Yugoslavia's official news agency and Filmske Novosti, Yugoslav film newsreel production company in Belgrade.

6. See Lawrence W. Martin (ed.), *Neutralism and Non-Alignment: The New States in World Affairs* (New York: Frederick A. Praeger), 1962.

7. Slobodan Stanković, "Tito and Non-Alignment," Radio Free Europe, December 6, 1967, http://osaarchivum.org/files/holdings/300/8/3/text/133-5-9.shtml. Accessed July 14, 2015. See Krishna Menon, India's Ambassador to the United Nations, response on American television in 1955:

into opposing blocs, the Non-Aligned Movement was effectively a "non-bloc bloc," a bloc that refused to understand itself as a bloc. The complexity of non-alignment in an age of alignment, its claims and demands, its modes of address and means of making public suggest a multivalent internationalism that complicates the combined and uneven processes of globalization characterized by Félix Guattari as "Integrated World Capitalism."[8]

The conjuncture of the digital, the institutional, the artistic and the theoretical set the stage for the

"We do not believe this division of the earth into camps of this kind is a good thing for stability and peace and the fortunes of all of us. If we think that, and we therefore do not like two blocs, how would we help by forming a third bloc?"

"Longines Chronoscope: A Television Journal of the Important Issues of the Hour," 1955, https://www.youtube.com/watch?v=7ylzRZA5-zs. Accessed July 3, 2014.

See also Modibo Keita's speech at the Political Bureau of the Sudanese Union RDA on the occasion of Tito's visit to Mali on March 26 1961:

"Is not a visit from a man like you, responsible for a state like Yugoslavia, one of the first initiators of the determined policy of non-commitment to either of the two blocs, is it not for us, the people of Mali, who firmly pursue the same policy, the policy of positive neutrality, an encouragement to persevere in that attitude?"

Obren Miličević, *With Friends in Africa* (Belgrade: Edition Jugoslavija, 1961), p. 47. See also Vijay Prasad, *The Darker Nations: A People's History of the Third World* (New York: The New Press, 2007). Jelena Vesić and Rachel O'Reilly's performance lecture *On Neutrality* at the Summer School at the Museum of Yugoslav History formulated a genealogy of the concept of neutrality.

See extracts on p. 297

8. Félix Guattari, "The Three Ecologies," trans. Chris Turner, in *New Formations*, Number 8 (Summer 1989), p. 137.

transdisciplinary grouping of *Travelling Communiqué* that approached the unedited images of the 1961 Conference from perspectives distinct from academic research and nationalist revisionism. The *Travelling Communiqué* project departed from the statements and positions addressed to the so-called Great Powers by the delegates. It expanded the form of the communiqué[9] beyond its standardized definition to include any public declaration articulated during the Conference in the form of an image, speech, sound, gesture, event, action or architecture that sought to internationalize the aims and objectives of Non-Alignment.[10] In 1961, the *communiqué* specifically referred to the letter signed by all twenty-five delegates, addressed to Nicolai Khrushchev and John F. Kennedy, the heads of state responsible for "a world at war."

Responding to the collectively signed letter prompted the *Travelling Communiqué* project to pose a question: Who is the addressee of the *communiqué* today? This question, formulated by Branimir Stojanović in the context of digitization, suggested a further proposition: What if the political demands made during the Conference of 1961, formulated in the collective letter, were active today, travelling into our present and confronting us now? The passage from 1961 into the present is staged in Milica Tomić's

9. The term *communiqué* is usually reserved for a press release issued by a government, political party or movement that summarises the contents of a closed meeting for use by the press in forthcoming articles.
10. The Museum of Yugoslav History was opened by Tito in 1962 under the name of the Museum of the 25th of May.

The Purloined Letter (2014) which was conceived as a "discursive operation in the form of a photograph"[11] in which Tomić descended the stone steps from the Mausoleum of Tito to the Museum garden carrying a life-size photograph of a section of the group portrait of the heads of state of Non-Aligned Countries.[12]

The digital prolongation proposed by the *Travelling Communiqué* project questions the political discourses that continue to consign the Non-Aligned Movement to the margins of Cold War historiography. To enquire whom the *communiqué* addresses today is to exceed the proper limits of political chronology maintained by bipolar historiography. To prolong the demands made by the *communiqué* is to articulate the interrupted continuities between the Global Cold War of 1961 and the permanent wars of the present. It is the unacknowledged correlations between the crimes of the twentieth century and the wars of the twenty-first century that cinema discerns in its depiction of the faces of children in Jean-Luc Godard's *De l'origine du XXIe siècle* (2000). A fragment from the extreme violence of the nineties'

11. According to Milica Tomić, *The Purloined Letter* departed from "the idea that the collective statements, images and sounds announced during the first Conference of the NAM in Belgrade in 1961 are still travelling."

See *Travelling Communiqué. Footnotes to an exhibition* (Belgrade: MYH, 2014), p. 33.

12. To prolong alludes to the sentence formulated in *Ici et Ailleurs*, Jean-Luc Godard, 1974 as

"... la guerre populaire prolongée ... prolongée ... prolongée ... jusqu'à la victoire... the popular war extended... extended... extended until victory of the Palestinian people..."

wars in the former Yugoslavia is arrested in *Je vous salue Sarajevo* (1994), seen in a photograph of a Serbian soldier aiming his boot at the head of a murdered civilian lying face down on the street.[13]

The normalized discontinuities between post-, ex- and former communisms, capitalisms, fascisms and nationalisms create historical voids and political silences that incubate incommunicative crises between generations. In this context, the perspective of the student takes on a significance beyond its immediate presence. In a sense, the demands of Non-Alignment make demands of us all.

Maja Hodoščeks *We Need a Title* (2014), in which teenagers from the debate club of the Grammar School Celje-Center in Slovenia compose a poem informed by their encounter with unfamiliar

13. See Sharon Sliwinski, *Human Rights in Camera* (Chicago: The University of Chicago Press, 2011), pp. 120–122: "The photograph of the Serbian soldier kicking the murdered civilian's body is one of the most memorable and provocative images of the Bosnian war. The detail that seems to draw the most indignation from spectators is the relaxed air of the soldier's left hand, the delicate way he holds a lit cigarette between his fingers as he kicks a woman in the head.

One's imagination has the capacity to animate the scene; spectators are compelled to envisage what is not actually portrayed: the sequence of shootings moments before, the women's momentary grief and terror at her husband's murder, the sound of the boot as it strikes." *Je vous salue Sarajevo* effectively animates the photograph by focusing on details of the photograph taken by photojournalist Ron Haviv who accompanied a Serbian paramilitary unit known as the Tigers as they murdered men and women from the largely Muslim town of Bijeljina in March 1992 as Godard laments that "the rule is to want the death of exception" and "the rule for cultural Europe is to organize the death of the art of living."

Yugoslav Partisan poetry, dramatizes the confrontation with the vacuum of the political. In *Jablanica Collection* (2014), Fabian Bechtle examines the memorial politics adopted by the Museum of the Battle for the Wounded on Neretva River in Jablanica, Bosnia and Herzegovina, to commemorate Yugoslav Partisan resistance to the Axis Powers in the Battle of Neretva in 1943.

In the context of their one-year project at the Dutch Art Institute (DAI) in Arnhem, post-graduate students developed individual and collaborative projects that experimented with non-alignment as a production process.[14] DAI students collaborated with artists from Netsa Art Village in Addis Ababa[15] to produce *Unfold* (2014), a newspaper whose first issue was entitled *MEGLET*.[16] "In bringing together various voices," the editorial of *Unfold* declared, *MEGLET* sought to explore the "links between the two Movements of Non-Alignment and Pan-Africanism" through a process of becoming a "student group of the Movement's emancipatory logic." Throughout the sixties, national liberation struggles were

14. The works exhibited in *Travelling Communiqué* by Jan Adriaans, Hanan Benammar, Katia Barrett, Anna Dasovic, Coco Duivenvoorde, Aziza Harmel, Monique Hendriksen, Marianna Maruyama, Laila Torres Mendieta, Celia Shomal, Aarti Sunder, Silvia Ulloa and Larraitz Torres Zumelaga could be understood as proposals for testing the claims of non-alignment in debates ranging from gender to geopolitics.
15. Netsa Art Village in Addis Ababa was founded and is run by artists Mihret Kebede, Tamrat Gezahegn, Helen Zeru Araya, Mulugeta Kassa and Tesfahun Kibru, each of whom produced works for *Travelling Communiqué*.
16. Amharic for "to turn a page" or "find something new."

internationalized by the militant cinemas of Algeria, Cuba, Bolivia, Egypt, Indonesia and India. Under what conditions could film screenings function as forms of solidarity? How could solidarity question its official protocols in and through spectatorship?

These questions framed the film program screened at the Academic Film Center in Belgrade throughout *Travelling Communiqué*.[17]

The encounter with voided histories took on different forms at the DAI, at Netsa Art Village, at the Academic Film Center, at the temporary Summer School within the *Travelling Communiqué* and at the Museum of Yugoslav History itself. Museum curators Radovan Cukić, Ivan Manojlović and Mirjana Slavković discovered a memorandum written in 1963 by artist and photographer Mirko Lovrić that indicated the origin of the Presidential Photo Service[18] and clarified its role within the now opaque hierarchy of the Press Department of the Cabinet of the President of the Socialist Federal Republic of Yugoslavia.

Josip Broz Tito died in 1980. The archives of the Presidential Photo Service were moved to the Museum of Yugoslav History in 2001. Reconstructing the structure of the Photo Service led the curators to retrace the organizational form of the Museum. Beyond its administrative structure, the Museum gradually became an author in its own right. The

17. See ANTICOLONIAL CINEMA on page 306.
18. On September 13, 1963, Mirko Lovrić, Head of the Photo Service of the Press Department of Tito's Cabinet from 1963 to 1971 presented a Memorandum to Tito's Chief of Cabinet Bogdan Crnobrnja. See p. 137.

curators analyzed its institutional context of production in the political life of Yugoslavia before and after 1980. In *Photo Archive of Josip Broz Tito: A view of the picture of political power* (2014), Cukić, Manojlović and Slavković compared photographs taken during Tito's diplomatic travels to Non-Aligned Countries such as Ghana with photographs of his visits to capitalist countries such as Japan, Mexico and the United Kingdom. What emerged from this visual study was an understanding of the "link between photographic protocols and the political network of a statesman" that raised the question of whether photography could be "an equal instrument" of a "political idea, on a level with political speech."[19]

The role of diplomatic photography as a visual form of political power returned in Armin Linke's *Staging and Servicing the Media* (2014). Linke studied German diplomatic missions undertaken throughout the European Union in 2014. This study revealed that the protocols operative in Titoist diplomatic photography persisted in the contemporary photography produced by the Press and Information Department of Germany.

The "digitalization of image production and media distribution," according to Linke, "does not seem to have changed the international codes and practice of photographers... ."[20] This insight into the unacknowledged continuities between the digital

19. Research Group of the Museum of Yugoslav History, in *Travelling Communiqué. Footnotes to an exhibition* (Belgrade: MYH, 2014), p. 6.
20. Armin Linke, in *Travelling Communiqué. Footnotes to an exhibition* (Belgrade: MYH, 2014), p. 11.

diplomatic photography of the present and the analog diplomatic photography produced during the Cold War revealed unforeseen continuities between ideologically opposed and historically differentiated political systems.

Reconstructing the six days and nights from the photographs of the 1961 Conference offers the possibility of specifying critical moments in the internationalization of the Non-Aligned Movement.

The first moment: shortly before 10 a.m. on September 1, 1961, twenty-five photographers capture the delegates as they settle into their chairs at the oval table of the Conference, marked with national nameplates.

The photograph of the photographers was catalogued "MYH K-179/30 Hall for Plenary Sessions on the opening day of the Conference of Heads of State or Government of Non-Aligned Countries, Belgrade, September 1, 1961. © Museum of Yugoslav History, Belgrade." MYH K-179/30 was copied in its thousands, sent by wire, distributed by press agencies, printed in newspapers and published in magazines within and outside of the Federal People's Republic of Yugoslavia. MYH K-179/30 acted as a reference for the prospective archive of the Conference.

The presence of the photographers anticipates the appearances of visual publics to be addressed by images that will travel across the planet. The noise of flash bulbs, television cameras, simultaneous interpretations heard through headphones and scraping chairs announces the moments before 10 a.m., when the Conference actually begins. It starts

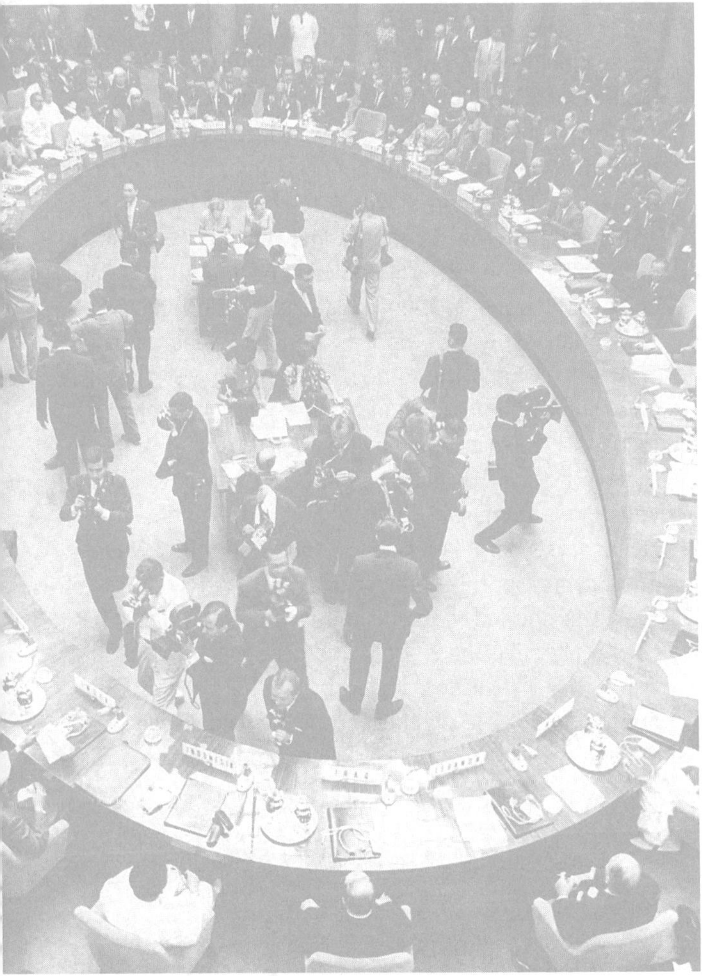

1961_179_0030 The Plenary session hall on the opening day of the Belgrade Conference of Heads of State or Government of the Non-Aligned Countries, September 1, 1961

with sixty seconds of dead silence that commemorated the women and men killed during Asian, African and Latin American anti-imperialist, anti-colonialist and anti-fascist struggles for the "liberty and independence of their people."[21] The collective silence could be understood as a special kind of *communiqué* that honored the transition from the era of liberation struggle to the epoch of the new nation states. The delegates invoked the continuities between the people's memories and the support for armed struggles in Algeria where the National Liberation Army was fighting against French settlers, in Angola, where the People's Movement for the Liberation of Angola fought the Portuguese armed forces, in Tunisia, against the French occupation of the territory of Bizerte and in Cuba, where the two year old Communist Party of Cuba demanded the closure of North America's Guantánamo Bay Naval Base at its South Eastern point.

The second moment: the letter, often described as a "collective message," was proposed by Nasser,[22] written by Nehru and signed by all the delegates on September 5, 1961. Sukarno and Keita delivered it to Kennedy while Nehru and Nkrumah delivered it to

21. *La Conférence des chefs d'État ou de gouvernement des Pays Non-Alignés Belgrade 1–6 September 1961*, published by JUGOSLAVIJA in 1961. Caption for photograph, unpaginated.

22. Nasser proposed that "this conference issues an invitation to the two sides to begin the negotiations. To give weight to this initiative which bears our idea in this matter, we propose that we address a collective message on behalf of this conference, which will be signed by all the heads of state or their representatives present here to Khrushchev and to Kennedy.

Khrushchev. The collective message[23] urged Khrushchev and Kennedy to acknowledge the "gravity of the crisis that menaces the world and the urgent need to avert the developments that may precipitate it." The crisis seemed to escalate throughout 1961. On February 13, after a delay of three weeks, the secessionist government of Katanga State led by Moïse Tshombe, announced the deaths of Patrice Lumumba, Prime Minister and Minister of Defense of the Democratic Republic of the Congo, Maurice Mpolo, Army Chief, and Joseph Okito, Vice President of the Senate.[24]

The message will be delivered by the heads of state present who will be chosen by the conference to assert to our peoples and the world peoples' intense concern and care for the future of peace."

See *Belgrade Conference Appeal*, September 4, 1961, on page 73. See also John F. Kennedy Presidential Library and Museum, Boston, Papers of John F. Kennedy, Presidential Papers, President's Office Files, 1961: August 28–September 5, folder JFKPOF-104-004, http://www.jfklibrary.org/Asset-Viewer/Archives/JFKPOF-104-004.aspx. Accessed September 4, 2013.

23. Kennedy's acknowledgement and reply to the Conference was sent from the White House on September 13, 1961. Khrushchev's acknowledgment and reply to the Conference was sent from the Kremlin on September 16, 1961. See note 22.

24. As Nkrumah wrote in 1963, "We cannot afford either to ignore the sinister chain of interests which unites events in the Congo and Angola to East and South Africa. These interests are also connected with the East-West battle for world supremacy and the frenzied efforts being made to drag the newly emerging countries of Africa into the orbit of the cold war. The contest for ideological influence over the new states of Africa is throwing into confusion and complicating even more what is already a complex enough struggle for freedom from imperialist political and economic dominance and the unification of the continent.

In April 1961, the U.S. launched a failed invasion against Cuba at Playa Giron in the Bay of Pigs. In August, the German Democratic Republic began construction on the Anti-Fascist Protection Rampart and closed its border with West Berlin.[25] On September 1, the news that the Soviet Union had resumed its nuclear test[26] program in Kazakhstan heightened the tension of the first day of the Conference.[27]

Any difference, any kind of fissure among Africans is seized and turned to the imperialist and cold war interests. The Congo offers perhaps the most striking example of how tribal dissensions and political careerism are exploited in order to fragment united territories and exacerbate divisions. The aim of the marionette control of local careerists like Moise Tshombe, beside the maintenance of economic power is to cut across the African determination to secure continental unity in full independence.

It was unfortunate that the United Nations was manoeuvred into a position where at one time it appeared to be weighting its influence against the legitimate Congolese government on the side of those who were responsible for throwing the country into upheaval and for the murder of Patrice Lumumba."

See Kwame Nkrumah, *Africa Must Unite* (London: Heinemann, 1963), p. 191. See also Jean-Paul Sartre, *The Political Thought of Patrice Lumumba*, in *Colonialism and Neocolonialism* (London: Routledge, 2001), pp. 175–223; Ludo De Witte, *The Assassination of Lumumba* (London: Verso, 2001), pp. 125–185; and Sven Augustijnen, *Spectres* (Brussels: ASA Publishers, 2011).

25. In his speech on September 4, Nehru stated that to "go ahead and to ignore a fact of life and a fact of contemporary politics means that you are ignoring something which indeed you do not desire. Such a thing in my opinion for the moment is (the situation—ed.) where we find the great city of Berlin divided by what may be called an international frontier." See note 22.

26. See Stanković, http://osaarchivum.org/files/holdings/300/8/3/text/133-5-9.shtml. Accessed July 14, 2015.

The third moment: On September 6, 1961, delegates finalized the twenty-seven points of the Declaration of Heads of State or Government of Non-Aligned Countries.[28] While the collective letter addressed the Kremlin and the White House, the Declaration addressed itself to the United Nations. It demanded that its points be "brought to the attention of all the Member States of the world Organization" and "forwarded to all the other states"[29] not yet seated at the United Nations. The transition from Moscow and Washington to the United Nations announced the Conference as a new kind of internationalism on the global stage. Neither an organization, nor a coalition, a third bloc or a Third World, it was a "non-bloc bloc" that focused upon the critical question of creating the conditions for "collective peace" in a context of intensifying nuclear tension. With East and West intent on escalating their

27. The collective letter provided the starting point for an initial version of *Travelling Communiqué* at *After Year Zero. Geographies of Collaboration* in Haus der Kulturen der Welt, Berlin from September 19 to November 24, 2013. See *Travelling Communiqué. Reading a Photo Archive (1948-80), Presidential Press Service, Yugoslavia* in Annett Busch and Anselm Franke (eds.), *After Year Zero. Geographies of Collaboration* (Berlin: Haus der Kulturen der Welt, 2015), pp. 135–138.
28. See *La Conférence des chefs d'État ou de gouvernement des Pays Non-Alignés Belgrade September 1–6, 1961* (Belgrade: Yugoslavija, 1961), in English, French, and Spanish. See also *The Five Summit Conferences of the Non-Aligned Countries Documents* (Havana: Editorial de Ciencias Sociales, 1979).
29. *Declaration of the Heads of State and Government of Non-Aligned Countries*, BEO/6, September 6, 1961. Archive of the President of the Republic, Belgrade.

so-called "nuclear test programme," the need to define and demand "peaceful coexistence" took on ever greater import. Theo Eshetu's montage *The Atom Bomb* (2014) connects the atmospheric nuclear tests of the sixties with the imperial atrocities committed by Italy against Ethiopia in the thirties. The diplomatic policy of peace and the struggle to mobilize around it was central to Non-Alignment discourse. Today, as Branimir Stojanović argues, political discourse has deleted the category of peace, preferring to normalize the state of proxy wars[30] depicted in *Syrian Voices* (2014), which focuses on the hidden violence visited on civilians by the Assad regime through Roza El-Hassan's collaborations with activists and photographers.

The first point of the Declaration of Heads of State or Government of Non-Aligned Countries articulated the "essential necessity for all non-aligned countries" to "participate in solving international issues" by a "concerted effort to put an end to all types of new colonialism and imperialist domination in all its forms and manifestations."[31] Because the Non-Aligned Movement, like the United Nations, insisted upon non-interference between independent sovereign nations, its delegates overlooked the imperialist domination practiced by its own member states over neighboring peoples and territories even as it denounced the neo-colonial regimes of Portugal,

30. See Milica Tomić in discussion with Branimir Stojanović and Olga Manojlović Pintar on p. 37.
31. *Declaration of the Heads of State and Government of Non-Aligned Countries*, BEO/6, September 6, 1961. Archive of the President of the Republic, Belgrade.

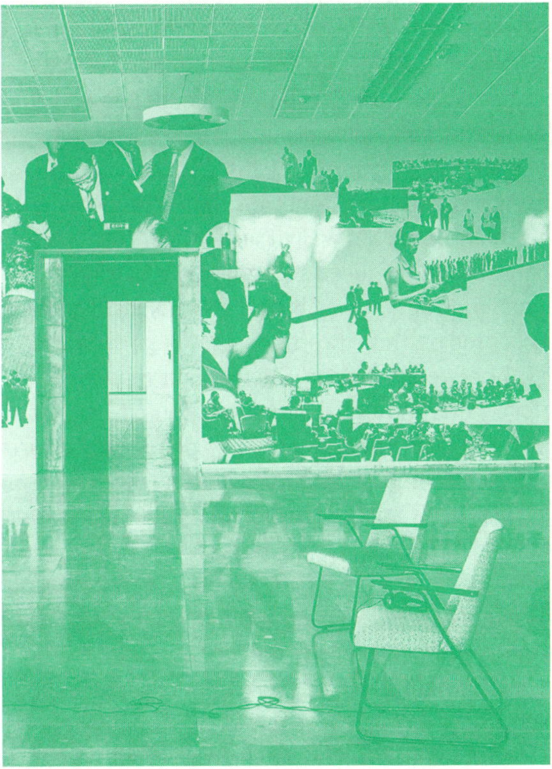

The Otolith Group, *Gather round me, my writers, musicians, artists: my name is NAM* (2014), installation view, Museum of Yugoslav History, Belgrade, 2014

Belgium, Rhodesia and South Africa operative throughout Central and South Africa. It did not intervene in the Eritrean War for Independence waged by the Eritrean Liberation Front against Ethiopia that began on the opening day of the Conference. The self-determination practiced by states often operated according to a logic that "preserves peoples by endangering persons."[32] The preoccupation with the duplicities of neo-colonialism authorized the domestic authoritarianism of many of the new nation states of Asia, Africa and Latin America that attended the 1961 Conference. Their conspiratorial tendencies were monitored and nurtured by America's Cold War political imagination which perceived Non-Alignment to be a contagion that threatened to undermine the division between the Iron Curtain and the Color Curtain.[33] It is the anti-Communist fantasy of Non-Alignment as an uncontrollable epidemic that informed The Otolith Group's *Gather round me, my writers, musicians, artists: My name is NAM* (2014). The work extracted gestures, expressions, technologies and architectures from digitized Conference photographs to assemble a fourteen-meter transhistorical frieze that occupied the central wall of the Museum.

In situating itself at the digital reconstruction of analogue photography, *Travelling Communiqué* provided space and time to analyze and visualize the protocols that had choreographed the images,

32. See HISTORY DOES NOT REPEAT ITSELF, BUT IT DOES RHYME on page 313.
33. Richard Wright, "The Color Curtain: A Report on the Bandung Conference, 1956," in Richard Wright, *Black Power: Three Books from Exile: Black Power, The Color Curtain, White Man, Listen* (New York: Harper, 2008).

speeches and texts of the Conference of 1961. This archaeological imperative existed in parallel with a tendency towards the proleptic. From this future oriented perspective, the encounter between the *communiqué* and its addressees was to be sustained in the form of proposals whose realization implied a duration beyond the time frame of the conventional exhibition format. Authors from artistic, cinematic, activist, spatial, theoretical, psychoanalytical and photographic fields were invited to articulate proposals that were printed in blocks of 1,000 sheets. Each proposal was placed on a table that drew attention to the interior volume of the Museum and the city skyline visible from the newly exposed Museum windows. To prolong the *communiqué* in this way indicated the unfinished project of *Travelling Communiqué*. Away from documents in vitrines.

Towards the work of articulating processes for making an exhibition. Away from expert perspectives.

Towards reading groups, screenings, discussions.

Towards working in groups based around friendships in Arnhem, Belgrade, Berlin, Addis Ababa, Cairo, London, Melbourne, Paris.

Towards those who decide to become addressees.

Those who responded to the *communiqué*.

Those who work with JPEGs and TIFFs, PDFs and TextEdits.

In files and folders and laptops and hardrives and shoulder bags.

In fragile exhibiting processes that continue to make matters public.

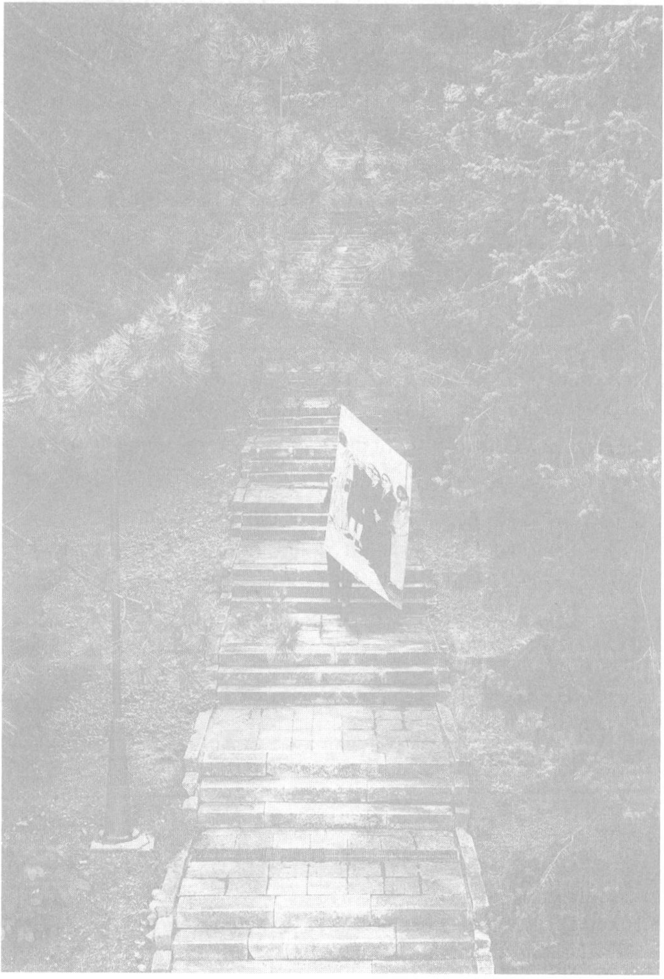

Milica Tomić, *The Purloined Letter* (2014), performance with lambda-print, 180x120cm, Museum of Yugoslav History, Belgrade, 2014

Belgrade, September 5, 1961.

CONFERENCE
OF HEADS OF STATE OR GOVERNMENT
OF NON-ALIGNED COUNTRIES

Your Excellency,

We, the Heads of States and Governments of our respective countries attending the Conference of Non-Aligned Countries held at Belgrade from September 1 to September 5, 1961 venture to address Your Excellency on a subject of vital and immediate importance to all of us and to the world as a whole. We do so not only on our behalf, but at the unaninmous desire of the Conference and of our peoples.

We are distressed and deeply concerned at the deterioration in the international situation and the prospect of war which now threatens humanity. Your Excellency has often pointed to the terrible nature of modern war and the use of nuclear weapons, which may well destroy humanity, and has pleaded for the maintenance of world peace.

Yet we are at the brink of this very danger that menaces the world and humanity. We are fully aware that Your Excellency is anxious as any of us to avoid this dreadful development which will not [...]

2/ ....

His Excellency Mr. John F. Kennedy
President of the United States of America
Washington

2.

[...] only end the hopes that we all have cherished for the advancement of our peoples but is a challenge to human survival. We are certain that Your Excellency will do everything in your power to avert such a calamity.

Having regard, however, to the gravity of the crisis that menaces the world and the urgent need to avert the developments that may precipitate it, we take the liberty of urging on the Great Powers concerned that negotiations should be resumed and pursued so that the danger of war might be removed from the world and mankind adopts ways of peace. In particular, we earnestly request for direct negotiations between Your Excellency and the Chairman of the Council of Ministers of the Union of Soviet Socialist Republics, who represent the two most powerful nations today and in whose hands lies the key to peace and war. We feel convinced that devoted as both of you are to world peace, your efforts through persistent negotiations will lead to a way out of the present impasse and enable the world and humanity to work and live for prosperity and peace.

We feel sure that Your Excellency will appreciate that this letter is written because of our love of peace and our horror of war and the compelling desire that a way out must be found before mankind is faced with a terrible disaster.

3/ ....

3.

We are sending a letter in identical terms to this to His Excellency Mr. N.S. Khruschev[5], Chairman of the Council of Ministers of the Union of Soviet Socialist Republics.

With assurances of our deep regard,
Yours sincerely,

Sardar Mohammad Daoud
Prime Minister of Afghanistan

Ben Youssef Ben Khedda
President of the Council of the Algerian Provisional Government

U Nu
Prime Minister of the Union of Burma

4.

Prince Norodom Sihanouk
Head of State of Cambodia

Sirimavo R. Bandaranaike
Prime Mnister and Minister of Defence and External Affairs of Ceylon

Cyrille Adoula
Prime Minister of Congo and Minister of National Defence

Dr. Osvaldo Dorticos Torrado
President of the Republic of Cuba

Archbishop Makarios
President of the Republic of Cyprus

5.

Haile Selassie I
Emperor of Ethiopia

Dr. Kwame Nkrumah
President of the Republic of Ghana

Beavogui Luis Lansana
Minister of Foreign Affairs of Guinea

Jawaharlal Nehru
Prime Minister of India

Dr. Achmad Soekarno
President of the Republic of Indonesia

6.

Dr. Hashim Jawad
Personal Plenipotentiary of the Prime Minister of Iraq and Minister of Foreign Affairs

Saeb Salam
Head of Government of Lebanon and President of the Council of Ministers

Modibo Keita
President of the Republic of Mali

King Hassan II of Marocco

Mahendra Bir Bikram Shah Deya
King of Nepal

7.

Sheikh Ibrahim Sowayel
Minister of Foreign Affairs and Personal Representative of King Saud of Saudi Arabia

Aden Abdulla Osman
President of the Somali Republic

Ibrahim Abboud
(Farik)
President of the Supreme Council for the Armed Forces and Prime Minister of the Republic of Sudan

Habib Bourguiba
President of the Republic of Tunisia

Gemal Abdel Naser
President of the United Arab Republic

8.

H.R.H. Seful Islam El Hassan
Personal Representative of H.M. Al Imam Ahmed the King of Yemen and the First Councellor of the Yemen Government

Josip Broz-Tito
President of the Federal People's Republic of Yugoslavia

CONFERENCE OF HEADS OF STATE
OR GOVERNMENT OF NON-ALIGNED
COUNTRIES
Beograd, September 1961

BEO/6
Original: English
6 September 1961

DECLARATION OF THE HEADS OF STATE OR GOVERNMENT OF NON-ALIGNED COUNTRIES

The Conference of Heads of State or Government of the following non-aligned countries:

1. Afghanistan
2. Algeria
3. Burma
4. Cambodia
5. Ceylon
6. Congo
7. Cuba
8. Cyprus
9. Ethiopia
10. Ghana Republic
11. Guinea
24. Yemen
12. India
13. Indonesia
14. Iraq
15. Lebanon
16. Mali
17. Morocco
18. Nepal
19. Saudi Arabia
20. Somalia
21. Sudan
22. Tunisia
23. United Arab Republic
24. Yemen
25. Yugoslavia

and of the following countries represented by observers:

1. Bolivia
2. Brazil
3. Ecuador

was held in Belgrade from September 1 to 6, 1961, for the purpose of exchanging views on international problems with a view to contributing more effectively to world peace and security and peaceful co-operation among peoples.

(2) BEO/6

The Heads of State or Government of the aforementioned countries have met at a moment when international events have taken a turn for the worst and when world peace is seriously threatened. Deeply concerned for the future of peace, voicing the aspirations of the vast majority of people of the world, aware that, in our time, no people and no government can or should abandon its responsibilities in regard to the safeguarding of world peace, the participating countries—having examined in detail, in an atmosphere of equality, sincerity and mutual confidence, the current state of international relations and trends prevailing in the present-day world—make the following declaration:

THE HEADS OF STATE OR GOVERNMENT OF NON-ALIGNED COUNTRIES

noting that there are crises that lead towards a world conflict in the transition from an old order based on domination to a new order based on cooperation between nations, founded on freedom, equality and social justice for the promotion of prosperity; considering that the dynamic processes and forms of social change often result in or represent a conflict between the old established and the new emerging nationalist forces; considering that a lasting peace can be achieved only if this confrontation leads to a world where the domination of colonialism-imperialism and neo-colonialism in all their manifestations is radically eliminated;

AND RECOGNIZING THE FACT

that acute emergencies threatening world peace now exist in this period of conflict in Africa, Asia, Europe and Latin America and big power rivalry likely to result in world conflagration cannot be excluded;

(3) BEO/6

that to eradicate the source of conflict is to eradicate colonialism in all its manifestations and to accept and practice a policy of peaceful co-existence in the world; that guided by these principles the period of transition and conflict can lay a firm foundation of cooperation and brotherhood between nations, state the following:

I

War has never threatened mankind with graver consequences than today. On the other hand, never before has mankind had at its disposal stronger forces for eliminating war as an instrument of policy in international relations.

Imperialism is weakening. Colonial empires and other forms of foreign oppression of peoples in Asia. Africa and Latin America are gradually disappearing from the stage of history. Great successes have been achieved in the struggle of many peoples for national independence and equality. In the same way, the peoples of Latin America are continuing to make an increasingly effective contribution to the improvement of international relations. Great social changes in the world are further promoting such a development. All this not only [...]

(4) BEO/6

[...] accelerates the end of the epoch of foreign oppression of peoples, but also makes peaceful cooperation among peoples, based on the principles of independence and equal rights, an essential condition for their freedom and progress.

Tremendous progress has been achieved in the development of science, techniques and in the means of economic development.

Prompted by such developments in the world: the vast majority of people are becomingly increasingly conscious of the fact that war between peoples constitutes not only an anachronism but also a crime against humanity. This awareness of peoples is becoming a great moral force, capable of exercising a vital influence on the development of international relations.

Relying on this and on the will of their peoples, the Governments of countries participating in the Conference resolutely reject the view that war, including the "cold war", is inevitable, as this view reflects a sense both of helplessness and hopelessness and is contrary to the progress of the world. They affirm their unwavering faith that the international community is able to organize its life without resorting to means which actually belong to a past epoch of human history.

However, the existing military blocs, which are growing into more and more powerful military, economic and political groupings, which, by the logic and nature of their mutual relations, necessarily provoke periodical aggravations of international relations.

The cold war and the constant and acute danger of its being transformed into actual war have become a part of the situation prevailing in international relations.

For all these reasons, the Heads of State and Representatives of Government of non-aligned countries wish, in this way, to draw the attention of the world community to the existing situation and to the necessity that all peoples should exert efforts to find a sure road towards the stabilization of peace.

II

The present-day world is characterized by the existence of different social systems. The participating countries do not consider that these differences constitute an insurmountable obstacle for the stabilization of peace, provided attempts at domination and interference in the internal development of other peoples and nations are ruled out.

All peoples and nations have to solve the problems of their own political, economic, social and cultural systems in accordance with their own conditions, needs and potentialities.

Furthermore, any attempt at imposing upon peoples one social or political system or another by force and from outside is a direct threat to world peace. The participating countries consider that under such conditions the principles of peaceful coexistence are the only alternative to the "cold war" and to a possible general nuclear catastrophe. Therefore, these principles - which include the right of peoples to self-determination, to independence and to the free determination of the forms and methods of economic, social and cultural development—must be the only basis of all international relations.

Active international cooperation in the fields of material and cultural exchanges among peoples is an essential means for the strengthening of confidence in the possibility of peaceful coexistence among States with different social systems.

The participants in the Conference emphasize, in this connexion, that the policy of coexistence amounts to an active effort towards the elimination of historical injustices and the liquidation of national oppression, guaranteeing, at the same time, to every people their independent development. Aware that ideological differences are necessarily a part of the growth of the human society, the participating countries consider that peoples and Governments shall refrain from any use of ideologies for the purpose of waging cold war, exercising pressure, or imposing their will.

III

The Heads of State or Government of non-aligned countries participating in the Conference are not making concrete proposals for the solution of all international disputes, and particularly disputes between the two blocs. They wish, above all, to draw attention to those acute problems of our time which must be solved rapidly, so that they should not lead to irreparable consequences.

In this respect, they particularly emphasize the need for a great sense of responsibility and realism when undertaking the solution of various problems resulting from differences in social systems.

The non-aligned countries represented at this Conference do not wish to form a new bloc and cannot be a bloc. They sincerely desire to cooperate with any Government which seeks to contribute to the strengthening of confidence and peace in the world. The non-aligned countries wish to proceed in this manner all the more so as they are aware that peace and stability in the world depend, to a considerable extent, on the mutual relations of the Great Powers;

(7)

Aware of this, the participants in the Conference consider it a matter of principle that the Great Powers take more determined action for the solving of various problems by means of negotiations, displaying at the same time the necessary constructive approach and readiness for reaching solutions which will be mutually acceptable and useful for world peace.

The participants in the Conference consider that, under present conditions, the existence and the activities of non-aligned countries in the interests of peace are one of the more important factors for safeguarding world peace.

The participants in the Conference consider it essential that the non-aligned countries should participate in solving outstanding international issues concerning peace and security in the world as none of them can remain unaffected by or indifferent to these issues.

They consider that the further extension of the non-committed area of the world constitutes the only possible and indispensable alternative to the policy of total division of the world into blocs, and intensification of cold war policies. The non-aligned countries provide encouragement and support to all peoples fighting for their independence and equality.

The participants in the Conference are convinced that the emergence of newly-liberated countries will further assist in narrowing of the area of bloc antagonisms and thus encourage all tendencies aimed at strengthening peace and promoting peaceful cooperation among independent and equal nations.

(8) BEO/6

1. The participants in the Conference solemnly reaffirm their support to the "Declaration on the Granting of Independence to Colonial Countries and Peoples", adopted at the 15th Session of the General Assembly of the United Nations and recommend the immediate unconditional, total and final abolition of colonialism and resolved to make a concerted effort to put an end to all types of new colonialism and imperialist domination in all its forms and manifestations.

2. The participants in the Conference demand that an immediate stop be put to armed action and repressive measures of any kind directed against dependent peoples to enable them to exercise peacefully and freely their right to complete independence and that the integrity of their national territory should be respected. Any aid given by any country to a colonial power in such suppression is contrary to the Charter of the United Nations.

   The participating countries respecting scrupulously the territorial integrity of all states oppose by all means any aims of annexation by other nations.

3. The participating countries consider the struggle of the people of Algeria for freedom, self-determination and independence, and for the integrity of its national territory including the Sahara, to be just and necessary and are, therefore, determined to extend to the people of Algeria all the possible support and aid. The Heads of State or Government are particularly gratified that

Algeria is represented at this Conference by its rightful representative, the Prime Minister of the Provisional Government of Algeria.

4. The participating countries drew attention with great concern to the developments in Angola and to the intolerable measures of repression taken by the Portuguese colonial authorities against the people of Angola and demand that an immediate end should be put to any further shedding of blood of the Angolan people, and the people of Angola should be assisted by all [...]

(9) BEO/6

[...] peace-loving countries, particularly member states of the United Nations, to establish their free and independent state without delay.

5. The participants in the Conference demand the immediate termination of all colonial occupation and the restoration of the territorial integrity to the rightful people in countries in which it has been violated in Asia, Africa and Latin America as well as the withdrawal of foreign forces from their national soil.

6. The participating countries demand the immediate evacuation of French armed forces from the whole of the Tunisian territory in accordance with the legitimate right of Tunisia to the exercise of its full national sovereignty.

7. The participating countries demand that the tragic events in the Congo must not be repeated and they feel that it is the duty of the world community to continue to do everything in its power in order to erase the consequences and to prevent any further foreign intervention in this young African state, and to enable the Congo to embark freely upon the road of its independent development based on respect for its sovereignty, unity and its territorial integrity.

8. The participants in the Conference resolutely condemn the policy of apartheid practised by the Union of South Africa and demand the immediate abandonment of this

policy. They further state that the policy of racial discrimination anywhere in the world constitutes a grave violation of the Charter of the United Nations and the Universal Declaration of Human Rights.

9. The participating countries declare solemnly the absolute respect of the rights of ethnic or religious minorities to be protected in particular against crimes of genocide or any other violation of their fundamental human rights.

(10) BEO/6

10. The participants in the Conference condemn the imperialist policies pursued in the Middle East, and declare their support for the full restoration of all the rights of the Arab people of Palestine in conformity with the Charter and resolutions of the United Nations.

11. The participating countries consider the establishment and maintenance of foreign military bases in the territories of other countries, particularly against their express will, a gross violation of the sovereignty of such States. They declare their full support to countries who are endeavouring to secure the vacation of these bases. They call upon those countries maintaining foreign bases to consider seriously their abolition as a contribution to world peace.

12. They also acknowledge that the North American military base at Guantanamo, Cuba, to the permanence of which the Government and people of Cuba have expressed their opposition, affects the sovereignty and territorial integrity of that country.

13. The participants in the Conference reaffirm their conviction that:

(a) All nations have the right of unity, self-determination.

and independence by virtue of which right they can determine their political status and freely pursue their economic, social and cultural development without intimidation or hindrance.

(b) All peoples may, for their own ends, freely dispose of their natural wealth and resources without prejudice to any obligations arising out of international economic co-operation, based upon the principle of mutual benefit, and international law. In no case may a people be deprived of its own means of subsistence.

(11) BEO/6

The participating countries believe that the right of Cuba as that of any other nation to freely choose their political and social systems in accordance with their own conditions, needs and possibilities should be respected.

14. The participating countries express their determination that no intimidation, interference or intervention should be brought to bear in the exercise of the right of self-determination of peoples including their right to pursue constructive and independent policies for the attainment and preservation of their sovereignty.

15. The participants in the Conference consider that disarmament is an imperative need and the most urgent task of mankind. A radical solution of this problem, which has become an urgent necessity in the present state of armaments, in the unanimous view of participating countries, can be achieved only by means of a general, complete and strictly and internationally controlled disarmament.

16. The Heads of State or Government point out that general and complete disarmament should include the elimination of armed forces, armaments, foreign bases, manufacture of arms as well as elimination of institutions and installations for military training, except for purposes of internal security; and the total prohibition of the production, possession and utilization of nuclear and thermo-nuclear arms, bacteriological and chemical weapons as well as the elimination of equipment and installations for the delivery and placement and operational use of weapons of mass destruction on national territories.

17. The participating countries call upon all States in general, and States exploring outer space at present in

particular, to undertake to use outer space exclusively for peaceful purposes. They expressed the hope that the international community will, through collective action, establish an international agency with a view to promote and coordinate the human actions in the field of international cooperation in the peaceful uses of outer space.

(12) BEO/6

18. The participants in the Conference urge the Great Powers to sign without further delay a treaty for general and complete disarmament in order to save mankind from the scourge of war and to release energy and resources now being spent on armaments to be used for the peaceful economic and social development of all mankind. The participating countries also consider that:

(a) The non-aligned Nations should be represented at all future world conferences on disarmament;

(b) All discussions on disarmament should be held under the auspices of the United Nations;

(c) General and complete disarmament should be guaranteed by an effective system of inspection and control, the teams of which should include members of non-aligned Nations.

19. The participants in the Conference consider it essential that an agreement on the prohibition of all nuclear and thermo-nuclear tests should be urgently concluded. With this aim in view, it is necessary that negotiations be immediately resumed, separately or as part of the negotiations on general disarmament. Meanwhile, the moratorium on the testing of all nuclear weapons should be resumed and observed by all countries.

20. The participants in the Conference recommend that the General Assembly of the United Nations should at its forthcoming session, adopt a decision on the convening either of a special session of the General Assembly of the United Nations devoted to discussion of disarmament or on the convening of a world disarmament conference under the auspices of the United Nations with a view to setting in motion the process of general disarmament.

21. The participants in the Conference consider that efforts should be made to remove economic inbalance inherited from colonialism and imperialism. They consider it necessary to close through accelerated economic, industrial and agricultural development, the ever-widening gap in the standards [...]

(13) BEO/6

[...] of living between the few economically advanced countries and the many economically less-developed countries. The participants in the Conference recommend the immediate establisment and operation of a United Nations Capital Development Fund.

They further agree to demand a just terms of trade for the economically less-developed countries and, in particular, constructive efforts to eliminate the excessive fluctuations in primary commodity trade and the restrictive measures and practices which adversely affect the trade and revenues of the newly-developing countries. In general, to demand that the fruits of the scientific and technological revolution be applied in all fields of economic development to hasten the achievement of international social justice.

22. The participating countries invite all the countries in the course of development to cooperate effectively in the economic and commercial fields so as to face the policies of pressure in the economic sphere, as well as the harmful results which may be created by the economic blocs of the industrial countries. They invite all the countries concerned to consider to convene, as soon as possible, an international conference to discuss their common problems and to reach an agreement on the ways and means of repelling all damage which may hinder their development; and to discuss and agree upon the most effective measures to ensure the realization of their economic and social development.

23. The countries participating in the Conference declare that the recipient countries must be free to determine the use of the economic and technical assistance which they receive, and to draw up their own plans and assign priorities in accordance with their needs.

24. The participating countries consider it essential that the General Assembly of the United Nations should, through the revision of the Charter, find a solution to the question of expanding the membership of the Security Council and of the Economic and Social Council in order to bring the composition and work of these two most important organs of the General Assembly into harmony with the needs of the Organisation and with the expanded membership of the United Nations.

25. The unity of the world Organisation and the assuring of the efficiency of its work make it absolutely necessary to evolve a more appropriate structure for the Secretariat of the United Nations, bearing in mind equitable regional distribution.

26 Those of the countries participating in the Conference who recognize the Government of the People's Republic of China recommend that the General Assembly in its forthcoming Session should accept the representatives of the Government of the People's Republic of China as the only legitimate representatives of that country in the United Nations.

27. The countries participating in the Conference consider that the German problem is not merely a regional problem but liable to exercise a decisive influence on the course of future developments in international relations.

Concerned at the developments which have led to the present acute aggravation of the situation in regard to Germany and Berlin, the participating countries call upon all parties concerned not to resort to or threaten the use of force to solve the German question or the problem of Berlin, in accordance with the appeal made by the Heads of State or Governments on 5 September, 1961.

The Heads of State or Government of non-aligned countries resolve that this Declaration should be forwarded to the United Nations and brought to the attention of all the Member States of the world Organisation. The present Declaration will be also forwarded to all the other States.

Armin Linke (AL) and Fabian Bechtle (FB)

NOTES TOWARDS A PHOTO ESSAY

with comments by Heike Behrend (HB), Radovan Cukić (RC), Dubravka Sekulić (DS), Sarah Poppel (SP), Philip Ursprung (PU), and Vanessa Vasić-Janeković (VVJ).

(PART 2)

1970_437_048

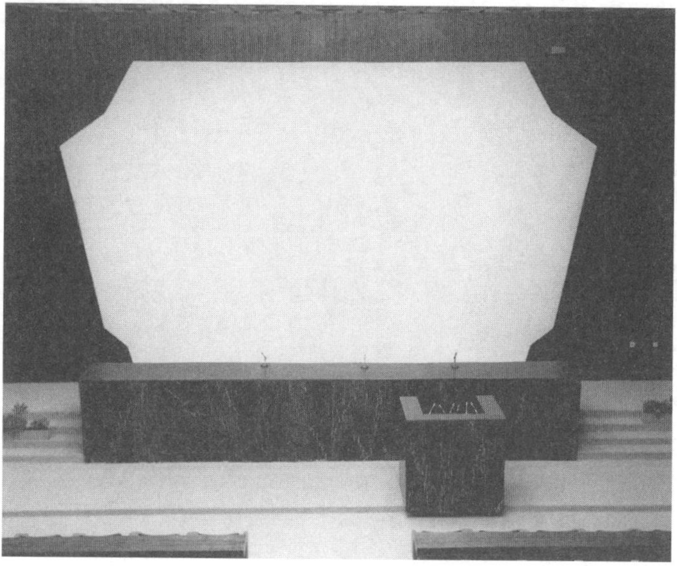

1970_437_048

Visiting the building of the Central Committee of the Communist League of the Socialist Republic of Macedonia. State: Yugoslavia (Macedonia); Location: Skopje; Keywords: Interior, League of Communists of Yugoslavia, Republic Authorities-Macedonia; Date: June 11, 1970

1968_365_058

Visiting the NHK TV and radio corporation studio set in Tokyo. State: Japan; Location: Tokyo; Keywords: Media-Radio and television; Bilateral Relations: Japan; Date: April 11, 1968

1968_365_058

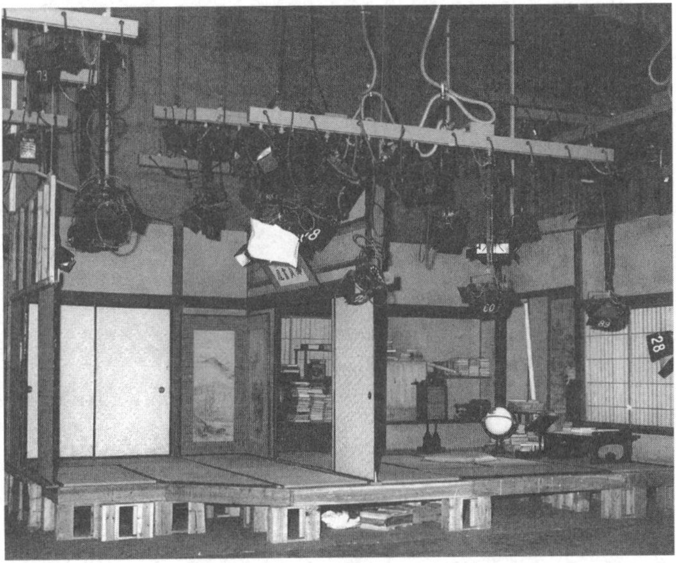

1971_469_071

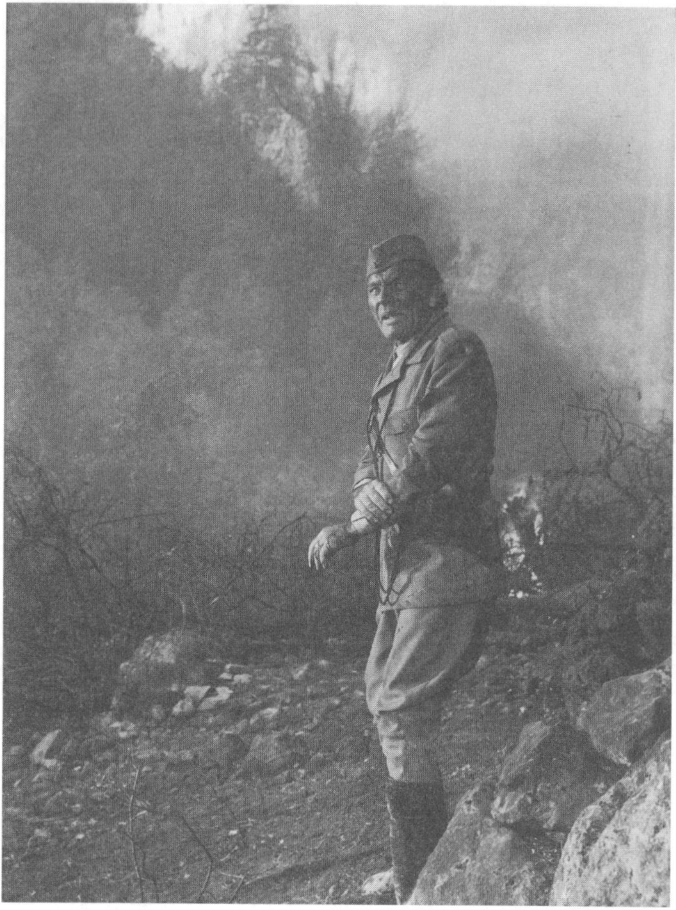

1971_469_071

At the filming of The Battle of Sutjeska (Sutjeska). State: Yugoslavia (BiH); Location: Tjentište; Personalities: Richard Burton; Keywords: Film, Anniversary, Veterans Associations of the People's Liberation War of Yugoslavia, Film workers; Date: September 5, 1971

FB — Sutjeska was one of the most expensive Yugoslav movies at that point; its very production reflected the international celebrity network Tito was cultivating. Burton plays Tito in this historical movie. He creates a fictional image out of the fictional image of Tito created by Tito himself—a movement of doubled fiction.

1971_468_215

Reception for local and international actors who worked on Sutjeska, on location in Tjentište. State: Yugoslavia (BiH); Location: Tjentište; Personalities: Richard Burton, Hardy Krüger, Jovanka Broz, Nikola Popović, Lijana Tambača, Ljubomir-Ljuba Tadić, Tomislav Pinter, Ružica Sokić, Relja Bašić, Ljubiša Samardžić, Neda Arnerić, Marko Vrhunec, Stipe Delić, Milan Vuković, Velimir-Bata Živojinović, Vlado Šegrt; Keywords: Film, Villa Sutjeska, Film workers; Date: September 4, 1971

1971_468_215

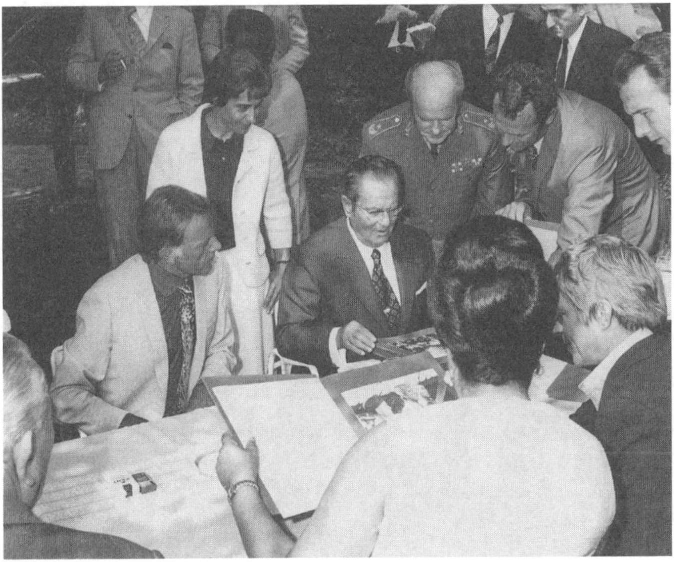

1968_352_136

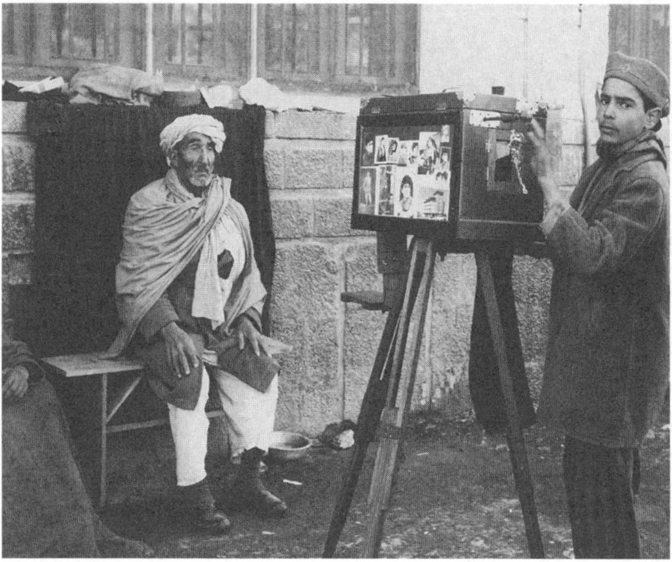

1968_352_136

Visit to Afghanistan: images from the streets of Kabul. State: Afghanistan; Location: Kabul;
Keywords: Panorama, Non-Aligned Movement; Bilateral Relations: Afghanistan; Date: January 8, 1968

HB — Here, the state enters the frame through the mobile, itinerant photographer: he takes passport photos for the state. These portraits then also enter the private domain, enacting a radical change. Before photography—especially in the Muslim countries—the dead were remembered only in space (the grave) and name. There were no images of ordinary people. Photography brought about a radical break, for the dead continue to have a face, a body—the very culture of death has been radically altered.

1968_365_152

Visit to Japan: the production lines in Matsushita Electric television factory. State: Japan; Location: Osaka; Keywords: Exterior, Receiving gifts, Book of impressions, Working collective, Industry-electronics; Bilateral Relations: Japan;
Date: April 12, 1968

AL — The mass of Matsushita workers is mass-producing mass media devices: television sets for the global market. To work in such an industry is to partake in a common script narrating shared aspirations of mass progress and consumption.

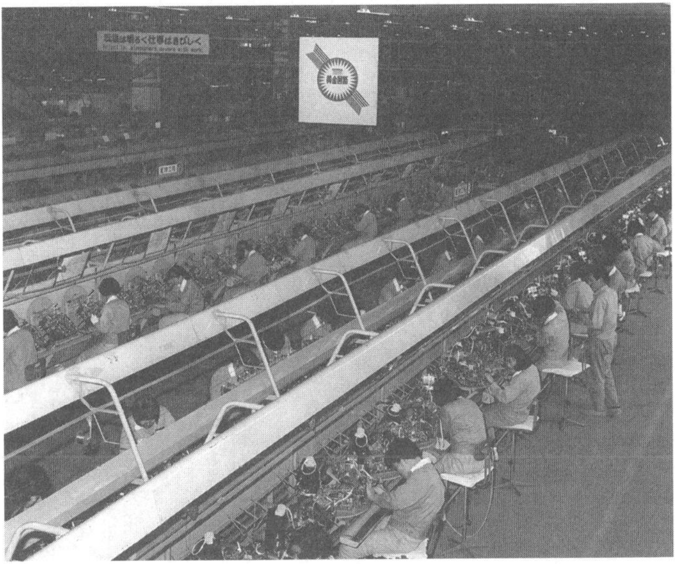

1959_108_0109

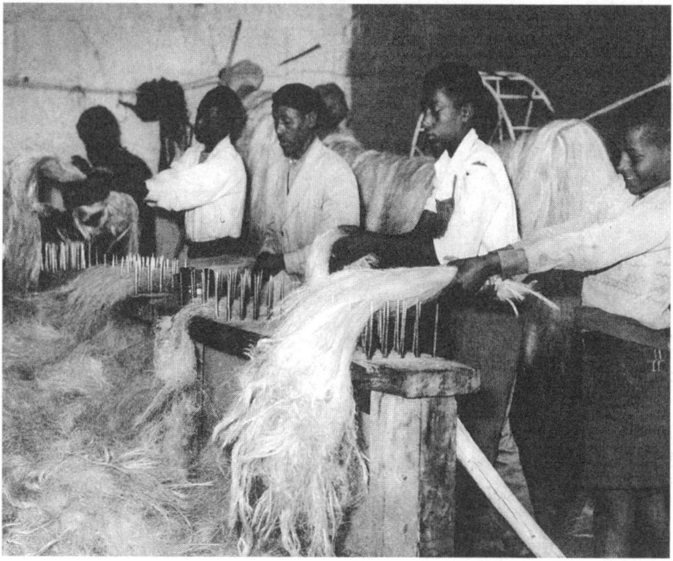

1959_108_0109

During Jovanka Broz's visit to a crafts school in Addis Ababa. State: Ethiopia; Location: Addis Ababa Keywords: Receiving gifts, Education, Crafts, First Lady; Bilateral Relations: Ethiopia; Date: February 12, 1959

AL — I see myself looking at these pictures with no tools to read them, as I belong to a generation that came fifty years later, and I am from a city. For me, the display of this technology seems somewhat exotic: it shows the dignity of traditional work. Though, perhaps at the moment this picture was taken, such display was a symbol of modernity and collective learning … we cannot know without exchanging information with those who know the context, who know how to read this image. I am interested in this contradiction and in this dialogue.

Armin Linke (AL) and Fabian Bechtle (FB)

NOTES TOWARDS A PHOTO ESSAY

PART 3 continues on page 193...

Elizabeth W. Giorgis

EMPEROR HAILE SELASSIE AND THE NON-ALIGNED MOVEMENT: IN CONTEXT

I set out to research Emperor Haile Selassie's role in the Non-Aligned Movement (NAM). During the research I came to realize the significance of the formation of the Organisation of African Unity (OAU) in this role. The broader framework of the Emperor's association with the NAM was shaped by different contestations preceding the ultimate realization of the OAU. The archive on this period is, similarly, a site of contestation, presenting quite a dilemma.

Selective silencing in the archives of contextually competing narratives forced me to look at the sixties from a different framework: childhood, revolution and exile, the destruction of an imperial center, seventeen years of repression and the allegorical context of radicalization. Such multi-layered significations adequately reflect the content and form of the historical, cultural and political implications that would comprehensively appropriate the past.

Interrogating the assumptions, implications and heuristics of the archive is therefore necessary for decoding its limits, structures of exclusion and the totality of temporal experience. The difference between archive and history is often not considered, indeed, one is often confused for the other. Archive as a space of deeply conflicting narratives offers possibilities for examining conflicts, which are, ultimately, the reason to engage in deconstructing the archival space. Deconstructing this skewed archive, however, requires sourcing other relevant archives. Where does one re-construct the archive from? This is particularly tricky in Ethiopia. A European archive of Ethiopia, of Ethiopian Studies, has historically, and "inclusively," had the European gaze, at times a racist, "noble savage" approach. Ethiopia had never been colonized. European archives reveal a troubling struggle to situate this "non-colonized subject" within a European discourse framed for a "colonized subject." There is a fascination amongst European scholars with the concept of Ethiopian mystic Christianity, distinguishing Ethiopia, supposedly an ancient Christian empire whose monarchs claimed to have descended from Solomon, as a "better African nation." Jules Leroy, one of the early European scholars writing on traditional Ethiopian art,[1] said

> Although the Ethiopian inhabits Africa, he is not an African in the usual sense in which the word is understood. His complexion, his physical features, as much as his language and original culture, declare him to be a Semite, related to the Arabs. It is this fact that Ethiopia is first and foremost a Christian country that gives her this individual character and ensures her a special place among the black African nations.

1. French specialist in the iconography of Near Eastern illuminated manuscripts and wall paintings, Jules Leroy, *Ethiopian Painting,* (London: Merlin Press, 1964), p. 35.

European scholarship thus frames Ethiopia within the contradictory narratives of exceptionalism and primitivism; the archive simultaneously denigrating as it "redeems" the Ethiopian subject. Despite such "redeeming" values, the archive rarely conceives the black Ethiopian subject as an independent creative subject.

The situation complicates with situating the Ethiopian archive in a position of power, as particularly apparent in the period in question. Neither the radicalization of the intellectual that inculcated the socio-economic impetus for the revolution, nor the central argument over territory and self-determination is discernible. Later archives attest to alternative frameworks: though also sites of contestations, they do signal a material foundation for different forms of inquiry.

I grew up in the sixties, in Addis Ababa, a time of transition from the colonial rule. After the global fall of colonialism, Ethiopia became the hub for the discourse of an African modernity in the making, a rallying site for Pan-Africanism,[2] with early writings of [W.E.B.] Du Bois and [Marcus] Garvey situating Ethiopia as the symbol and pride of black people.

In later movements, Aimé Césaire positions Ethiopia as a symbol of African Unity in his poem *Mon Ethiopie*.[3] This quest for continental unity and

2. In the African and African American imaginary, Ethiopia had always been a powerful nostalgic place of ancient society that spoke a written language and successfully drove off European colonization when the first black army defeated Italian attempt of colonization at the Battle of Adwa.
3. See also Fikru Gebre Kidan's *Bond without Blood*

integration took root in Addis Ababa in 1963, at the historic founding meeting of the OAU. Questions of power and agency of decolonization changed both the African geopolitical landscape and the politics of African culture and identity; the decolonization movement, charged with a radical popular consciousness, set the ground for innovations in theater, literature and art throughout the continent. In Addis Ababa, now a cultural intersection, vibrant Ethiopian literature and art movement emerged in seminal works such as Dagnachew Worku's *Adefres*, Bealu Girma's *Ke-Admas Bashager*, visual art of Skunder Boghossian and plays by Mengistu Lema and Tsgaye Gebre Medhin.

My older brothers were part of the decolonization movement galvanizing a supposing of a theory of social change, not necessarily or primarily against the colonial powers cultural hegemony, but against the ambiguities of modern citizenship in the Ethiopian state. Evening conversation in my parents' home revolved around historical, cultural and political conditions of the time. Too young to understand the historical order obliging such intellectual enterprises among my brothers and their friends, I was enthralled by the proclivity for debate on justice for humanity, by the impetus of attempting to achieve a fair and just organic unity between the cultural, moral, political and social spheres of African life.

Ethiopian intellectuals addressed central questions of modernity: the political divide of

(Ewing Township, NJ: Africa World Press, 2004), where he historicizes Ethiopia as a rallying imaginary in the movement of Pan-Africanism.

modernity and the emancipation of individuals and society from exploitation and political oppression. A new politics of knowledge was reflected in new ideals of state and nation: a budding intellectual student movement including my brothers thought Marxism a way to modernity. They challenged the Emperor's patronage of African anticolonial resistance, his rhetoric of "official nationalism" paradoxically reducing Ethiopian sovereignty to imperial ideology of the State and imperial institutionalization of Ethiopian nationalism. This group defied imperial rule in order to indict social inequalities. They produced texts informed by dissent, most notably Yohannes Admassu's *Este Teteyeku* [Let us ask you], Daganache Worku's *Adefres* [One who disturbs], Abe Gubegna's *Alewoledem* [I am not going to be born].

We must examine Emperor Haile Selassie's contribution to the NAM and his commitment to the OAU against this backdrop. Both movements had multiple manifestations of the decolonial episteme. Significantly, both served as strategic positions to quell opposing domestic and regional political projects. Examining them, not only in order to comprehend their corresponding desires, but also to fathom the Emperor's political intentions, is a difficult task. Most official archives, replete with daunting silence about domestic political troubles, positioned the Emperor as the creator, nurturer, and protector of the nation, as well as the emblem and torchbearer of African Unity. The Emperor played an important role in the OAU, remarked Andreas Eshete:

> In respect to Africa's liberation, it might suffice to cite: the moral, diplomatic and material support extended to liberation movements, among them, Mau Mau and the ANC; furnishing training and safe haven to freedom fighters; championing collective support to liberation movements, including a regime of the sanctions against South Africa; provision of a scholarship program to bring African Students for higher education to Ethiopia, following a pledge made at the 1958 Conference of Independent African States convened by Kwame Nkrumah in Accra. Similarly, extensive work was undertaken toward the making of the OAU: persuasion, in person or through distinguished envoys, of influential African leaders and Pan-African groups to embrace the idea; reconciliation of groups with rival conceptions and strategies for the realization of African unity.[4]

Whilst his contribution to the formation and evolution of the OAU is incontestable, abundant official archival representations situate the Emperor in an extravagant nationalist and internationalist discourse and imagination, as a spokesperson and vanguard for decolonization, disarmament and freedom of smaller nations to exercise their rights. In the opening speech of the second conference of the OAU, the Emperor said:

4. Andreas Eshete, "The Contribution of Emperor Haile Selassie and his Government to the Making of the OAU," speech given at the fiftieth anniversary of the OAU, July 27, 2013, Africa Hall, Addis Abbaba.

> Africans wanted to eradicate the dangers of Nuclear and thermo Nuclear war and were hoping for the success of this discussion by big powers in the United Nations. However, the failure of this discussion has worried all Africans. One cannot divide peace. For our countries to develop, peace is imperative. The limitation of armistice is important for Africans to have peace and we all need to work on that. While the discussion by big powers to create peace is important, smaller nations should also play vital roles.[5]

In September 1961, two years before the founding of the OAU, although with negotiations underway,[6] the Emperor attended the first NAM summit in Belgrade.[7] The summit centered on Cold War politics, emphasizing the need for self-determination and independence. The Emperor stated his position on self-determination thus:

> We are to discuss during this Conference, the right of peoples and nations to self-determination, a right which is an issue in various

5. *Addis Zemen*, January 1964.
6. Among the statesmen were Sukarno, President of Indonesia, Kwame Nkrumah, President of Ghana, Gamal Abdel Nasser, President of the Arab Republic of Egypt, Jawaharlal Nehru, Prime Minister of India, Josip Broz Tito, President of Yugoslavia and Emperor Haile Selassie of Ethiopia.
7. The Emperor had already visited Yugoslavia and Tito in 1954, setting the foundation for a long friendship with Tito, who visited Ethiopia in January 1956.

> regions of the world today. We are also called upon to reaffirm our respect for the sovereignty and territorial integrity of states and the principle of non-interference and non-intervention in their internal affairs, principles which have demonstrated their essential worth and validity in the field of international relations many times over and to which we believe all here are wholly dedicated.
>
> We deign to suggest that there is some inconsistency, some internal contradiction between these principles when closely linked together, whereas considered separately and apart, none would deny them at least lip service. Can a Government which overtly or covertly supports the violation of the territorial integrity of another state justify its actions on the ground that it seeks only to implement the principle of self-determination for all or a portion of the people of that nation? We think not. To contend contrariwise is to adopt the thesis of Adolf Hitler, who contended, in support of the action of the Third Reich in incorporating Austria into Germany, that "It is obvious that an idea embracing the entire German people and arising from its depths cannot be stopped at the frontiers of a country."[8]

These attempts to instill into public memory a representation of a conceptually insightful and progressive monarch are contrasted by three

8. Retrieved from http://www.black-king.net/haile%20selassie%2007e.htm.

important, if less well represented, political sequences: the failed 1960 coup and subsequent mobilization against the Emperor, and the Eritrean and Somali self-determination and independence struggles against the Ethiopian Empire.

The Emperor was discredited by the 1960 coup attempt orchestrated by Brigadier Mengistu Neway, Commander of the Imperial Bodyguard and his brother Garmame Neway, Cambridge University political science graduate. Mengistu Neway allegedly said at the time that, "Ethiopia shall never be the same again. Once we start the fire, it will burn on by itself."[9] The coup, which the Emperor stopped short by murdering its participants, radicalized intellectuals who later formed the Ethiopian Students Movement. As Andreas Eshete says, "the coup awakened the generation coming of age to the vulnerability of imperial rule and its claims to legitimacy."[10]

The second sequence culminated in the 1962 annexation of Eritrea by the Ethiopian empire, following ten years of political and armed resistance.[11]

9. Richard Greenfield, *Ethiopia: A New Political History* (New York: A. Praeger, 1965), p. 430.
10. Eshete, *Ibid.*
11. The history of Eritrea and Ethiopia had always been contested and contentious. Until 1950, Eritrea was under British military administration, following the Italian surrender in the Second World War. The British and the U.S. favored relinquishing Eritrea to Ethiopia, despite consistent requests by the Independence Bloc of Eritrean Parties to the UN General Assembly that the issue be decided in a referendum. In 1952, the UN resolution to federate Eritrea with Ethiopia went into effect. Militant opposition to this incorporation began in 1958. By 1962, the opposition was contained and Eritrea annexed.

Having failed to secure international support for their independence claims, Eritrean independence movements worked clandestinely in the late fifties; in 1960, students and intellectuals openly established the Eritrean Liberation Front in Cairo, signaling the start of guerrilla warfare.[12]

The third sequence lay in "Similar challenges [that] had arisen from Somalia with the establishment of a liberation movement seeking self-determination for Somalis inhabiting the Ogaden region."[13] Italian Somaliland was placed under British protectorate, which returned a part of it to Ethiopia. Just like in Eritrea, several movements continued opposing this throughout the sixties.[14] Eshete contextualizes the significance of these factors in shaping the role of Emperor Haile Selassie's vigorous involvement both in the OAU and in the NAM:

> Against this grim background, it should not come as a surprise that Haile Selassie should seek an African organisation that would honor the sanctity of existing borders and rule out in advance sub-national claims to self-determination, and intervention by any state in matters of internal governance. Admittedly, this stance and its defining stands were already

12. In the late sixties, the movement split, leading to a splinter group forming the Eritrean People's Liberation Front in the seventies; this left wing rebel movement conducted a guerilla activity until the EPRDF came to power in Ethiopia in 1991.
13. Eshete, *Ibid.*
14. Though guerrilla activities were sporadic after Somalia gained independence in 1960.

> embraced by the Non-Aligned Movement; and they were congenial to many African states, basking in newfound independence and vulnerable to sub-national cleavage and contest, and hence reluctant to allow limits on sovereignty.[15]

In many of his later speeches, the Emperor repeatedly emphasized the necessity for Africans to participate in the NAM and the OAU, not only to determine their own destiny, but also to curtail European interference in African internal affairs, perhaps most crucially in Ethiopia, where the disenchantment of young Ethiopian intellectuals began engendering the tumultuous history of Ethiopia that followed.

The Ethiopian Student Movement started out in 1960 with university students organizing in support of the failed coup. Ethiopian students' organizations such as the University Students Union in Addis Ababa (USUAA), Ethiopian Students World Wide Federation and the Ethiopian Student Union in North America (ESUNA) evolved out of this support. By the late sixties, these organizations emerged as Marxist opposition, advocating creation of a people's government. Their paper *Struggle* called for a violent revolutionary uprising against the Imperial regime. This movement also contributed to the coming of the Ethiopian Peoples' Revolutionary Party (EPRP) and All Ethiopian Socialist Movement (MEISONE), with key roles in the revolution of 1974.

15. Eshete, *Ibid.*

However, the 1974 revolution was hijacked by the Derg "socialist" military junta introducing seventeen years (1974–91)[16] of gruesome, Soviet-sponsored rule. Competing histories of Marxism went underground through various splintered armed movements of the Ethiopian Student Movement. The EPRP took to guerilla fighting against the Derg; MEISONE initially allied with the military junta, but later fell out. In 1979, the junta launched what is known as The Red Terror, supposedly to wipe out reactionaries detrimental to the revolution. Some of us were forced to flee into exile. Many remained, only to become witnesses of genocide, struggling, even today, to comprehend the losses of an exuberant time that failed its promises.[17]

The intellectuals of the fifties and sixties who changed Ethiopian modern history, were determined to modernize their country, free it from the shackles of poverty and ignorance. With an urgency to define the realm of the critical and ethical, they concentrated on subverting the dominant ideological

16. The Coordinating Committee of the Armed Forces, Police, and Territorial Army, or the Derg (Committee), was formed in June 1974 by military officers, following a mutiny by the military against the Emperor. There were originally 120 committee members, but the number fell as some members were expelled or killed. Mengistu Hailemariam was its chair.

17. This onslaught was mainly aimed at the momentum gained by the EPRP in guerilla warfare conducted both in the countryside and in the urban areas. Young students suspected of being EPRP members were massacred: Amnesty International estimated the deaths at over 500,000. Groups of people were herded into churches and burnt; women were systematically raped by the soldiers.

structures of society. While their concerns were crucial, necessary and candid, they unfortunately rethought history and human agency through a linear and teleological understanding of Marxist history. In the sixties, Marxism as a philosophy had provided several African governments with a moral order and a set of values. In Ethiopia, the paradoxical metaphors of the intellectual subject within this dynamic of Marxist-Leninist thought not only failed in questioning the Ethiopian present, but also did not perform, negotiate, or challenge the plurality of Marxism in various contexts or its multi directional flow of ideas at the global level. The revolution of 1974 emphasized a Marxist approach imbued with narrow empiricism and a penchant for broad Marxist theoretical generalization. No crisis in Ethiopian history has been as profound as this introduction of Marxism.

The reckoning of the social and political imaginary of decolonization was also gradually subsumed by different kinds of subordination in those African countries that, including Ethiopia, served as battlefields and proxies for the contradiction between the Soviet Union and the U.S. Values, ideologies and histories of decolonization were gradually fragmented. Decolonization, however, produced moments of inspiration and promise that linger in our political imaginaries. The founding of the NAM and the OAU were of such conceptual significance. While the OAU helped make more concrete the idea of Pan Africanism, the NAM established a decolonial perspective based on critical dialogue between various perspectives and insights of the global South.

While Emperor Haile Selassie played a pivotal role in the ethical and political projects of both movements, it is also important to critically reflect on the period from a broader canon of thought. Even though the archives[18] attempt to portray the Emperor as a magnanimous leader who fought tirelessly for previously colonized African countries and nobly agreed with the ideals of the NAM, it appears that his country's unique political trajectory more urgently dictated the conditions and extent of his involvement. Ethiopia's involvement in the NAM could not have been as significant had it not been for the Emperor's vigor and political whim, but the coordinates that recover the past should be open to possibilities of inquiry even as the recovery subverts overriding historical images.

I do not aim to conclude with the claim that strategy swallowed the symbolic and visionary. Despite the deep domestic disappointment, Emperor Haile Sellassie's masterful midwifery of the birth of the OAU is undoubtedly a jewel in his long, illustrious international career; moreover, the OAU's birth remains an enduring contribution to the Pan-African cause by the educated Ethiopian elite that then served the crown.[19]

18. I looked into all newspapers that pertained to the Non-Aligned Movement and the Organisation of African Unity. There are no books written on the Non-Aligned Movement. The formation of the OAU is referenced on various sources. Researched documents on the formation of the OAU could not be attained. Therefore, my main archival sources were newspapers such as the official state newspaper *Addis Zemen* and magazines published by the Ministry of Information such as *Menen*.
19. Eshete, *Ibid*.

Branimir Stojanović

PARTISAN HYSTERIA— THE TRUTH OF YUGOSLAV COMMUNISM

Subsequently on love

Have we loved, we who spoke so seldom of it,
for whom love was not a blinding drunken whirl
so you do not see and do not shout: against whom
the cavalry, against whom the gallop;
what are to you the nails and pliers, these shins and
that drill?

Have we loved, to whom the urgent always more
urgent would be;
than song and tale, when urgent were, more urgent,
proclamations and leaflets;
we busy by night, marching, by day sleepy, with a
song that stings
and sinks into sleep and flesh—like a bullet in the
body, unincisible?

Was that it—when you, before leaving, angled the
button to its loop
and lingered, felt the other blood, which can be felt
but beats not;
was it that—when you were, alone with yourself, both
eloquent and persuasive,
then in a meeting, in farewell—irrecuperably dry and
stuttering; ....

Radovan Zogović, 1943

"All resistance is a rupture with what is. For the one engaging in it, resistance begins through rapture with oneself. The philosophers of Resistance have already indicated that this fact is in relation of the order of thought.

For this is the end signification of [Georges] Canguilhem's "resistance by logic." *Stating what is and drawing conclusions from that statement represent a process of thought, for an illiterate peasant as well as for a philosopher.* [Emph. B.S.] This operation, though entirely natural and practical in its Real, does not refer to objective analysis of social groups or to previously formulated views. Those who do not participate in rebellion, save the collaborationist clique whose non-participation is a conscious choice, are simply those who do not wish to clearly state their views on the situation, not even to themselves. To claim they do not think is no exaggeration. More accurately, they do not think the Real of the present situation, they refuse to accept that the Real could be, for them personally, a bearer of possibility, as is every Real when our thought, as [Sylvain] Lazarus states somewhat later, is in a relation of it."

(Alain Badiou, *Abrege de metapolitique* [Seuil, 1998], p. 16, translation into Serbian by Branimir Stojanović.)

This quote is part of the conclusion of Alain Badiou's text on French Resistance, or rather, on philosophers of the Resistance movement, introducing a collection of texts entitled *Kratak kurs metapolitike* [A Short Course in Metapolitics]—*Abrege de metapolitique.* It drew my attention as the first contemporary philosophical thematization of politics of Resistance to Nazism in the Second World War; or rather because it leans onto a simple, to me very familiar, axiom, one that Badiou's teacher expressed twenty years after the war in his farewell to [Jean] Cavaillès, the great French mathematician and epistemologist, his comrade in the Resistance, with these words, "Cavaillès was resistant by logic." I heard this stance on resistance by logic, formulated at about the same time as Canguilhem's, from my father, an engineer and mathematician. At that moment, he was dressed in the Territorial Defence uniform, mobilised in the then Yugoslavia as part of a preventative, defensive state manoeuvre following Soviet occupation of Czechoslovakia. When he appeared in our flat, in uniform, holding a weapon, I asked, frightened, "How will you go to war? You are not a soldier, you are an engineer." He replied, "I have already been to war, as a young man." When I asked, "Why did you go to war as a child?" he replied, "It was logical."

If resistance by logic existed in Yugoslavia as an operation of thought, what about philosophers of Resistance, do they exist and did they exist? There are no philosophers of Resistance today, but, to add to confusion, there exist in Serbia philosophers of counter-revolution who, for some reason, use

Badiou's language of the critique of counter-revolution. I am referring here to the translation of and the confusion over the translation of Badiou's *Abrege de metapolitique*. The book appeared in Serbian translation in 2007, titled *Pregled metapolitike* [The Overview of Metapolitics]. This translation reeks of ideological formaldehyde, archaisms and newly coined phantasmatic language, to such an extent that I had to translate the conclusion anew (the part I needed), for Badiou's words sounded like a Slavoserbian liturgy held in an eighteenth century provincial church in Vojvodina.

The very translation of the title *Abrege de metapolitique* into *Pregled metapolitike* is the first misunderstanding of Badiou by the translator and the publisher. Moreover, this translation eloquently presents the tragic circumstances of current cultural production in Serbia. By avoiding to translate the title as *Kratak kurs...* [A Short Course], as was obviously Badiou's intention, an allusion to the left political imaginarium he is part of, the translator and the editor acted out of fear that this would sound Stalinist and repulse the audience it was intended for: the political and intellectual body of the most extreme representative of the Thermidore of Yugoslav revolution, as well as of revisionism and denial of the outcome of the Second World War. Even more confusingly, Badiou's *Abrege de metapolitique* is a polemic with current political and philosophical ideologies participating in the politics of Thermidore and counter-revolution. It is a paradox of progressivist ideology that the philosophers of counter-revolution have imported the critique of counter-revolution. This ideology today speaks the language of the right and counter-revolution. Even in Socialism, in which it was forged, its function was, as it is now, to overturn the logic of revolutionary politics into the calm waters of bourgeois ideology.

The introductory text of *Abrege de metapolitique*, "Philosophers of Resistance," has a dual function: to show that when it comes to politics, the philosopher is, as any human, hung only and alone onto a simple operation of thought in relation of the Real, coinciding with his stated stance of refusal of what is, and his logical deduction of consequent conclusions from it; or rather, Badiou in 1998, when writing this text, applies this simple stance of refusal to the moment of articulating his own thought-Real relation through which he breaks with the political reality of France then, and yet, more so of France today in her renewal of Pétainist ideology. The text itself is a call to resistance through the axiom: resistance is logical and all resistance is resistance by logic against what is.

Even more importantly for us: what happened to that simple axiom in the former Yugoslavia, the axiom I heard from my father when he said: "It was logical?" "It was logical" referred to a high school pupil joining the Partisans and participating in the People's Liberation Struggle (PLS).

The difference between the time in which my father put his engagement in the PLS as "logical" and the time in which local counter-revolutionary intelligentsia speaks in the language of the critique of counter-revolution is the difference between the times of two theses—at the end of the sixties it was:

"all of Serbia was resistant," whilst in 2007, when Badiou's book was published, the opposite held: "all of Serbia were *Nedićevci*."[1] The two statements are not simply false; they are devoid of any sense. Resistance by logic, expressed in "rebellion is logical," belongs to rare moments of production of politics of truth, irreducible to numbers and statistics, or to belonging to an exclusive social group; nor is it recognizable in universal logical quantificators: on the contrary, this stance is an exclusively personal act, stripped of any connection with the collective; it draws its certainty from itself, at the cost of rupture with itself and through the necessity of rupture with itself; it is, therefore, not a phenomenon of class or ethics, even less so of a moral position—it is a matter of logic.

If it is, however, utterly clear why neo-Nedićist ideology today refuses to face the meaninglessness of "all of Serbia were *Nedićevci*," what about "all of Serbia was resistant," the statement that has in Yugoslavia been masking any practice of "rebellion is logical," and what are the conditions of speaking about it today?

PERIODIZATION

How do we relate to the PLS today when collaborationist ideology has become the dominant ideology of the states established on the soil of former Yugoslavia? When they either vehemently

1. Nedićevci were members of the quisling regime and its military/police apparatus in power during the terror of occupied Serbia, from 1941–44. They were named after Milan Nedić, their Prime Minister.

distance themselves from the PLS, and criminalize it, or attempt to Europeanize and normalize it through a newly created antifascist matrix? The People's Liberation Struggle is a forgotten and excluded political sequence of their shared history, the only political event in the twentieth-century history of all the Yugoslav peoples. Where does, then, this ambivalence towards the PLS stem from?

It is the thesis of this text that the PLS was, strictly speaking, already excluded as a political sequence in the epoch of socialism, through traditionalization and rituals of celebration, precisely because the nature of politics it produced excludes domination and exclusivity of the Party-State. The PLS is, therefore, a political sequence that saturates and questions the Party-State. Oskar Davičo[2] noted this erasure at the height of Yugoslav self-managing socialism, as early as 1967, when he said, "There are no more revolutionary communists today. The nationalists took over the state apparatuses in culture, and we must ascertain that the revolutionary communists have lost the political battle." The syntagm revolutionary communist referred to those faithful to the PLS, those engaged in political struggle against nationalism, which was growing within the Communist Party elites. At the same time and at the height of the Cultural Revolution, Mao Zedong said, "Under socialism, the bourgeoisie has reconstituted and reorganized itself within the Communist Party."

2. Leading Yugoslav novelist and poet (1909–1989), the most acclaimed Serbian surrealist writer and a revolutionary communist activist.

However, a question arises that is not only historical, but a very current political question: what gives unity to a politics if it is not directly guaranteed by formal unity of the state? The basic, fully standardized historical narrative of the PLS presumes that the PLS was a political-military formation of the guerrilla type, which, led by the Communist Party, defeated German National Socialism and quisling regimes created through occupation; after the war, the Communist Party carried out a socialist revolution, took over the state apparatus and formed the Socialist Federal Republic of Yugoslavia (SFRY). This historical account, accurate in any case, agreed upon by all, presumes an inevitable link between the PLS and the SFRY; or rather, without the SFRY the PLS would not have been a political sequence with its own logic; or rather the PLS necessarily presumes the state to be direct product of its political activity. In other words, PLS begins with the Communist Party declaration calling for uprising against the occupation in July 1941, and ends on May 15, 1945 with victory over National Socialism.

This standardized version of the history of the Second World War is the official historiographical version of the history of the Communist Party. It is also the official version of the history of the SFRY. It remains unproblematized and non-thematised, even by its political enemies. This periodization of the PLS is only viable if we accept it from the perspective of the SFRY state history, from the perspective of the Party-State with its own criteria: civic stability, productivity, certain stability at the top of administrative leadership, and unity and cohesion of the army. However, if we use as a criterion the collective thinking of politics that the PLS sequence is, which is a feature of emancipatory politics *par exellence* or of politics as invention, the periodization is entirely different. In that case, the PLS is a separate political sequence lasting from December 1941 to May 1943. This is the revolutionary sequence of the PLS, tied to political activity of the masses, their own words, forms of organizing and places. Politics of the Communist Party in this period is revolutionary politics—it is only in this sequence that the Communist Party is entirely distanced from the Stalinist Party's formalist and terrorist model. For the PLS has, even as it ceased to exist as a political sequence, imparted a lasting and constitutive tear into the Party-State of the Stalinist type. Moreover, the revolutionary sequence of the Communist Party is also its political sequence, but its example had to be forgotten after the war, given the Party-State tendency to ban politics, especially politics that bring masses into politics. In another register, the PLS politics begins with *Dijalektički antibarbarus*[3] [Dialectical Antibarbarus] by Miroslav Krleža,[4] in 1939, continues in Radovan Zogović's[5] 1941–43 cycle of

3. *Pečat*, No. 8-9 (Zagreb, 1939).
4. One of the most significant Yugoslav authors of the twentieth century (1893-1981), certainly the most significant intellectual of the Yugoslav left.
5. One of the greatest Yugoslav poets (1907–1986), a communist activist, co-founder of the Partisan movement and member of the General Staff of the PLS, Zogović fell out of favour with the Communist Party in 1948 and spent over a decade under house arrest, until a semi-rehabilitation in the sixties.

poems and ends with Oskar Davičo's politics of faithfulness to the PLS, from 1967–79, or rather with the philosophical sequence of the *Praxis* school between 1950 and 1960, but this is another history, one that this text will not be engaging with.

The PLS is then, a thorough implosion of all the axiomatic party principles. The PLS is, moreover, the bearer of or the other name of politics in which it is no longer possible to uniformly signify neither the action by the revolutionary mass, nor its organizational phenomena, nor the strict logic of class representation—all that the formalist terror of a Stalinist Party rests upon. The PLS is the greatest secret of the later socialist state, a secret that had to be hidden and its effects and practices ritualized and traditionalized—as in [Maurice] Merleau-Ponty's "tradition is the oblivion of origin"—so as to return to standard forms of class representations of the "workers' state," traditional forms of political organization, and especially to forget that masses ought to be included in politics. Instead of involving the masses in politics, the Communist Party had, after the war was over and the state stabilized, brought the masses into governance of the state, the industry and the economy, but excluded the possibility of political subjectivation.

KOZARA 1943

Official historiography and post-war psychiatry agree that Partisan war neurosis, later termed Partisan hysteria, appeared among partisan troops on the Kozara mountain[6], in late spring and early summer of

1943, afflicting young, immature, uneducated and, as referred to in some psychiatric reports, "primitive" fighters in Partisan units. This is how Hugo Klajn, a psychoanalyst and psychiatrist from Belgrade, the author of the only book on Partisan hysteria, titled *Ratna neuroza Jugoslovena* [Yugoslav War Neurosis] described an appearance of Partisan hysteria:

> The neurotic lays on the ground ... screams, "Attack! Forward proletarians, brothers, fighters, comrades!" or a similar battle cry. Eyes closed, his breathing is loud and fast and whilst lying on the ground, he raises his knees, kicks his chest, his head stuck to the ground, he waves his arms with fisted hands. He imitates the positions, movements and sounds of shooting from a rifle or another weapon, bomb throwing; he lies back down and moves his legs as if marching, running or jumping. ... He takes prisoners, knocks the enemy to the ground, shoots him, slits his throat... he swears, shouts, telephones, sends telegraphic messages, drives a truck, drinks alcohol, to good health of his dead comrades. Some, once they are calmer, talk about their comrades, remembering their sacrifices and achievements and complain about those who do not treat them in an appropriate manner.

This account of Partisan hysteria concerns one of over two hundred cases Klajn encountered directly during his research, testifying to the epidemic

6. Western Bosnia.

proportions of the illness. From its appearance in 1943 to its disappearance in 1947, thousands of Partisan fighters were taken ill.

Significantly for us, it was within this complicated and unexplored sequence of modern Yugoslav psychiatry, in the early phase of forming the new SFRY state mechanisms, that the psychiatry and the Party forged and constructed the discourse and ideology of enlightenment and progressivism—they became the closest, most significant partners in the operation of normalizing, traditionalizing, primitivizing and folklorizing the PLS. Though for different reasons, both the Communist Party and Yugoslav psychiatry agree that this illness represents "teething troubles of the new order." It follows that the PLS fighters hit by neurosis are immature, illiterate, primitive and mainly young people who cannot adapt to new conditions, to the needs of forming new state that now faces great tasks for which she needs mature, literate, enlightened citizens. Both military and civilian psychiatry hold that the primitive hysteric ought to be subjected to a process of education and cultivation, and freed from his symptom (civilian psychiatry became involved because of the high caseload).

What is, however, the symptom of Partisan hysteria? It is an excess of belligerence, which the subject knows not what to do with under new conditions. Accounts of treatment attempts in psychiatric institutions show that any such attempt brings about annihilation of mechanisms that define an institution. Almost at once, fighters rebel, self-organize, obstruct hospital hierarchy and take control over the institution they were brought into. The type of solidarity and personal bonds forged among Partisan fighters is, simply, destructive for any system attempting to separate or individualize them. Dr. Nadežda Jeftić reports on an interesting case[7] involving three female and a male fighter brought together from the battlefield with the same symptom: refusal to be separated and gender segregated, despite many (failed) attempts by hospital staff. Attempts to explain hospital rules of gender separation induced eruptions of fury: the four fighters attacked staff, destroyed wantonly, and thoroughly obstructed the functioning of the hospital system. During the rare, brief separations, the three female fighters slept in the same bed and would not communicate with staff until the male joined them. The Communist Party saw in the afflicted fighters a potentially dangerous enemy whom it characterized as politically illiterate, with suspicious political positions, an easy prey for political manipulation, completely ignorant of the Party history and the body of Marxist ideas, belonging primarily to the peasantry, not the workers—in brief, the hysterics do not understand the Party language...

Neither the Party nor psychiatry understands Partisan fighters; the psychoanalyst Hugo Klajn alone does. His study *Ratna neuroza Jugoslovena*, though written in 1945, was not published until 1955; censored by military authorities, it only existed as an internal report he wrote for the Military Medical Academy in Belgrade. Klajn was the first to refer to

7. Arhiv Srbije [The Archive of Serbia], G-222, K-120, F-20888 (Belgrade).

the Yugoslav war neurosis as hysteria. Other psychiatrists were more inclined to refer to this illness neutrally as war neurosis, even pseudo-epilepsy. For us, it is important to ascertain that the diagnosis of hysteria remained under military censorship and that the book had been unknown outside the very narrow professional circles until as late as 1991, when it was published again.

Hugo Klajn understands that excess belligerence remains non-thematized as the main symptom in Partisan hysteria. Klajn circles around it in his text, but does not manage to conceptualize it outside the language of the standard conflict of the hysterical patient, his complicated libidinal economy of guilt and his demand for recognition. In other words, Klajn understands that excess belligerence and demand for recognition are in direct relation, or rather, that the hysterical subject is trapped in the logic: the more recognized, the less satisfied; or there is no recognition that could satisfy Partisan hysteric. Hysteric is the subject of desire *par exellence* and no object is good enough to him. His economy is hung on an impossible demand: I want this and that, but only provided it does not exist; or translated into the field of social discourse: I want a master on the condition that there isn't one. Following the failure by all objects to satisfy his desire, one radical demand remains, not to not desire anything any longer, but to desire: nothing. Hysteric is a radical nihilist. His radical nihilism, however, is merely a reaction to traumatic desubjectivation, the moment of interruption in the flux of desire. In other words, what does the Partisan hysteric desire and what does he mourn?

To us, Partisan hysteria is, therefore, an indicator of the ceasing of a type of subjectivity, of radical desubjectivation of the political subject forged in the PLS. Hysteric is the place of rupture of this political subject and of its transfer into another regime of production of politics. Primitive, young, uneducated and violent hysterics were nothing but a remainder of a political subjectivation within the regime of "resistance by logic" or the logic of rebellion through which they constructed radical conclusions: their own words, slogans, political declarations, places, forms of organizing, theatre, newspapers and their own logic of functioning that, whilst placing them within the regime of revolutionary politics, transcended each of them individually. Hysteric is thus the index of a radical collective thinking of politics, equally, as Badiou puts it, "for an illiterate peasant as well as for a philosopher." Partisan hysteric is but the materialization and the place of transition and demobilization of the revolutionary subject—political subject *par exellence*—and at the same time the place of traumatic memory of disappearance of the flux of desire, disappearance of political subjectivity. He is the site at which the rituals mourning the loss of political subjectivity are enacted by playing out the most traumatic moments of the Partisan war through loss representable to others: acting out mortal danger, losing comrades, mobilizing for attack, slaughter...

The truth of Partisan hysteria is simple: the political subject of the PLS was dismantled in May 1943. It left behind a form of hysterized individual who then, without a political subject and in the only way left at his disposal, acts out and conveys the truth about its existence through materialization in a symptom: belligerence. Hysteria is a reaction to the moment of renaming the subject of politics: Narodno-oslobodilačka borba [People's Liberation Struggle] into a military formation: Narodno-oslobodilačka vojska [People's Liberation Army]. The renaming operation caused a tear in the political subject, dislocating it dramatically—from the revolutionary mass and popular movement into the military formation. Through ritualized belligerence, Partisan hysteric testifies that PLS, the political subject, is lost and that Partisan struggle or politics production has been replaced by a military formation. This is why Partisan hysteric is basically in the right, and this is the moment of the analysis that Klajn leaves unthematised: hysteric will never receive the recognition that he participated in creating a political subject, for the revolutionary political subject is anonymous. All other recognitions on offer belong to a wholly different plane and utterly miss the flux of his desire for recognition.

Partisan hysteric is a figure of politics with two simultaneous significations: there is revolutionary politics and (unfortunately) there is no longer any. This ambivalence was built into the SFRY construct, and it was her permanent subjective condition. Namely, the SFRY was always hung on a single subjective condition: there is revolutionary politics. In other words, she was not even a state, but a temporary site of demobilization of the political subject of the PLS, or the site of hysteric's ambivalence. When it became clear that the SFRY had surpassed the ambivalence built into her foundation, when she definitely decided that she is a state, or rather when she started believing she is a state and took a thoroughly cynical attitude to her key subjective condition—there is revolutionary politics!—she lost the reason to exist and, in reality, lived through what the Partisan hysteric acted out in his ritualized performances of the loss of political subjectivity: death, killing, suffering, destruction... no longer, however, in the modus of political subject, but in a modus of counter-revolution—collective serial killers murdering the weakest, the poorest and the most powerless civilians, in fact, those that the progressivist ideology had described, forty five years earlier, in treating hysterics, as illiterate, young, primitive peasants throughout the SFRY.

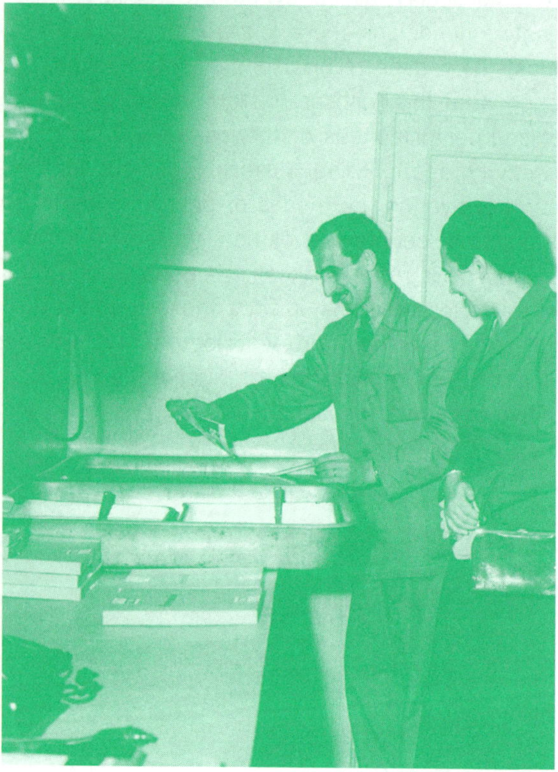

1956_056_016 Jovanka Broz visiting the Press Department of the Cabinet of the President of the Republic, May 19, 1956

MEMORANDUM
Attn: comrade Bogdan Crnobrnja

At your request, I will set forth the shortcomings in the functioning of the Photo Department in the order of phases of the work process and offer suggestions on how to overcome them.

RECORDING is done using three different techniques:
Recording on black and white film,
Recording on color slides and
Recording on three-dimensional color slides.

Recording on black and white film is the main activity and is carried out for the purposes of
archive documents,
sets of photographs for comrade President,
sets of photographs for guests,
meeting the requirements of the press
books and publications and
propaganda material.

The archive contains a large number of recorded negatives, very few of which are usable, because the photographing was entirely done only with the aim of recording the events, without the sense of spotting and highlighting crucial moments. There are hundreds of negatives where comrade President is stepping on the ship, stepping off the ship, getting in and out of the car, shaking hands with people whose identity is unknown and in neither of these pictures can be seen whether the events took place in Belgrade, Cairo, or in India.

Recording is done without taking the setting or the time of events into account which, in addition to the protagonists, are the main factors in a picture. Such an approach is a consequence of the low level of general education of news photographers. Even when some aesthetic quality is found, it is due to chance, rather than the outcome of a conscious pursuit within the limits of the possible.

Great quantity, which is inevitable, especially on journeys, because of special circumstances, should result in quality.

Recording should be regarded as creation of a serious and comprehensive chronicle of one's time, where every major event is to be a well-rounded entity, as far as content is concerned and whose most important moments are to be highlighted.

The place and angle of recording must be chosen on the spot, taking facial expressions and movements of chief protagonists into account—these are the aesthetic qualities that should be consciously insisted on.

RECORDING TECHNIQUE

The department has more than ten different cameras for recording, only five of which are usually usable. None of the news photographers is issued cameras, instead, they all use the ones that are in working order together.

It is absolutely necessary that every news photographer has his own cameras and gear, allowing successful recording of events at a greater distance (even up to 250 m), as well as at normal and very small distance (recording in crowds and in cramped rooms. Every news photographer should be personally issued with these items, which will ensure better care and maintenance of equipment.

A news photographer brings at least four different cameras when recording major events (which leaves a tremendous impression on the uninformed). Every camera requires its own exposure, methods of rewinding and changing the film, even holding and operating the device, which is determined by its technical construction. Simultaneous use of different types of cameras makes the photographer very distracted for these genuine reasons, which is one of the causes of poor results.

This approach to work must yield high quality results too. Given the seriousness and historic importance of our activity, technical issues must not affect the results. The modernization of technical equipment is inevitable.

RECORDING MATERIAL—FILMS—is procured depending on the current availability on the market, rather than on technical specifications and experience.

The same type of films of the highest quality should constantly be used, since that is the only way to discover its potential.

It is absolutely necessary to introduce the use of high sensitivity films that appeared on the market four years ago. In this way, the flash would no longer be used, wherever there is enough light. (Many world famous news photographers do not use the flash at all). Before these films appeared, the flash had been adopted in the domain of photography as the necessary means of lighting the scene. It has numerous limitations, but let us mention just the following:

— It creates frontal flat lighting which deadens the atmosphere and deprives the picture of its natural setting.
— Its use makes the people in the picture look unnatural after the first flash. They lose their natural movements and posture, so the photograph looks unreal, arranged—and not like a frozen natural moment in time, which is the aim of contemporary photography.
— Medical specialists are qualified to talk about adverse effects of the flash on the eyes. Experience shows that a strong flash makes the eyes briefly incapable of seeing light from other sources.

The flash should remain in use only in darker rooms.

COLOR RECORDING has been done in a small 24x36 mm (Leica) format up to now. According to the experts on printing color photographs, this format is too small. The needs of the graphic industry require a bigger format, such as 6x6 or 6x9 cm.

This problem is latent for now, because we still do not have magazines that publish color photo reports. However, when building up an archive, the development of the visual means necessary for communication in the future must be taken into account. (Illustrated papers are replacing text-oriented ones a bit and color television is becoming the most important means of communication with audiences).

In order to achieve high quality color photographs, photographers must learn the basics of art education, which means that they have to be familiar with color as an aesthetic phenomenon, the symbolism of color and its other characteristics.

It is absolutely necessary to master the process of recording on color negatives and developing color photographs. Color has its own expression and brings qualities into photography that are incomparable to the black and white technology. Black and white photos will eventually be treated in the same way as we treat silent films today.

THREE-DIMENSIONAL TECHNOLOGY. This technology is used for recording on color slides, which is commendable as a far as adopting the latest technological advancements is concerned. However, adopting a technical procedure in an unqualified manner, instead of consciously mastering it, does not lead to progress. The appropriate technical innovations should be used as a means of putting certain ideas into action, rather than creating fancy effects.

Three-dimensional technology should be used for recording the events taking place in wide spaces with a lot of depth (rallies, motorcades, walks through crowds of people, deep landscapes) since, this kind of event can, in fact, be represented in the most realistic way possible by using this method.

RECORDING is a creative activity that in addition to the compulsory high level of craftsmanship requires a sense of spotting the most important and most suitable moments. Photographers should have a solid general and political education in order to be able to fully represent, in the form of photographic documents, the importance of the events that are being dealt with. They must continuously read professional literature and prepare for every major event in advance.

WORK IN THE LABORATORY

The work is done in the most primitive of ways. Films are developed by hand, which causes the emulsion to become damaged by nails and leads to a wide variety of chemical errors (smudges, stains and the like). Because of the huge scope of work, negatives often dry in the corridor and in the rooms, which leaves them exposed to dust.

The chemicals used for work are prepared in an unprofessional way, without taking into account the principles of photo chemistry.

Since such an approach to work does not ensure that proper technical procedure is adhered to, the entire organization of work in the laboratory needs changing. The work process should be organized in accordance with the highest achievements of contemporary photo chemistry. The laboratory must make provisions for the negatives to be kept up-to date and make sure that their chemical durability is not compromised; these are its most important tasks.

The work in the laboratory is a craft, which requires laboratory technicians to have knowledge of the fundamentals of photo chemistry and be immaculately tidy and clean in the process of developing negatives and making photographs.

MAKING SETS OF PHOTOGRAPHS

Stricter criteria should be applied when preparing the albums given to the guests of comrade President. Insignificant photographs should not be insisted on.

Previous practice consisting of putting photos in book-shaped boxes should be replaced by placing them in well-designed albums.

ARCHIVE

The work in the archive has not been done in a timely manner, due to the illness of comrade Zdenka and the current scope of activities. Just systematizing the whole of the archive, by gluing contact prints into albums, and their synchronized marking in chronological order is a task that would take one clerk around four years to complete. The entire archive consists of over one hundred thousand photographic recordings. It is necessary to bring at least the files on current events up to date.

The best negatives should be immediately set aside and their duplicates made. These copies should be used for everyday purposes, while the originals are to be put in some secure safe and guarded as the most authentic historical facts. This is necessary because negatives gradually deteriorate due to prolonged use and because accidental loss of the original negatives is utterly irreparable. (The French keep the original negatives made by their photographers who won national acclaim for their artistic achievements in the safes of their national bank. We still have not developed the tradition of creating such archives that are, in fact, the most credible witness of the development of our society. The original photographs of the works on the Brčko–Banovići railway have already become a rarity today, while the negatives of the 1946 May 1st celebrations held in Belgrade can be found only in our archive in Belgrade).

The activities in the domain of archiving should be broadened to include collecting the best photographs of comrade President, made by the photographers of local and foreign newspapers.

ORGANIZATION OF WORK

The organization of work should be completely changed, because the process of making photographs implemented in an ordinary photographer's shop cannot meet the needs of a modern department like ours. The system of work, where the same individuals are both news photographers and laboratory technicians cannot ensure efficiency in a situation where there is a huge and diverse need for shooting and printing photographs. This is the main reason for tardiness and poor results.

In addition to a laboratory organized in accordance with modern principles, an organization of work that would be modernized in its entirety and based on the use of the latest methods for performing tasks quickly and conforming to quality standards is required so that our needs can be met.

The work in the laboratory should be done in two shifts and recording separated from laboratory work. This would solve a number of current problems.

The ways of putting our archive to a wider use should be devised, with the aim of informing the public better. Some material should be used for putting on exhibitions on current topics (especially in the course of journeys), while colour slides should be shown during lectures on the same themes. This is how the archive would become more dynamic and functional. Naturally, special attention should be paid to quality as part of these activities.

I have proposed the majority of these ideas, aimed at improvement and continuous development of photography in the country at the working meetings at the Press Department, but since they have been rejected every time, I would like to ask you for a face-to-face conversation when you have read this memorandum.

September 13, 1963
Belgrade

M. Lovrić

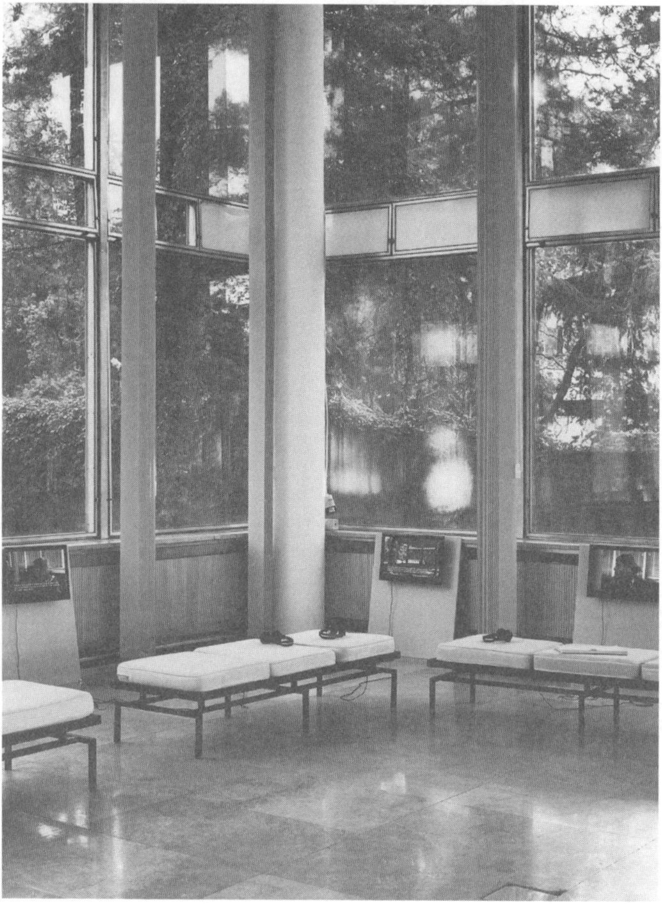

In Conversation, a series of recorded interviews (2012–2014): Mirko Lovrić and Olga Manojlović Pintar, Fabian Bechtle; Miroslav Mladenović and Radovan Cukić; Momo Cvijović and Milica Tomić; Katarina Živanović and Fabian Bechtle; Pramod Kumar and Armin Linke; installation view, Museum of Yugoslav History, Belgrade, 2014

IN CONVERSATION WITH MIRKO LOVRIĆ
Olga Manojlović Pintar

Museum of Yugoslav History,
Belgrade, July 2012

Mirko Lovrić was one of the official photographers of Yugoslav President Josip Broz Tito. In the sixties he was documenting his life and activities, accompanying him on numerous travels in Yugoslavia and abroad. He developed precise professional standards for the Photo Service of the Press Department of the Cabinet of the President of Yugoslavia. This interview with Mirko Lovrić, made for the Travelling Communiqué project, deals with the methodology of his work and the organization of the Photo Service. It was based on a Professional Note written by Mirko Lovrić to the General Secretary of the President's Cabinet, in which Lovrić proposed technical improvements, archiving of photographic materials, as well as professional training for photo reporters and other associates.

Olga Manojlović Pintar: Your first positions after graduation were in the Četvrti juli publishing house and in the 25 May Museum.[1]

Mirko Lovrić: I wanted to work with *Politika* or *Borba*, then the leading daily newspapers here. However,

1. Muzej 25. Maj, established in 1962 in order to exhibit and care for presents given to President Josip Broz Tito, whose birthday was celebrated on May 25. The Museum is now part of the Musem of Yugoslav History.

they couldn't employ me immediately. A colleague thought it unlikely they would employ me at all, as their photo department chiefs had no formal photographic education and might fear I would jeopardize their positions. He told me, "You know, I have a relative working for the *Četvrti juli* magazine and he says they need a photo reporter. Go talk to them, they will employ you immediately." I didn't have any money and I wanted a job, so I went to see them and they employed me. I worked there for several months.

In the meantime, Bogdan Crnobrnja, who was the General Secretary to the [Cabinet of the] President of the Republic, recommended me for the presidential Photo Service. Crnobrnja was a Partisan war commander in the area we lived in during the war. He commanded my brother, my sisters and my father, and they later socialized in Belgrade. Crnobrnja even attended my graduation celebration. He knew me and knew my work.

As it happened, during a presidential visit to South America, a colleague employed by the presidential Photo Service made a mistake, a gaffe —and you know that South American countries observed the strictest protocol, akin to the early nineteenth century court protocol. The hosts laughed; it was quite an embarrassment, and Tito was very sensitive. He objected to Crnobrnja for not having chosen better associates. Tito said, "By Mother of God, how can we not, in this country, among so many millions, have a single educated photographer who can behave in society?" Crnobrnja replied: "Well, there happens to be one, he has just graduated, and has strong photographic education."— "Please, bring him here tomorrow!"

Of course, it couldn't happen overnight. When they did call me, I left *Četvrti juli*—they were unhappy, angry even, as they had only just established their photographic department. I was first invited to work as a curator at the 25 May Museum. I understood this was to give them time to inspect my soul and my social circle, my propriety, for no one could come near comrade President unless they had been thoroughly checked. The director of the museum was [Vladeta] Petrić, a sculptor. He put me to work on cataloguing — measuring and describing relay batons[2] for the museum records. It took several months until certain comrades determined I was an utterly correct person, from an appropriate, revolutionary family. Only then could I join the Photo Service. My first assignment was photographing the new Indian ambassador [Kewal] Singh, later a famous Foreign Secretary, presenting his credentials. My new colleagues did not accept me eagerly: I differed somehow, was not from the same milieu. We did work together and performed our duties successfully, or as well as it was expected.

OMP: Could you tell us more about the organization of the Service itself?

ML: When I joined, Miloš Rašeta, Aleksandar Stojanović and Dragoslav Grbić were already working there.

2. Relay batons were carried in the *Relay of Youth*, a relay race held every year to mark Tito's birthday. The museum houses the collection of these batons.

After a few months, Grbić went to *Politika*'s photo department. That left three of us in photography, working in the lab at the same time. Later on, the service employed a laboratory assistant, photographer Mileva Pilipović. We also trained a lady, named Mara, I don't recall her last name, who was a cleaner, in some basic lab tasks, such as rinsing and drying photographs. At first, our offices and photo lab were on the third floor. During a subsequent renovation, I proposed new office space and an entire plan for the organization of work in the Photo Service. I visited photo departments in the Belgrade press, in Zagreb's *Vjesnik* daily, at the Secretariat of the Interior Affairs in Zagreb, *Delo* in Ljubljana, and requested information on the organization of large photo departments in the world. I prepared our program on that basis. Our Photo Service was part of the Press Department of the President's Cabinet, headed by Tihomir Stanojević, which had two journalists and a typist, a secretary.

I was made the head of the Photo Service, formed as a new small organization. We moved into new offices, with better conditions: a very practical, spacious laboratory in which we could print large quantities of photographs. Protocol courtesy meant that we sent photographs to all who were photographed with Tito on May 25, his birthday, for example, or on his visits to working communities[3]

3. "Radna zajednica" denotes a community of people working together. English language authors of works on Yugoslav self-governance use either "work collective" (Susan Woodward) or "work community" (Dennison Rusinow). We chose "community" as closer to the original meaning encompassing the collective (as in "agricultural collective," for example).

around the world. All of Tito's guests, heads of state from around the world, received large sets [of photographs] during their visits. We would print the photographs while they were still here and bind them into books, with captions. They would then be given to their Protocol Offices, before their departure.

For example, Iranian Shah [Reza] Pahlavi sent a message through the protocol, alongside a large sum of money to me as a gift, because I photographed his visit to Yugoslavia. He said that when he gave it to his wife, Empress Farah Diba, who couldn't join him because she was pregnant, she said, "I feel like I was there with you, I can see how well you were welcomed!"

We were able to print a thousand photos in a day then. Two of us, or even all three, worked in the lab—one would expose, the other would process, the third one rinse, and we had big rollers for drying. The photos were then all sorted and sent to people who appeared on them with Tito. Of course, many made quite a name for themselves on the back of such photographs. For them Tito was like an emperor, this is how they treated him. Tito had something of an aura of a deity, of course, mostly among his associates.

> OMP: After a year at the Photo Service you wrote a professional note,[4] addressed directly to Bogdan Crnobrnja. There you expressed your views of the situation in the Photo Service and made precise proposals for upgrading and

4. See MEMORANDUM, p. 137.

professionalizing its work. This document covers several aspects, from your attempt to make qualitative changes in your work, ranging from technical conditions, to put it that way, to direct changes in photographers' or photo reporters' way of thinking and working, to the way of archiving these documents.

ML: I detected some weaknesses in our way of working. Although more of an artist by inner impulse, more interested in problems relating to the essence of the photographic medium, I did master the basics of photo reportage and documentary photography. My job then was related, in fact, to what is today known as news photography or photojournalism, to creating comprehensive visual documentation. I advocated for an authentic document with answers to the five journalist's questions—where, who, when, why, how—so that it can be immediately clear to anyone looking at the photo who the main figures are, where it is taking place, etc.

I also tried to bring in some of my artistic desires, so to speak, so that this visual chronicle attains another dimension, now known as metaphotography; so that other layers could be found beneath the surface layer and read through a different analysis. Perhaps this would then be from an aesthetic perspective, having exhausted the possibilities of the documentary, the authenticity, the character of the basic carriers of an event, as we would say then. Photoreporters the world over use the term, as in "I'm going to an event."

I endeavoured to enrich our activity, to function

beyond an authentic testimony, to be a richer visual chronicle or presentation of everything we photograph. To achieve that, one must master the technical aspects of photography, its technology: this means cameras, it means films, it means expanding the laboratory, etc. It means to turn the flash off where possible, because the flash strongly unifies the surroundings, it unifies the event itself.

Photographing, for example, in Tito's big cabinet, in front of the big painting that is here [in the Museum] now, would be photographing an event with the highest regard for protocol, such as the presentation of credentials. Tito stands on one side, and the formally attired ambassador on the other. He introduces himself to Tito and presents him with the documents. The only change [from photograph to photograph] is the ambassador. Everything else is there and one could easily do it in Photoshop today, just change the characters. However, I always advocated ambient atmosphere for each event, I wanted to weave it into the fibre of all our photographs. I have always maintained that a photograph should be a note of the entire atmosphere of the event. That's why I had this idea. I knew Crnobrnja to be an educatod, open-minded man, a revolutionary not just by profession. I was very lucky to have had him as a boss, so we could achieve some minor things. To achieve more, I needed colleagues with ideas at least similar to mine, similar educational experiences, but also similar attitudes to art and photography. Unfortunately, not all that I have envisioned could be realized. You know the situation then, personnel changes were not easy, and there was a lot of work. It was a golden age of news photography in the world and all the great magazines, such as *Life*, *Paris Match*, etc., German magazines were on the rise too, wanted photos of Tito and Jovanka [Broz].

The improvements were mostly technical. We were always given the cameras we requested. It was hard work being a photo reporter in those days, especially when travelling, it was complicated and physically exhausting. We always carried three or four cameras, big heavy flashes with batteries, as well as back-up batteries, because we would have to shoot up to a thousand photos by noon. We usually shot in six by six format, mainly using Rolleiflex cameras, a normal Rolleiflex and one with a wide-angle lens. We had to have a back-up camera, and we usually shot slides on a Leica. I guess those slides were preserved..

Photo reporters from big agencies and papers often came to visit us. That is how I first came into contact with Magnum photo reporters. I also met Lord Snowdon, brother-in-law to the Queen of England, who came to photograph Tito. World famous photographers came, such as Yousuf Karsh, who came to photograph a movie co-production, and secured a permission, through the Canadian ambassador, to take photos of Tito. He made very good portraits of Tito, which must be here somewhere. He shot them in large format, fifty by sixty, thirty by forty? They are very good portraits, typically Karsh in style, with very sharp facial characteristics. That was the first time I could talk with photo reporters of world renown.

I selected photographs for foreign magazine requests. The procedure was such that one received the original note of request and a demand from the protocol to make a selection of photos and slides, which would then be given to Tito to review. A sentence would be written, usually, "I agree" and his signature. You certainly have many of those documents around. I was in charge of this selection for years and Tito never had any objections.

> OMP: You had a clear idea of the kind of photos he liked and preferred to be made public. Could you tell us what kind of photos they were, what did he confidently release to the public eye?

ML: He permitted publication of any photos pleasant to the eye, shall we say, photos that had some content, that looked good, he didn't have any special demands. But I knew it was appropriate to send to England photos of his meeting some English actors, or to send to France photographs of a meeting with [Jean-Paul] Sartre or French actors; that the Italians would be eager to see Mario del Monaco with Tito, and I paid attention to such matters.

He did not have any immediate demands. As a somewhat eccentric man, an artist, and all artists are a little weird, I had some of my own ideas, but those were met without objections. I was frequently in contact with Tito and sometimes I helped him in his laboratory on the island of Vanga [Brijuni, Croatia]. He had a laboratory in Belgrade and a laboratory on Vanga. Of course, I was told a hundred times, to only answer questions, and not state my opinions and ideas. It was a general order to all the associates allowed to accompany him.

> OMP: In the description of your duties it states that, among other things you do, you take photographs with Tito's camera. Does it mean you took some photos which...

ML: ...which are on his camera? Yes. He liked to take photos, he did it himself, but he often gave his camera to his photographer and said, "Take a photo of all of us here now."

Tito would address me formally, as "vi" [personal pronoun you, as in French "vous"], which made me feel uneasy in the presence of other ministers or generals, whom he usually addressed informally as "ti" [or the archaic "thou," as in French "tu"]. I said to Crnobrnja on one occasion, "You know, I feel uneasy when the President addresses me formally, he addresses all of his other associates informally." And he told me, "Shut up, you fool, others would give both their hands for your status, it means he truly appreciates you and your work."

Later on, I wanted to go freelance, for many reasons that I do not wish to mention now. One of the important reasons was that during the Cairo conference I contracted some sort of African liver inflammation, and barely survived. I spent several months at the Military Medical Academy. I wanted, in fact, to be an artist. It was never my idea to be a photo reporter, a documentary chronicler of, I don't know, society. There was little scope for the mini revolution I wanted within the Photo Service, because my co-workers were not interested. Instead, there were opponents, demanding that everything be kept at the level already established, using fixed practices. The art of photography was on a tremendous upwards curve, undergoing technological, visual, aesthetic development. I wanted for us to follow that development, to create a service at a certain level. I resigned and had some difficulties, for everybody thought me insane: a big limo would pick me up for a shoot, I had a relatively good salary and the like, why leave? Not to mention that everyone in the old Yugoslavia tried very hard to get as close as they could to comrade President.

However, I arrived to the service as a formed artist. It was not a launching pad for my art career at all. I had an established photographic practice [outside the Photo Service]; I was in demand by many architects in Belgrade and working for some of the famous TV shows. I could work twenty-four hours a day and still have a lot of work at all times. Finally I left the Photo Service.

OMP: One gets the impression, in fact, that you had more difficulties in working with your colleagues in tho service. Were there any directions, any kind of censorship, or any cloar signs as to what was not desirable? Were any negatives left out or not included in the archive?

ML: There was no such control, or any directions, as the Central Committee would put it, because we were making a visual chronicle of events that had already been through the filtering. The only thing we were being told by these guardians of souls was to keep reiterating to comrade President that chemicals used in color photography were very poisonous so as to put him off his idea of making color photographs. In fact, these party ideologues, or whatever they were, held that he wasted too much on photography. Otherwise, no direct bans were imposed, no destruction of material.

> OMP: I have a technical question. When you had to send photos to national and foreign press, did you send negatives, copies of negatives or did you send prints?

ML: We would only send prints, with the exception of the leading international color magazines, to which we sent slides. Sometimes these slides were returned, sometimes not. We would only lend negatives to Tanjug [Yugoslav news agency], those that would be printed in the daily press. For example, if comrade Tito meets with Sartre today, and the only photo reporter present is from the Photo Service, then the film is processed immediately and index prints are ready an hour and a half later. We pick one or two best shots, and wait for the courier from Tanjug to take them, so that Tanjug can send photos to domestic press, and wire associated agencies around the world.

> OMP: In this note we mentioned, you discuss, among other things, the preservation of documents. One can see how aware you are of the significance of preserving negatives and of

the need to archive them. Did your co-workers support you in this?

ML: My co-workers supported me in a sense that they were, despite lacking somewhat in education, aware of the fact they were creating historical material. This was an extremely important aspect, this knowledge that what they were photographing was a testimony of a kind. And they also endeavoured, at my insistence, not to take photos in a primitive sense, only of the main figures of an event, but to encompass a somewhat wider environment. That is why you can see in all those photos, say, of hunting in Karađorđevo [Serbia], wall decorations, the arrangement of the dinner table for the diplomatic corps, etc. We photographed the surroundings, which, in fact, contributed to the main content [of the photograph].

OMP: You insist that quantity does not always mean quality. You have demanded that the work of the photographer does not remain fixed at the level of continued accumulation of photographs, but to rely on an active contribution, thinking on the part of photo reporters on which moments to capture and how. Did you have the opportunity to suggest a certain photo to Tito, to place him in a certain spot, or did photographs always depend on his attending to his activities?

ML: It happened very rarely. We made large portraits of him collectively: we told him to sit down, to stand in certain spots and so on. Or, for example, if a newspaper asked for photographs of Tito at his home, for new, unpublished photographs, then we would come and take photos of him in his study and the like, of Jovanka reading, or the two of them looking at something, their poodles or similar. We could, in those cases, ask him to move here or there, turn this way or that. Otherwise, we were only able to take photos as the events in front of us unfolded. There weren't many moments when we could place him anywhere or anything of the sort.

OMP: When you compare yourself, for example, to you colleagues from Tanjug, *Politika*, or *Vjesnik*, in the former Yugoslavia, were your work conditions better or at the same level?

ML: They were better. We were privileged. We could ask for new cameras, make a lab that absolutely fits required standards. They would always reply to our requests. And, finally, we were paid better than photographers in the press.

This interview is an extract from a conversation conducted by the historian Olga Manojlović Pintar, in July 2012. The interview was conceived in collaboration with Armin Linke, Ivan Manojlović, Doreen Mende, Mirjana Slavković and Milica Tomić. Mirko Lovrić died in June 2013.

CONVERSATION BETWEEN RADOVAN CUKIĆ, IVAN MANOJLOVIĆ, SARAH POPPEL AND VANESSA VASIĆ-JANEKOVIĆ

Ivan Manojlović: Opening the MYH to artists, especially in the frame of the *Travelling Communiqué* exhibition/project has created a strange, yet liberating position for the museum: it gave up its role of being the sole interpreter and transmitter of the archive, becoming, instead open to new views and readings. Working sessions with artists offered an expansion of possible views or readings of photographs. From our perspectives as researchers or curators, we tend to look at photographs as visual documentation.

We were questioning our approach, as we started with this memo by Mirko Lovrić that we found in the Archive of Yugoslavia (as well as other textual documents that we exhibited), which elaborates the problems photographers faced when covering diplomatic events. We can read between the lines that Lovrić's intention was to provide the broader context of events, that somehow photographs should visualize even the political relations between countries whose statesmen visit each other. He succeeded in some elements—looking at his photos from Tito's visit to Japan, for example, which we exhibited as part of our contribution, he managed to depict the highly complex relation between the two statesmen, Tito and the Japanese Emperor Hirohito.

Lovrić wanted the viewer to be able to recognize the kind of relationship Yugoslavia had with each country at the time these photographs were taken. Of course, this may be a goal set too high, but in some elements, on some of the visits we analyzed, this relationship is obvious.

> Radovan Cukić: We selected eight of Tito's travels in total: to the United Kingdom in 1953, France in 1956, USSR in 1956, Ghana in 1961, Mexico in 1963, Japan in 1968, China in 1977, and to the U.S. in 1978. We wanted to present relations with the Eastern bloc and the Western bloc, as well as with the Non-Aligned Countries, to present the differences in protocol and behavior during these encounters.

IM: Yes, we selected these travels as they cover the Eastern and the Western bloc countries, as well as some Non-Aligned Countries. Tito travelled as one of the promoters of the Non-Aligned Movement, so we selected events in order to cover aspects of diplomatic activity and show how they cover diplomatic relations, but also as events historically important for Yugoslavia. We tried to find a pattern of moments within these events, to see how these moments are connected to pre-scripted diplomatic activities.

We realized that by consulting programs of diplomatic visits in the Archive of Yugoslavia, we were able to predict what kinds of photographs we would find in our archive. We wanted to show this connection between an archive of written documents and our archive of photographic records, so we extracted photographs for our contribution in this way. Then, simply by comparing photographs of different events/visits, we obtained some basic insights: for example, you can see how the body of the ruler, of the president, is presented in the photographs. Radovan wrote about this too.

When we extracted photographs from the archive for the exhibition and positioned them next to each other, by certain moments, we could see differences in Tito's attitude towards different statesmen. There is a marked difference between his body language and communication with African leaders, and the leaders from, let's say, Western countries.

Sarah Poppel: How would you describe the difference?

IM: It is obvious that Tito felt closer to the African leaders, the relations are more friendly than diplomatic—this is a matter of diplomatic tradition too, but it also speaks about Tito's relationships to certain leader. There is another crucial aspect to this distinction. When they took Tito sightseeing in Non-Aligned or Eastern bloc countries, they would usually take him to see factories, or construction sites—scenes of the renewal of the country, whilst in the Western countries they would usually take him to see traditional heritage: operas, museums, etc. I am generalizing a little, but this pattern is clearly observable.

Vanessa Vasić-Janeković: This really delineates the post-colonial condition, does it not?

IM: Yes, in a way, and there is a logical explanation, this is something that Radovan, Mira [Mirjana

Slavković] and I talked about. Tito saw the countries of the Non-Aligned Movement as a huge market. As you know, Yugoslavia did a lot of construction work in these countries, especially in Africa. This opportunity for another market is now being recognized by historians and economic historians studying Non-Alignment: as some Yugoslav products were not meant to be sold in the West because of the political situation, but also as not competitive enough for those markets, Yugoslavia had to find new markets.

VVJ: It seems to chime with that part of the idea of the Non-Aligned Movement that concerns independent economic development...

IM: Yes, of course, and this economic cooperation was very welcome in the Non-Aligned Countries. Accepting goods and products from Yugoslavia meant avoiding to be seen as being colonized all over again.

This conversation between Radovan Cukić, Ivan Manojlović, Sarah Poppel and Vanessa Vasić-Janeković was held in May 2015.

IMAGES FROM *A VIEW OF THE PICTURE OF POLITICAL POWER* (2014)

A selection from the MYH Research Group's contribution to the *Travelling Communiqué* exhibition.

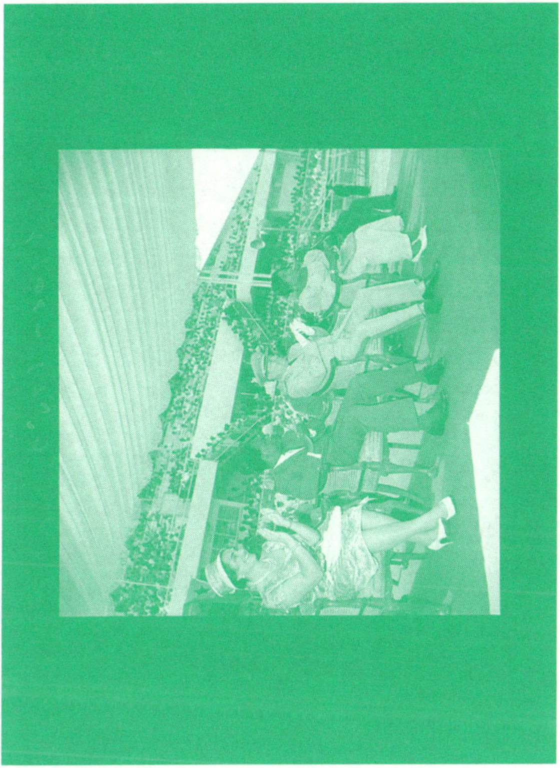

1961_151_0095
Visit to Ghana: a parade of social organizations in Accra, March 1, 1961

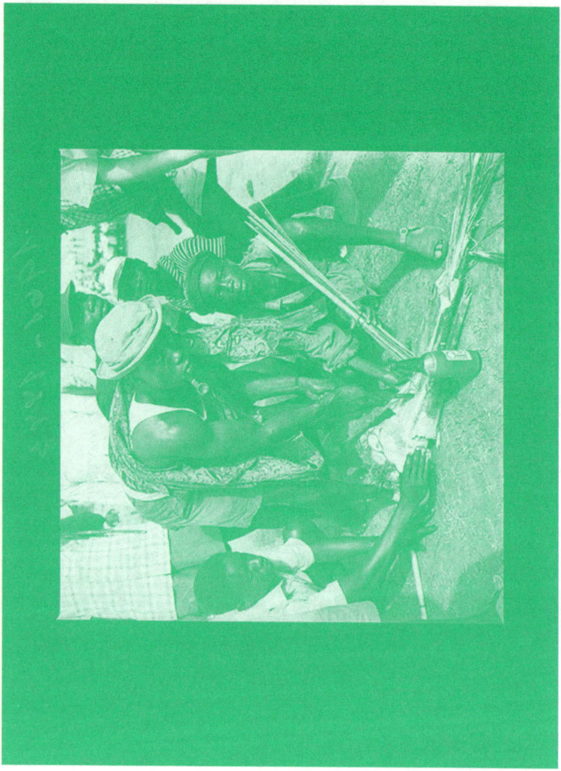

1961_128_3488_1443 (contactsheet only)
Visit to Ghana: a parade of social organizations in Accra, March 1, 1961

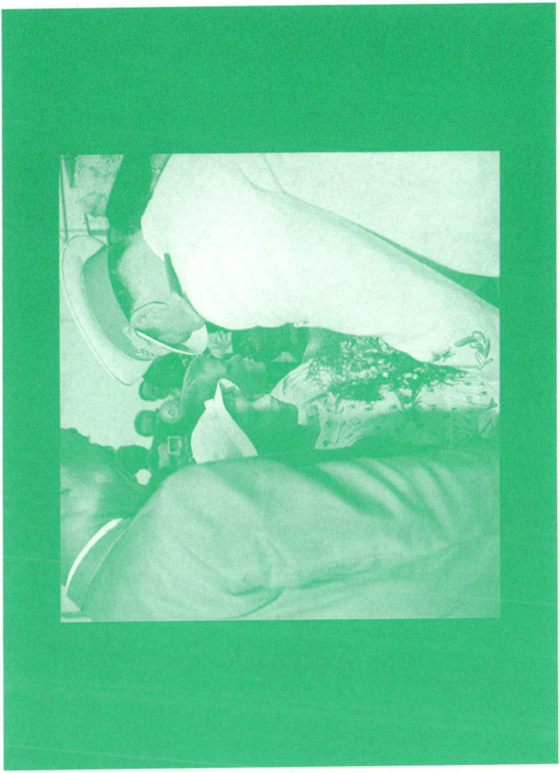

1961_151_0095 (contactsheet only)
Visit in Moscow: visit to a Moscow car factory and speech at a rally in the factory, June 5, 1956

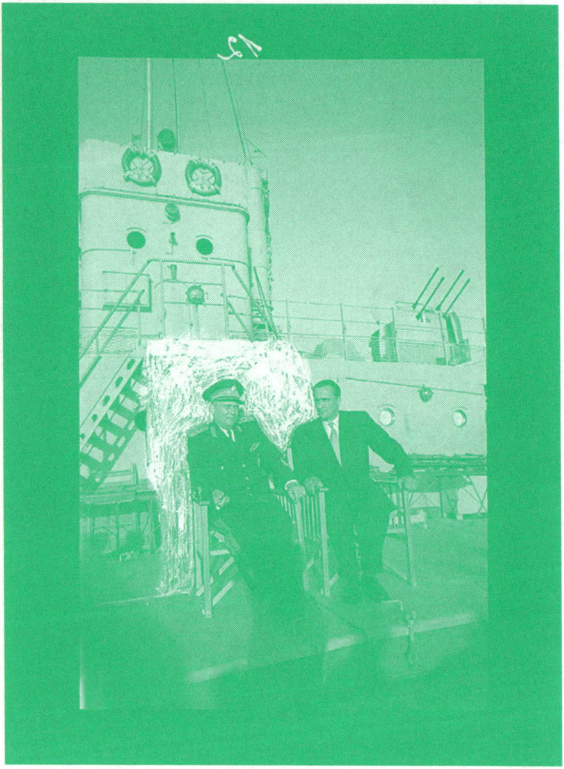

1953_025_859_012 (contactsheet only)
On "Galeb" [the presidential ship], returning from Great Britain, March 29, 1953

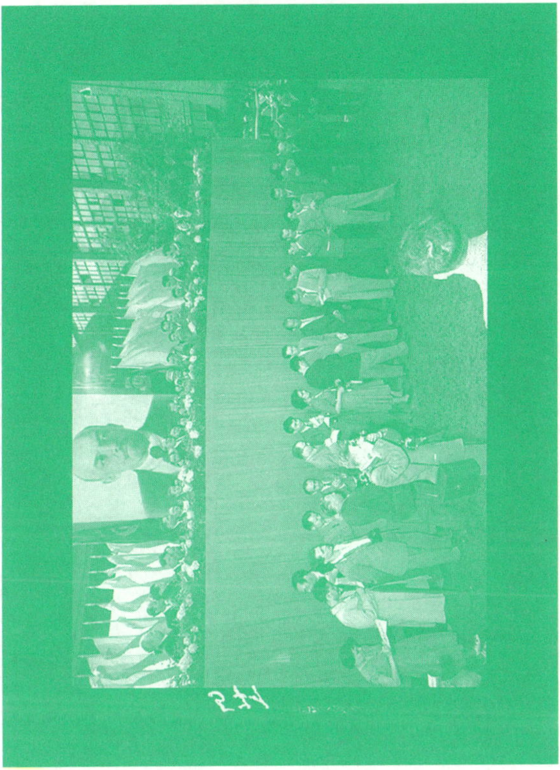

195E_058_081 (contactsheet only)
In Moscow: visit to a Moscow car factory and speech at a rally in the factory, June 5, 1956

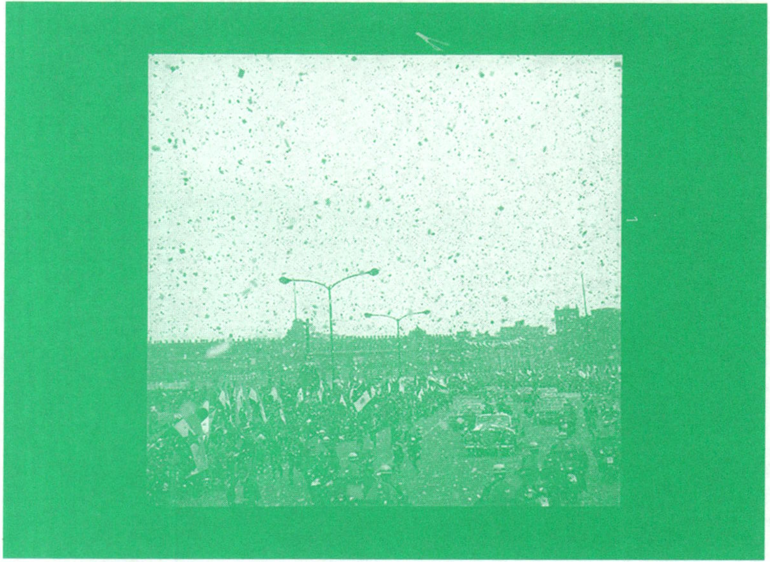

1963_228_046 (contactsheet only)
In Mexico: at the ceremonial welcome at the airport in Mexico City, meeting President Lopez Mateos and driving through the city, October 4, 1963

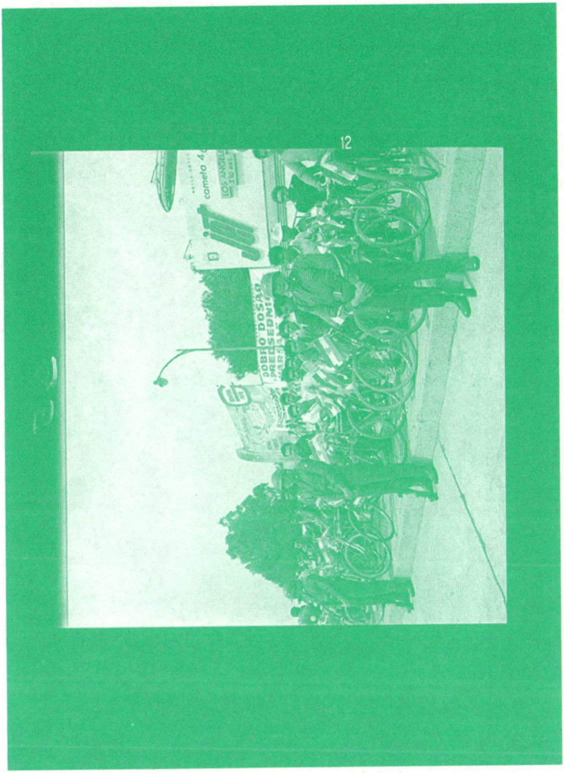

1963_182_4582_025
Visit to Mexico: welcome by crowds on the streets of Mexico City, October 4, 1963

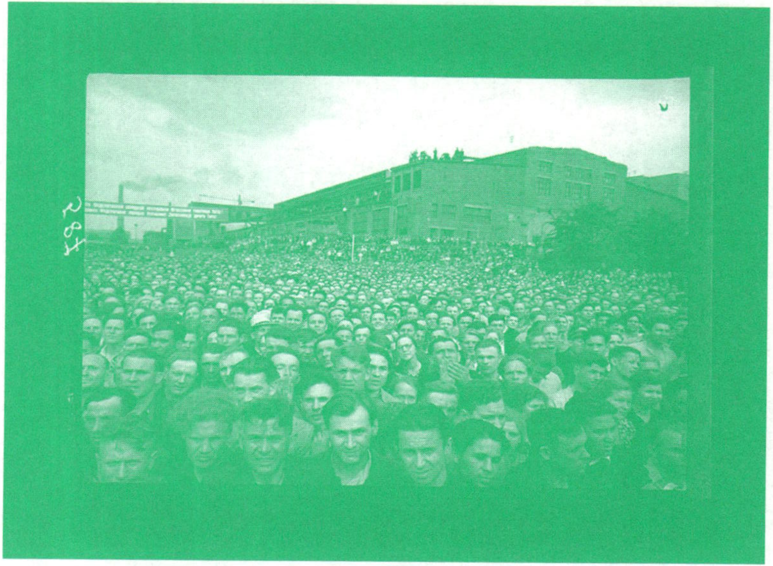

1956_058_081 (contactsheet only)
In Mexico: at the ceremonial welcome at the airport in Mexico City, meeting President Lopez Mateos and driving through the city, October 4, 1963

Ivan Manojlović

THE PHOTO ARCHIVE OF JOSIP BROZ TITO A VIEW OF THE PICTURE OF POLITICAL POWER

Photo Parade

In many aspects, documentary photography is the dominant form of the twentieth-century photographic language. With documentary photographs commonly regarded as "evidence" of an event, documentary photography is perceived as a truthful and objective way of representing historical events. Adjectives such as disputed, problematic, emotional and disturbing usually accompany the subject matter of documentary photographs: poverty, social and political injustice, war, crime, destruction, disasters, suffering. A photographic image is taken to be a faithful reproduction of reality that, at the very moment of exposure, already becomes the past and, as such, unavailable. As documents, photographic images are windows into a world that has already been lost from the point of view of the beholder.

A great delusion has thus always accompanied the photographic medium: the opinion that the camera cannot lie. This deeply rooted belief, though explicable by the very nature of the medium, would cast photography in the role of a machine for documenting the past, a means of creating an objective account of history. This illusion was fostered by a failure to consider social and cultural context in which photographs are produced, or, indeed the position of the photographer who is not a neutral, passive operator.

By the very nature of its medium, photography appears to share an identity with memory (as history). The mechanical nature of images seems to imbue photography with unlimited authority. Technical principles and characteristics of the analog photographic medium endow it with the ability to capture more than the visual record of an event: photography captures tiny fragments of the past itself.[1] By reflecting off what surrounds us, light acts upon the photosensitive material and this makes it possible for a photograph to also physically contain light particles of the reality it documents.

If we accept an identity between photography and memory as history, can we reverse the order? Namely, are history and photography one and the same thing? Various theorists and philosophers of photography, including Roland Barthes, Susan Sontag and Vilém Flusser, seem to hold that this correspondence exists. We place unconditional trust in photography because of its seemingly objective recording of reality. Our faith in its cold, technological objectivity puts photography before our own living memory. We feel justified in believing that photography is more reliable at the task of preserving memories (namely, history). Photography offers means of control over what to remember and what to discard (unlike our memory which hardly ever affords us such control). Photography is thus a more

1. Susan Sontag, *On Photography* (Belgrade: Cultural Centre of Belgrade, 2009), p. 77.

sophisticated means of remembering than our own, individual memory: the process begins with selecting what to remember, deciding which moment is worthy of being photographed. Control over memories would thus turn into control over history. Sometimes a photograph attains immense significance. It is then that such a photograph becomes iconic. This process involves abstraction of meaning, in which photographs lose connection to the context of their production, with the circumstances in which they were made—with where, when and how of their recording.

The notion of photography as history is, in this sense, a construct: from framing the shot, through processing (either in the dark room or using computer software), to the possibility of manipulating images. This procedure poses no problem when followed by one and the same person constructing their own memory as their own history, from their point of view. Problem, however, arises when the photograph is made by someone else who then becomes extremely important as the recorder of memories we eventually accept as *shared*. Why? Their viewpoint, first of all, is certainly not the same as ours. His/her views and mind-set are most likely different to ours. The gap made by these differences renders the process of transforming photographs made by someone else into our own history and memories very complex.

Following the Second World War, in newly socialist Yugoslavia photography was seen as the matrix of new popular culture, modelled on the Soviet practice. "In the monumental project of aestheticizing the new political system, photography had a prominent role, second only to film," as written in the editorial of the first issue of the 1948 *Fotografija* magazine."[2] Milanka Todić further argues that "photographs capturing spectacular mass games in Yugoslavia from 1945 to 1958 provide an ideal model of the relation between the ideology of totalitarianism and mass media."[3] The very conception of a society of mass spectacles, which Yugoslav society was, implied continuous production of images reflecting the reality of an idyllic society. Photographs of mass festivities, such as the celebration of Tito's birthday and the International Workers' Day parade, as well as organized mass activities such as voluntary youth labor campaigns, occupied a special place as carriers of the communist allegory.

Mirko Lovrić, a "recorder of memories"

The archive now housed at the Museum of Yugoslav History grew out of the work of the Photo Service of the Cabinet of the Marshal[4] of Yugoslavia, Josip Broz Tito. It was founded in mid-1947 by Dragutin Grbić, a well known news photographer with the Telegraphic Agency of New Yugoslavia (TANJUG),[5] as part of the Press Department of the Cabinet. Four photographers were employed by the Photo Service: Dragutin Grbić, Aleksandar Stojanović, Miloš Rašeta and Mirko Lovrić. Their cameras captured Tito's journeys in the country

2. Milanka Todić, *Fotografija i propaganda 1945–1958* (Banja Luka-Pančevo: Helicon, 2005), p. 110.
3. Todić, p. 117.
4. Office of the President.
5. Archive of Yugoslavia, the Cabinet of the President of the Republic, file VI–16.

and abroad, visiting foreign heads of state and government, meeting world famous people from all walks of life, attending international meetings and conferences, as well as moments from his daily life.

The Photo Service was reorganized in the mid-sixties, after Mirko Lovrić in 1963 submitted a series of proposals for improvements.[6] Lovrić was made the new head of the Service. Although essentially an artist,[7] primarily concerned with the essence of photography as a medium, Lovrić mastered the art of news photography at the very beginning of his professional life. He argued that the Photo Service must produce photographs of documentary quality, as authentic as possible, each providing the answers to the basic journalist's questions; extending to the viewer a clear picture of the location, of the protagonists and even the moment in which it was made. Lovrić strived to enrich his approach to documentary photography with some of his artistic criteria, to introduce another dimension into photographs, which Lovrić referred to as metaphotography.[8]

The aim of Lovrić's method was to render the layers of photographic content more complex, so as to enable decoding other angles. Photographic recording was to provide a richer visual representation, extending its testimonial potential. It

6. See MEMORANDUM, p. 137.
7. Lovrić graduated at the School of Applied Arts in Zagreb, the Department of Art Photography, after which he earned his BA in Art History from the University of Belgrade, Faculty of Philosophy.
8. See IN CONVERSATION WITH MIRKO LOVRIĆ, p. 145.

was thus necessary, according to Lovrić, to also capture the ambiance of a scene, to make it possible to recognize the context of the events depicted in photographs. Lovrić drew an analogy with the Dutch painter Vermeer, highlighting the fact that Vermeer's paintings offer a clue as to the time of the day "in the painting." Adopting a similar approach in photography would allow us to, based on the shadows cast by buildings and other objects, work out the time of the day at which an event took place. Lovrić firmly held that photographs must not merely mirror that which is in front of the lens, but rather provide a snapshot of the entire atmosphere.

It would be interesting to consider at this point what the contemporary theorist of photography Gerry Badger refers to as "the quiet photograph." Freed from any form of authorship or artistic intention, such photographs have, for many years, been considered to be mere documents. Badger elaborates on the way in which such photographs are created.

> Quiet photographs demand a high degree of intellectual rigor, awareness, and purpose on the part of their makers—and I use the word maker rather then taker advisedly. Furthermore, quiet photographs also require work on the part of their viewers in order that their subtleties might be fully appreciated. The quiet photograph is neither document nor aesthetic object nor simulacrum nor fictional tale, but combination of all four, a different combination in the hands of every individual photographer.[9]

Photographs that are now part of the collections of the Museum of Yugoslav History had a utilitarian, documentary purpose, both prior to and following their musealization. We learn from Lovrić's testimony[10] that these photographs, produced by the Photo Service, were reprinted by media, various local and foreign news agencies, but also given as gifts to foreign diplomats at the end of their official visits. Some of these photographs were made for Josip Broz Tito. Now in a separate photographic collection, they have also played the role of a unique family album.

A VIEW AT THE PICTURE OF POLITICAL POWER.

This separate collection is today known as the Photo Library. It consists of around 135,000 black and white 18 x 24 cm photographs, kept in 702 boxes resembling books, and categorized by event and year. Since the beginning of their life in the museum, in 2003, they were mainly used to complement narration as part of exhibitions and publications, but also in research, as a means of obtaining additional information related to a historical event or figure.

The entire collection was scanned and digitized in 2012, and uploaded onto the MYH website for unlimited public access.[11] The photographic archive of the Museum of Yugoslav History has thus become a unique historical resource for understanding,

9. Gerry Badger, *The Pleasures of Good Photographs* (New York, 2010), p. 219.
10. See IN CONVERSATION WITH MIRKO LOVRIĆ, p. 145.
11. See www.foto.mij.rs.

interpreting and deconstructing the official history and popular myths related to the personality of Josip Broz Tito and the country whose leader he had been for thirty-five years. Through the museum's engagement with scientific and artistic research and exhibitions we are developing points of departure towards a method of de- and re-contextualization: by inviting the academic community and the wider public to participate in the practice of working in/with national historical archives, we are promoting public dialogue about recent history.

Recent photography theories have enabled us to read something more into documentary photographs. We now perceive in them relationships that were not their subject matter, creating new interpretations, which may not be relevant for scientific research, but are especially interesting as artistic reactions and interpretations.

The availability of photographic images from this unusual collection in both the physical and the virtual environment today puts us under an obligation to ask ourselves certain questions. What do these images tell us today? Why was it important to digitize this photographic material, offer new interpretations of it and make it available to the widest possible public? What will be the significance of the photo archive of the Museum of Yugoslav History for future generations? The answers to these questions become increasingly important in view of the historical outcome of the events that took place in the last decade of existence of Yugoslavia and the post-Yugoslav conflicts.

In attempting to find answers to at least some of these questions, we applied an almost forensic approach to our research into the photo archive of the Museum of Yugoslav History. By taking apart the entire photographic fundus, we wanted to uncover its constituent parts and typological units, such as, for example, Josip Broz Tito's travels. We custom-developed a methodological process highlighting the connection between sequences and moments, for testing the context by inserting selected images into recognized categories, for understanding the language of these photographic images and examining the relationship between archival and media potential of photographs.

The visual analysis was conducted not only with the aim of exhibiting this extensive photographic material, but also in order to determine the possibilities for changing the perception and understanding of a particular museum collection. By comparing photographic material with its textual archival counterpart, we set predefined moments (determined by state protocol) as typological units determining the structure of families of photographs, on which the work of the official photographers of the president of the Socialist Federal Republic of Yugoslavia was based.

By extending our research to Yugoslav media archives, we inspected the channels through which photographs of Josip Broz Tito became available to the citizens of the Socialist Federal Republic of Yugoslavia, imposing themselves as iconic representations of a statesman.

Radovan Cukić

THE PHOTO ARCHIVE OF JOSIP BROZ TITO: Yesterday, Today, Tomorrow

Though the use and experience of photography mutated often during Yugoslav socialism (1944–90), in line with its ideological and political oscillations, the Communist Party's monopoly in control over all segments of the state was the one constant element. In time, this supervision had waned, but not disappeared. This decline in ideological domination and instrumentalization of photography by the Party propaganda began in 1952; the Party's grasp on the use of photographic medium in artistic practices disappeared altogether after 1958.[1] And while the period between 1945 and 1958 is commonly singled out as the one during which the rhetoric of photography as mass visual medium was most markedly instrumentalized by propaganda, Milanka Todić rightly points out that this was but a step in the development of mass communication, mass culture and the society of spectacle that began between the two world wars.[2]

A multitude of radiant, happy heroic faces of the anonymous builders of the new society beam from

1. See, for example, Milanka Todić, *Fotografija i propaganda 1945–1958* (Banja Luka-Pančevo: Helicon, 2005), p. 36.
2. "For Debord, Dada and surrealism 'marked the end of modern art.' According to him, the advent of the society of the spectacle should be placed in precisely the late 1920s, when the zone of 'pure art' was abandoned in favor of a mass culture and the society of the spectacle." Todić, p. 21.

the photographic records from that era, intended to inspire the same or similar beliefs and sentiments in citizens living or working in conditions different from the ones proclaimed by the propaganda. Such closely controlled and directed creative application of photography reached its peak in this period. These shots of beaming faces bear no trace of commentary, or even a hint of a question, a scene differently arranged or an arbitrary moment that might question the official version and the status of the person portrayed. The individual is secondary, what matters is the idea of glorification of work. Only the head of the Party was photographed close up, though in a strictly predefined way. These canons were followed when taking photographs and when publishing them.[3]

Given such attachment to the importance of photographic medium, it is somewhat surprising that it took over two years after the end of the World War Two before a photo service was established at the Cabinet of the Marshal of Yugoslavia, Josip Broz Tito, in order to document his activities. As if the pre-war habits of illegal political activities were still too strong among Yugoslav communists, despite their complete hold on power. Even the photographic records of Tito's official inter-state activities in this period can only be found in photo albums received through other countries' protocol services. Even after the Photo Service was finally formed, its most imposing

3. Jovan Despotović, "Slika i informacija 1945–1990," in Miodrag Đorđević, *Fotografija kod Srba 1839–1989* (exhibition catalogue) (Belgrade: Galerija SANU, 1991), pp. 122–23, 127.

activity—preparing sets of photographs for Tito—can only be followed from mid-1948 onwards, coinciding with the culmination of the break up with Stalin.

Owing to Tito's lifelong stay in power, photographers tasked with covering his activities (four in total over thirty-three years: Dragutin Grbić, Aleksandar Stojanović, Miloš Rašeta and Mirko Lovrić), took several hundred thousand shots. Over the decades the collection of 18x24 cm black and white photographs, selected and printed for Tito himself and presented to him at the end of each year in specially designed boxes, grew to a total of about 132,000.

How do we attempt to correctly understand a photo archive that was in becoming between 1947 and 1980? How did its functions change with the flow of time? We will try to offer a reply to these questions.

Firstly, we must make a clear distinction between the negatives archive (including contact copies) and the collection of photographs selected for Tito himself, the so-called Fototeka.[4] Despite the huge difference in the number of photographs, it could be said that Fototeka consistently conveys the structure of the archive. By this we mean to say that all the events covered by the archive are literally transferred into Fototeka, with the same captions, though fewer images. Of course, a selection took place (and it would be legitimate to examine the criteria used), and in most cases, this probably meant simply choosing the most successful shots. As

4. The term Fototeka points to a room in Tito's residence housing book-like boxes with photographs.

mentioned, Fototeka only includes events documented since mid-1948, although the photographic recording started a year earlier, in mid-1947. There is also the separate issue of possible (or rather probable) discrepancies between negatives and photographs: as various negative formats were used, certain elements of the original shots were cut out. Finally, we must address the accessibility of the archive and Fototeka—their completely different museal life. The archive was, in post-Titoist socialist Yugoslavia, and later on, until 1999, (selectively) open to researchers, for they could request to see contact copies of particular events.

Today, it is closed within the Museum depot and rarely used, almost exclusively by the curators of the Museum of Yugoslav History (MYH). Fototeka has, however, after Tito's death, become the sacrosanct part of his home open to visitors, but without true access to its content, even for curators. From 2002, however, this access has been granted to curators and external researchers. From that moment Fototeka has, as smaller and more manageable, and, owing to its medium (prints as opposed to negatives) more accessible, acted as a surrogate for the archive. Though a satisfactory surrogate, it is still a surrogate.

This notion became even stronger during the process of digitizing—in 2013 the whole of Fototeka was digitizing and made accessible on the MYH website (www.foto.mij.rs)—requiring the support of a comprehensive research project in order to enable online search functions. The terminology used in this text reflects this: when not explicitly stated otherwise, archive is to denote Fototeka, for it is only the fundus of Fototeka that we have completely at our disposal.

Documents on the work of the Photo Service list as its functions the creation of photo documentation about President's activities; providing photographs for publication in the press; preparing "presidential sets" of photographs, as well as sets for his guests. Given that the service was part of the Press Department, we can assume that its main task was creating a desirable public image of the President. Milanka Todić states that to study, analyze and present photography as the exponent of political power in the epoch of socialism means having to [only] work with the official records, for only officially approved state-produced[5] photography appears in public.[6]

The work of the Photo Service is the ultimate example of this. However, not all the photographs created by this service were intended for publication. At a certain level this meant a careful selection of the most successful photographs to be presented in the press, sending a strong and monumental propaganda message, within which there was no space for "inappropriate" scenes. At another level, photographs with lower media potential were also made, not intended for publication, or perhaps intended for selective publication. Their function can only be comprehended within the framework of this selected collection of photographs, a personal/family album of sorts, a grandiose version of the common practice among American and European bourgeois families

5. By official state news agencies and media.
6. Todić, p. 8.

from mid-nineteenth century onwards, of offering some of family memories to visitors.[7]

Researching photographs [from the archive] that were published in the press media thus represents a significant segment of our work on the archive. This was one of the presentation procedures applied to our participation in the *Travelling Communiqué* exhibition, at least when it comes to official state visits. The most present are photographs of splendid welcomes prepared for Tito abroad and official meetings of the so called summit diplomacy. In Yugoslavia, photographs created as part of propaganda served, Milan Ristović points out, as the concrete proof of the "unity of people and the leader" on their path to achieving "progressive" society. Parades, mass games, mass rallies and other mass manifestations were among the motifs exploited to this effect, and so were the images of newly built residential, industrial, schools and medical buildings (when opened or visited by Tito), and "jubilant" welcomes and farewells [prepared for Tito].[8]

Yugoslavia's great incursion into world politics at the beginning of the fifties heightened the importance of presenting a desirable image of the Yugoslav President abroad. Some of the photographs from the archive, especially genre scenes from his private life, were probably first intended for publication in the

7. Ritzenthaler/Munoff/Long, p. 15.

8. Milan Ristović, "*Od tradicije do modernosti: 1878–1990,*" in Marko Popović/Miroslav Timotijević/Milan Ristović, *Istorija privatnog života u Srba: od srednjeg veka do savremenog doba* [History of the Private Life of the Serbs from the Middle Ages to Modern Times] (Belgrade: Clio, 2011), p. 556–63.

West, rather than in the still poverty stricken Yugoslavia. Some of his favorite hunting images, on the other hand, gradually became unacceptable for publication in the West, where the public became sensibilized to the killing of animals.

We cannot infer from available documentation whether the founders of the Photo Service had, besides their clearly set out tasks, some long-term aims in mind. We can state at the least that they were not explicitly set out. A programmatic document[9] created in 1963, however, clearly states the idea that the work of the Service ought to be understood as creation of a serious, all-encompassing chronicle of its time. Its author was Mirko Lovrić, the head of Photo Service. Lovrić remarks that the work of documenting Josip Broz's activities has unfolded exclusively as photographic registration of events, without consideration of the main moments, the ambiance or the time of each particular event. Such practice was, according to him, the result of the low level of photographer's general education. Subsequently, only a small number of the great mass of negatives was usable, and any aesthetic quality the result of coincidence, instead of conscious striving. Photographic recording ought to be organized, according to Lovrić, so that it results in records that retain contextual unity, whilst emphasizing the most important moments of each significant event. The idea of creating authentic historical records carries within itself the logic of care for their preservation: Lovrić makes a number of constructive proposals for

9. See MEMORANDUM, p. 137.

organizing an archive of photographic records.[10] Although many of Lovrić's objections are legitimate, it is important to consider that photoreporters had to also satisfy daily press demands for images. Photographs were made in series, in quick successions of exposures with insufficient regard for composition, and consequently, with uncertain qualitative outcome.

The most significant of Lovrić's objections relate to establishing the archive as a serious, all-encompassing chronicle of its time. We ought to, however, consider other factors besides photoreporters's low levels of education, on which Lovrić put the emphasis—factors that might have affected quality and objectivity of documenting. Though camera can see what the eye misses, the human eye chooses what will be recorded through framing and additional work and selection. Political photography represents (and more so than any other type of photography) power relations of political life, rather than proffering an image of reality as it was.[11] Photographs of strict protocolar events, such as presentations of credentials, for example, seem to have come closest to Lovrić's proclaimed ideal. These rather static situations could almost always be recorded in the same code of several shots depicting handshakes and presentation of credentials, a courteous conversation and a group portrait with clearly determined positions. Though inter-state visits

10. Archive of Yugoslavia, Cabinet of the President of the Republic, folder VI-8.
11. Milanka Šaponja, *„Do istine na novinskim stupcima,"* in Đorđević, p. 127.

are far more dynamic events, they are, nevertheless governed by firmly structured protocol, and as such, also probably easier to cover. This was the theme of the segment of the MYH participation at the *Travelling Communiqué* exhibition. Interestingly, on assignments abroad, the photographers gave themselves far more freedom in presenting the wider context of events. Some of their photographs, especially those shot in Africa, are excellent examples of travel or even anthropological photography. It is certainly worth considering their motivation for photographing such scenes, for taking such photographs in Yugoslavia is almost unthinkable.[12]

Lovrić's objections to the way in which domestic political events were being photographed are largely justified. Even those regarded as significant determinants of Tito's epoch are recorded in such a way that an observer from the future, relying only on what can be found in the archive, could not obtain an insight into their significance, or would obtain a crudely distorted insight. Let us single out documentation of two sessions of Yugoslav political leadership, both featuring "confrontation" with political opponents. Though their political and historical significance was immense, it would appear that the complexity of these events had overwhelmed the reporters to the extent that it affected the way in which they recorded them. One of these events was the Twenty-first Session of the Presidency of the League of Communists of Yugoslavia (LCY), on December 1, 1971, in Karađorđevo. It featured

12. See, for example: foto.mij.rs/site/gallery/4257/photo/10, or: foto.mij.rs/site/gallery/4259/photo/52.

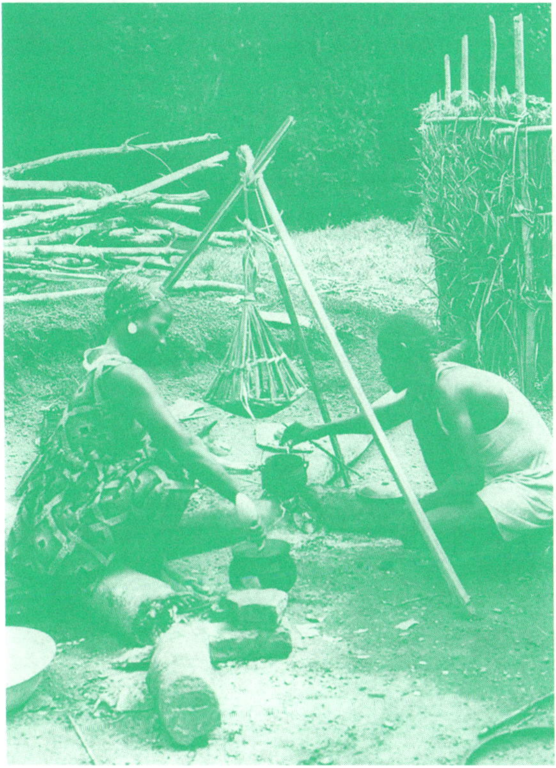

1961_156_0052 Visit to Liberia: photographs of settlements between Totota and Kokota, March 17 1961

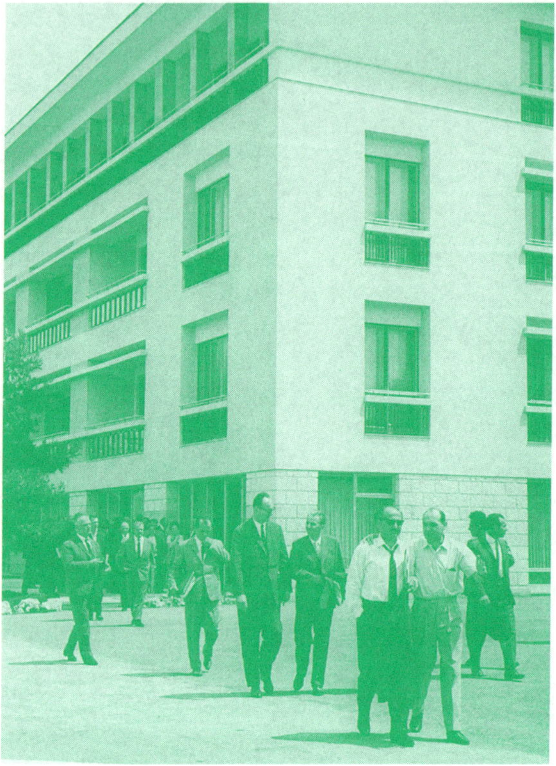

1966_306_133 The Fourth Plenum of the Central Committee of the LCY: during a break, July 1, 1966.

13. See, for example: foto.mij.rs/site/gallery/8112/photo/133.
14. 1966_306_133 The Fourth Plenum of the Central Committee of the LCY: during a break, July 1, 1966.

condemnation of Croatian leadership that had far-reaching consequences for political life in that republic, as well as in the rest of the country. Even so, we only find four photographs of this event in the archive, and its main protagonists are, apart from Tito, barely visible on any of those photographs.[13] Much more drastic, however, is the example of the famous Fourth Plenum of the Central Committee of the LCY (July 1, 1966), the confrontation with Aleksandar Ranković as the exponent of the "hard line" of the LCY, following accusations of unauthorised surveillance of Tito, and his subsequent disgrace and removal from the political scene. Ranković was, until then, the first man of the State Security Administration [UDBA], the vice-president of the state and the designated "heir to Tito."

In this case, documentation conveys the dramatic charge of the plenum, the bitter outbursts and pauses between them, during which delegates grouped for discussions. Rather unbelievably, Ranković does not appear on any of the thirty two photographs: there is no record of the speech in which he defended himself, of his presence in the rather small hotel conference hall, or during the break in front of the hotel;[14] akin to covering a trial without once mentioning the accused. Such examples tell us that Lovrić's expected outcome of creating contextual unity of a record, whilst emphasizing the most significant moments, was, certainly when documenting complex events, far from routine. Despite the volume of photographic material, this narrow perspective led to missing an opportunity to create a chronicle of time and state, and not just one person.

As the function of this photo archive changed in step with our reality changing, so has the way in which the archive is viewed. By tracing the process of its musealization over the past two decades, we could say that it was firstly forgotten and displaced out of the reach of curators, to then be perceived as newly unearthed treasure. Search ensued for a portion of "privacy" of the ruler now rediscovered for the interested public, as well as for some of the splendour of the bygone epoch. Curators and researchers have been trying to see in the archive something that it is not: the chronicle of a time and a state. This seems to be facilitated by its new accessibility, organization and the level to which it is preserved (often not the case with big photo archives in the region).

A great research undertaking underlies the process of digitizing the archive and placing it online, aiming to enable movement through the archive; to enable various searches by determining temporal, spatial and thematic coordinates; as well as by identifying persons appearing in photographs. In order to fully contextualize the archive, however, our tasks in the MYH would have to be set more ambitiously. It would be necessary to, through factually supportable descriptions of depicted events, present their wider meaning, hyperlink them to other content, such as photo documents or information about published photographs. Only in this way would it be possible to obtain a more complex picture: of the depicted events, of the way in which the archive came to be, of the practice of photographic documenting of an epoch and of the various functions of the archive.

Armin Linke (AL) and Fabian Bechtle (FB)

NOTES TOWARDS A PHOTO ESSAY

with comments by Heike Behrend (HB), Radovan Cukić (RC), Dubravka Sekulić (DS), Sarah Poppel (SP), Philip Ursprung (PU), and Vanessa Vasić-Janeković (VVJ).

(PART 3)

1968_367_0107

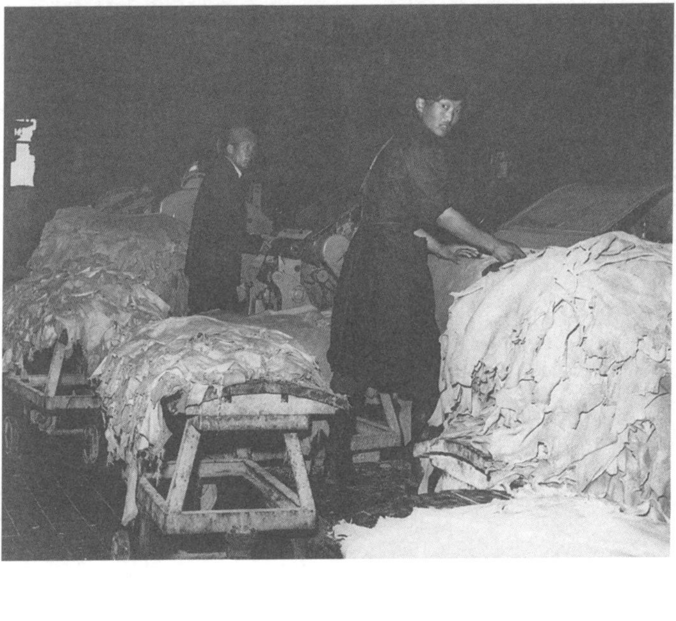

1968_367_0107

Visit to Mongolia: in a leather goods factory.
State: Mongolia; Location: Ulan Bator; Keywords: Book of impressions, President of the Government, Party general secretary, Industry: leather and footwear; Bilateral Relations: Mongolia; Date: April 17, 1968

1961_155_0050

Visit to Liberia: at a reception in honour of President Tito and Jovanka Broz, in Monrovia.
State: Liberia; Location: Monrovia; Personalities: Jovanka Broz, Wiliam Tubman, Antoinette Tubman, Wiliam Tolbert, Lazar Koliševski, Veljko Mićunović, Milan Žeželj, Isidor Papo, Zvonko Perišić;
Keywords: Speech, Ceremonial reception, Folkloric performance, President of the State;
Bilateral Relations: Liberia; Date: March 13, 1961

HB — Viewed through the lens of folklore studies, tradition has been perceived as static, as not historicized and open to the future. The term tradition has often been used as modernity's opposite—modernity and tradition belong together.

But the idea that tradition is inflexible has since been deeply criticized. We know now that tradition has a history: nothing is more modern than tradition. Tradition and history are integrated in modernity. This is very important when we view images on which many differences are staged. We must look at them against the view of tradition as inflexible, we have to historicize them, view them from the outset with awareness of how quickly people react, inventing traditions in a flash.

1961_155_0050

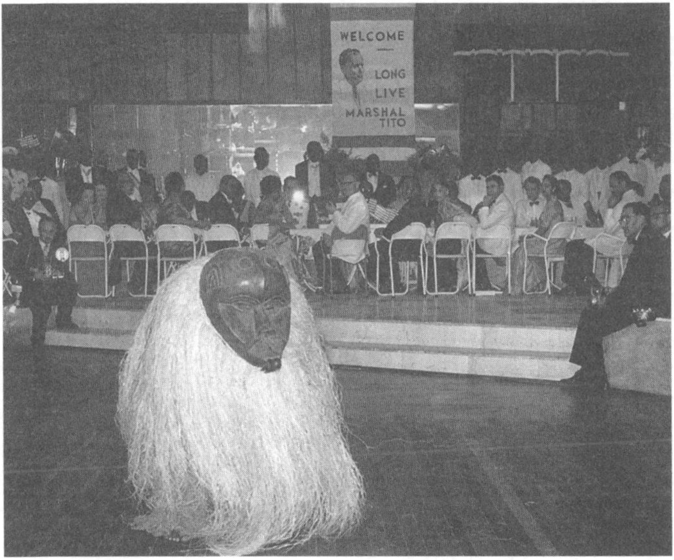

1961_155_0051

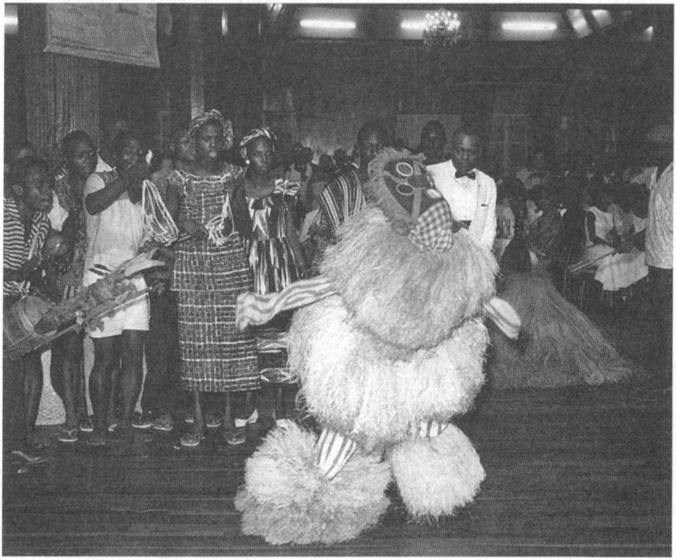

1961_155_0051

Visit to Liberia: at a reception in honour of President Tito and Jovanka Broz, in Monrovia.
State: Liberia; Location: Monrovia; Keywords: Speech, Ceremonial reception, Folkloric performance, President of the State; Bilateral relations: Liberia; Date: March 13, 1961

AL — We have been wondering whether something such as a notion of "self-exoticism" exists?

HB — I do not think they would see this as self-exoticisation. They are showing their traditions marked in this mask. Mask society and secret societies have been present in Liberia from far back. The impact of globalization processes through colonialism and otherwise has been so strong that people would often integrate something from the outside. They might keep it as foreign or really take it up, so as to become part of their own tradition.

1961_155_0053

Visit to Liberia: at a reception in honor of President Tito and Jovanka Broz, in Monrovia.
State: Liberia; Location: Monrovia;
Keywords: Speech, Ceremonial reception, Folkloric performance, President of the State;
Bilateral Relations: Liberia; Date: March 13, 1961

HB — Traditions are being permanently reworked. The girl's skirt is open in the front, exposing her naked thighs. Normally, the skirts develop wonderful ornaments and patterns, but are never this length. This is a kind of a sexy modernization.

In that context tradition is becoming a commodity. But there is also a reversal of commodification going on, a sort of reautentification. Some people have decided to have no media presence at all, to revalue the secrecy. There is no single trajectory here, but breaks, returns, other uses and ways of defining authenticity. Strategy of commercialization has its counterpart in processes of decommercialization.

1961_155_0053

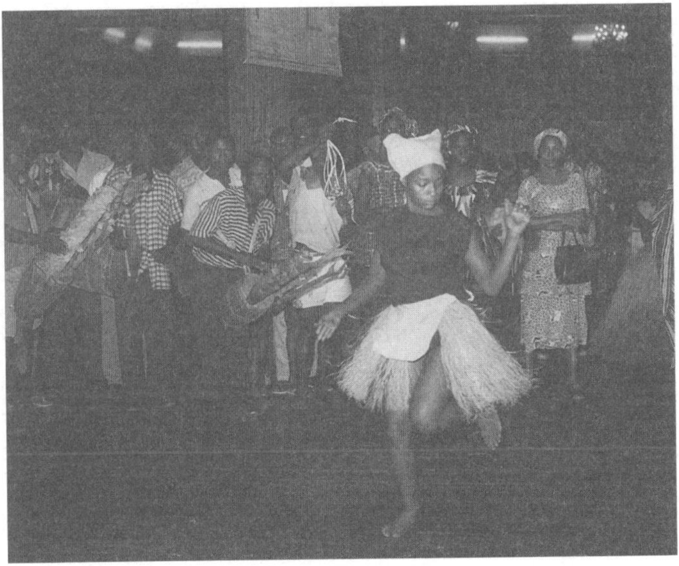

1965_266_055

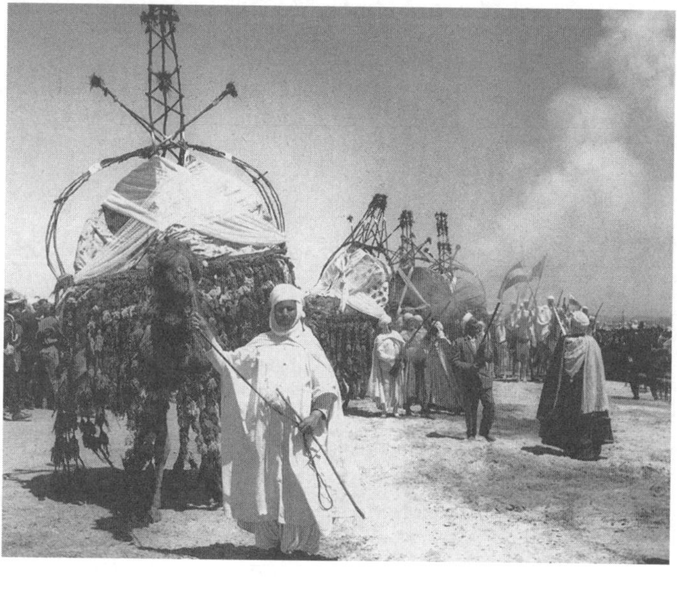

1965_266_055

Visit to Algeria: the performance of Bedouin fantasy near Laghouat. State: Algeria; Location: Laghouat Keywords: Welcome, Journey, Automobile, Panorama, Parade, Folkloric performance, Traditional dress, President of the State, Non-Aligned Movement; Bilateral Relations: Algeria; Date: April 18, 1965

AL — Do we read this as a mediatic spectacle staged for a diplomatic event or as traditional ceremony?

HB — I have seen something like this on a beach in Morocco, but involving horse racing. These are tents, I think. Inside the tent there should sit a woman, not to be shown. So you have a display of something that is inside, as I said, a woman not shown. A secret then, both concealing and exposing; both are always there, but here this is really explicit.

1968_355_198

Visit to Cambodia: the Legend of Angkor Wat Sound and Light Show. State: Cambodia; Location: Siem Reap; Keywords: Fireworks, Historic-cultural monument, Monarch, Folkloric performance, Non-Aligned Movement, Play; Bilateral Relations: Cambodia; Date: January 19, 1968

HB — This is more of a re-enactment of history, with folkloristic elements, of course, and it seems commercialized.

1968_355_198

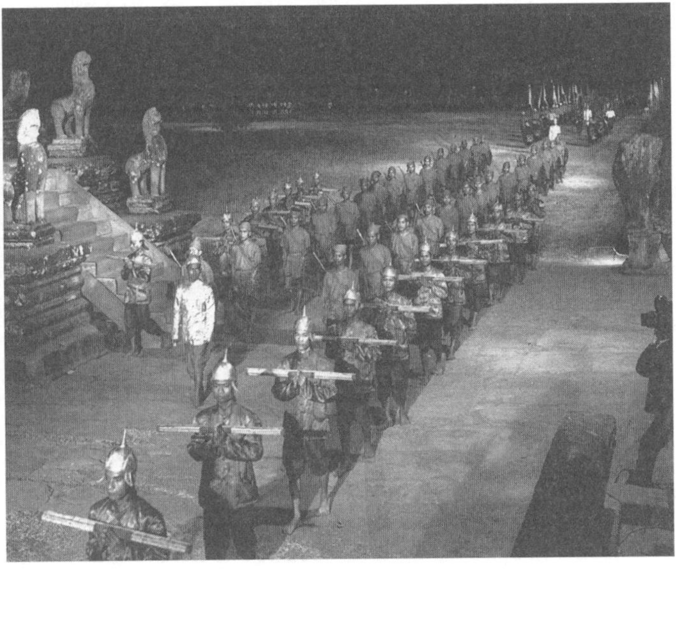

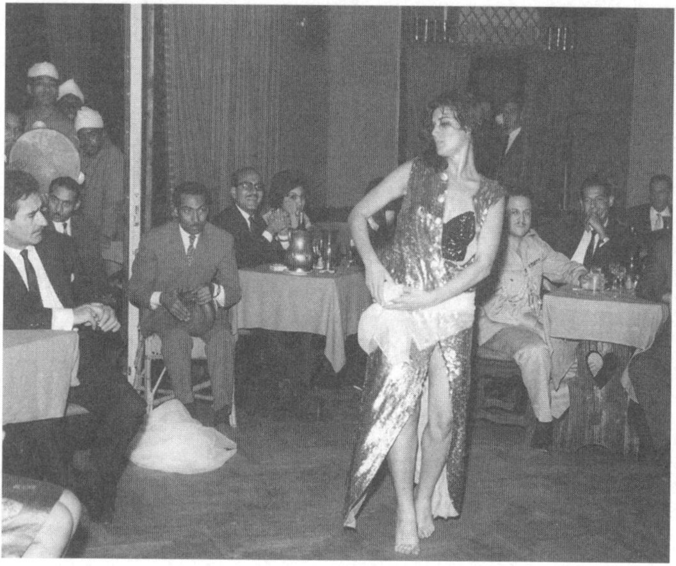

1964_255_0062

Cairo, after the Second Non-Aligned conference: dinner at a restaurant. State: UAR (Egypt); Location: Cairo; Personalities: Jovanka Broz, Vladimir Popović; Keywords: Music, Entertainment, Non-Aligned Movement, Restaurant; Bilateral Relations: UAR; Date: October 12, 1964

AL — This looks like a cabaret in Cairo, following dinner in a restaurant.

HB — Is this belly dance? With unveiling? It is a veil?
Yes, it is a veil… and there would be more, I'm sure. Perhaps this is striptease?

AL — So, more of a Western adaptation…

HB — I would say it is rather the orientalizing of stripteaze…

AL — It is very dangerous to look at images, isn't it?

1968_360_0015

Visit to Ethiopia: in front of hunting lodge tents. State: Ethiopia; Location: Bako; Keywords: Folkloric performance, Non-Aligned Movement, Camping; Bilateral Relations: Ethiopia; Date: January 30, 1968

HB — They seem to be staging the killing of an animal, played by this man. This is very interesting, for, symbolically, when Tito goes hunting, he connects to this tradition of kings killing animals and humans as an act of sovereignty.

1968_360_0015

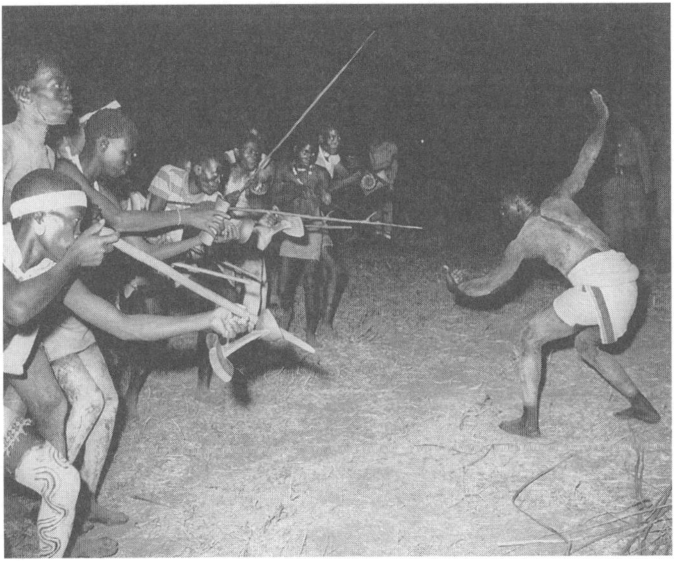

1968_357_0166

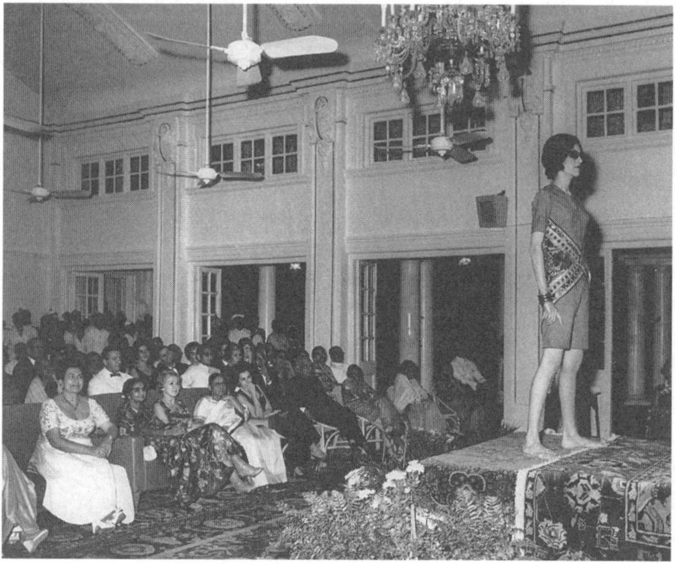

1968_357_0166

Visit to India: Jovanka Broz at a fashion show in Mumbai. State: India; Location: Bombay (Mumbai); Personalities: Jovanka Broz, Lijana Tambača, Zora Nikezić, Sloven Smodlaka, Nada Komar, P.V. Cherian; Keywords: First Lady, Fashion, Non-Aligned Movement; Bilateral Relations: India; Date: January 24, 1968

AL — This fashion image attracted me because it points to the notion of the dress as a kind of contemporary identity tool. This, then, is the tradition of the present.

1970_429_0108

Visit to Libya: official bilateral talks in People's Palace in Tripoli. State: Libya; Place: Tripoli; Keywords: Residence, Exterior, President of the State, Official talks, Non-Aligned Movement; Bilateral Relations: Libya, Date: February 26, 1970

DS — During a recent Zurich bound flight from Belgrade I spoke with a gray haired man sporting a chic sash and a hat, on his way to London. I mentioned that I am a PhD student in Zurich, working on a thesis on Yugoslav construction companies's work in the NAM countries. My travel companion said, "Ah, Libya and Iraq! In the eighties, I was the financial director of one of the largest of such companies from Belgrade. I could tell you many stories, but much of what we did was classified. As for the rest: a lot of the money never reached Yugoslav banks."

In the seventies and eighties, Libya and Iraq were among the most profitable markets for Yugoslav companies working mainly for military contractors on classified infrastructure projects. These companies would sometimes even accept contracts on which they lost money in order to also be able to showcase unclassified projects, such as Energoprojekt's redevelopment of Al-Khulafa street for the NAM Summit planned for Baghdad, but relocated due to the Iraq-Iran war.

1970_429_0108

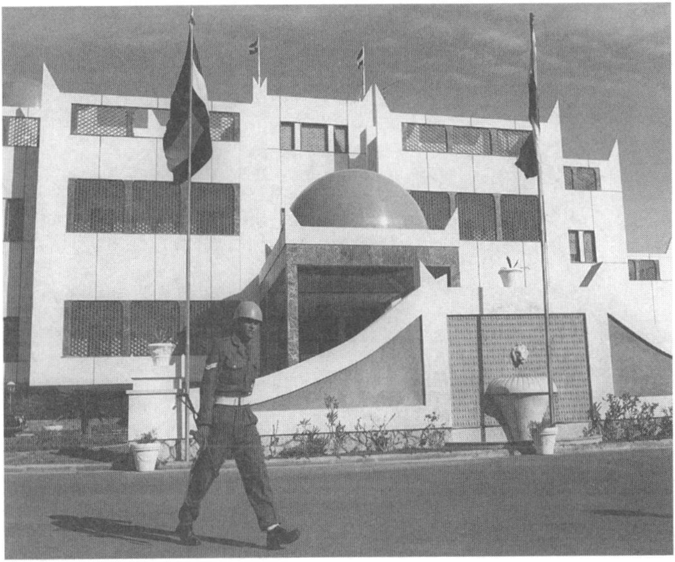

1961_153_0109

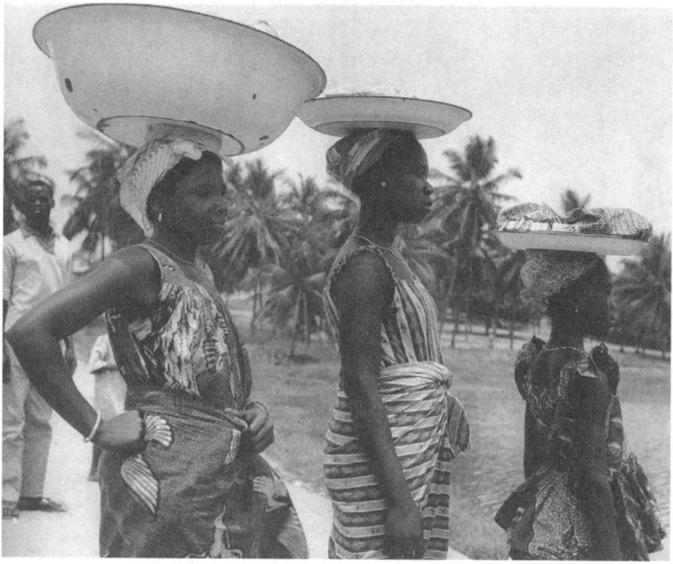

1961_153_0109

Visit to Togo: women of Togo in traditional dress. State: Togo; Location: Palime; Keywords: Traditional dress; Bilateral Relations: Togo; Date: March 6, 1961

HB — They are wearing a cloth called kanga, mainly produced on the East African coast, but, in fact, absolutely cosmopolitan. Women designed the prints and their designs were in the process of colonization produced in Manchester and the Netherlands, to then be exported back to Africa. Nowadays, most of the production takes place in India—so there is a truly cosmopolitan history to this cloth. Some African Americans identify this cloth with their African heritage, but this heritage has a history that is absolutely global and full of contradictions.

PROPOSALS

The proposal-concept was conceived by Doreen Mende with the contributions *Décollage* by Kader Attia, *Future Remake* by Tarek Elhaik and Kriss Ravetto-Biagioli, *Testimonies, Protests and Photojournalism* by Heba Farid, *Manifestation of the Right to not be Understood* by Flaka Halliti, *Algeria 1961: The Paradigm of Counterinsurgency* by Samia Henni, *Triple Juncture* by Doreen Mende, *A Belgrade Version of Love* by O'Tam Pulto, *Black on White: How to Continue Without Oneself* by Branimir Stojanović, *This Film Was Created Out of Love for Man as a Protest Against Violence and Destruction* by Subversive Film, *Družina A: The Non-Aligned Movement and its Relation to Art and Society* by Milica Tomić, *Alternative Cartographies and the Decolonization of Europe* by Françoise Vérges, and *On Neutrality* by Jelena Vesić and Rachel O'Reilly.

The typography was designed by Žiga Testen with James Oates. The twenty-one meter table-display was designed as an architectural intervention by exhibition architect Milica Lopičić.

Originally displayed as take away posters in A2 blocks, some of the proposals are adapted for this publication on the following pages.

PROPOSAL BY SUBVERSIVE FILM

Subversive Film is a cinema research and production collective founded in 2011. It is based in Ramallah, occupied Palestine and London, UK.

This Film Was Created Out of Love for Man as a Protest Against Violence and Destruction

We want to write a "storyline" from formal and non-formal narratives.
We want to write a narrative by reading public and private archives.
We want to do this by borrowing on memories from a grandfather, a state, a system of world order that once was, and a system of political cinema that once was.
We wish to propose an idea for research for a film we came up with very recently.
We are curious to see whether it would be possible to create this narrative by observing physical, emotional, and electronic impressions and documents of certain moments, events, places, time and people. It seems a very complex task to us, considering this involves moving in time and space, both personal and collective. We don't know what to expect from this research.
We don't know yet whether the narrative, or the storyline will be fiction or non-fiction.

See IN CONVERSATION WITH MIRKO LOVRIĆ, p. 145.

What we do know however, is which characters we would like to pursue: an event, a film, historical figures turned ephemeral, and real characters turned fictional. Something connects them, a certain thread, or threads that hold(s) them together with such an extraordinary simplicity, to a point of utter complexity. This thread, or threads will remain unrevealed here, in this document, because it is precisely there that the narrative/storyline we search for lies.

Subversive Film, June, 2014

NON-ALIGNED MOVEMENT, THE FIRST CONFERENCE

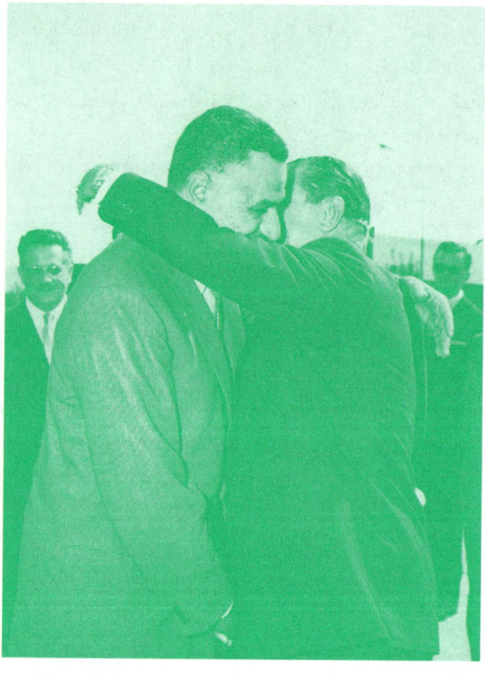

The Non-Aligned Movement[1] was officially formed in September 1961, in Belgrade, where twenty-five nations met for the first NAM conference., The movement was anticolonial in its essence and acted as a response to the bipolar distribution/division of global power. Josip Broz Tito and Gamal Abdel Nasser were among the key minds conceiving the movement.

1 — Up until 1976, the Non-Alignment Movement was referred to as Conference of Heads of State or Government of Non-Aligned Countries

KRV I SUZE / BLOOD AND TEARS

Krv i Suze (Blood and Tears), 12 minutes long, is a film produced in 1970 by Filmske Novosti, a Yugoslav state owned newsreel production body. The film crew consisted of

Stevan Labudović (camera),
Mirko Aksentijević (writer),
Voja Korijenac (editing),
Branka Mihić (selection of music), and
Boško Mratinković (director).

The film is narrated in several languages.

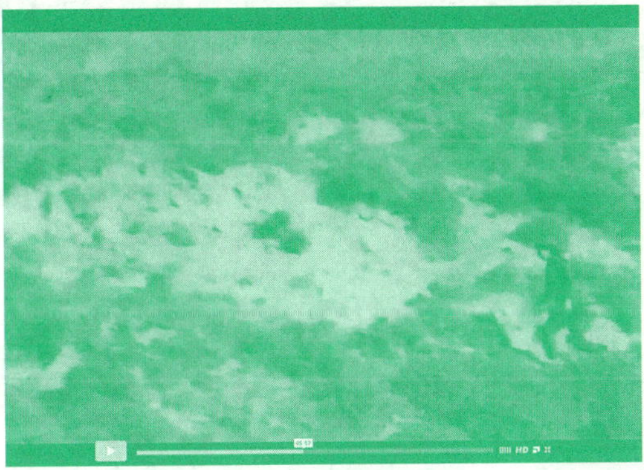

The crew, or part of it, traveled in 1970 to Jordan, from where the Palestinian revolution has been operating since 1968.

Up until the Black September War in 1970, Palestinian refugee camps in Jordan were the hubs for various militant movements struggling towards liberation of Palestine.

Krv i Suze was shot shortly before the Black September, one of many films made during that stage of Palestinian revolution by filmmakers and artists who arrived to the revolution to produce films in support of a liberation struggle and in protest against colonial projects across the world.

The film portrays the early years of the Palestinian struggle for liberation as a political, militant and social movement. Alternating between shots of life in refugee camps and military training camps, *Krv i Suze* renders the Palestinian revolution as a people's struggle and as a national effort towards liberation.

> "The lifetime of a people is not measured by time but by sacrifices. We do not say this because we like war, but because we are concerned. Man is in danger." (minute 12:09–12:18)

ABU OMAR

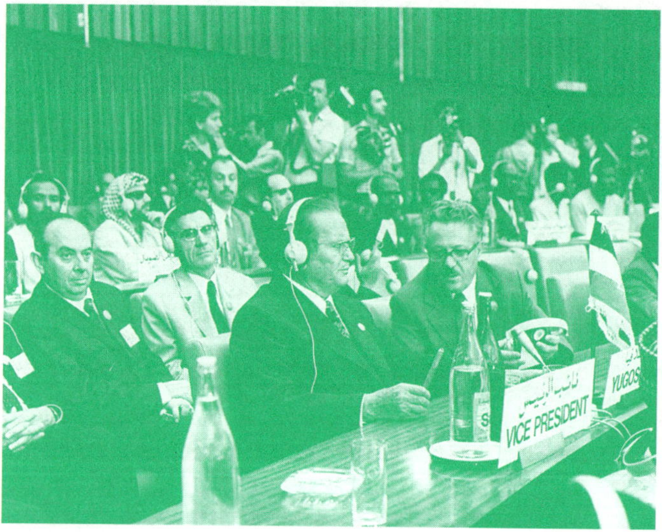

In 1969, Abu Omar, presented as a high-ranking member of the Palestinian FATAH movement, meets with two Yugoslav officials. Abu Omar spends his days in Belgrade staying with a Palestinian student.

In his late thirties, he is short, with closely shaved beard, dressed casually in dark pants, light shirt and a light summer jacket. He wore dark sunglasses during the first half of the meeting.

During the meeting with the two members of the League of Communists of Yugoslavia, he requested that Yugoslavia provide military help to FATAH and its armed struggle for the liberation of Palestine. He asked that the Yugoslav government provide Palestinian fighters with arms and training. The meeting ended with the hosts hesitant to agree to any of Abu Omar's requests. He shook their hands and left very disappointed.

Days later, the Yugoslav officials received information about Abu Omar's true identity.

He was Yasser Arafat.

YOUNG JNA/UNEF SOLDIER IN RAFAH, GAZA

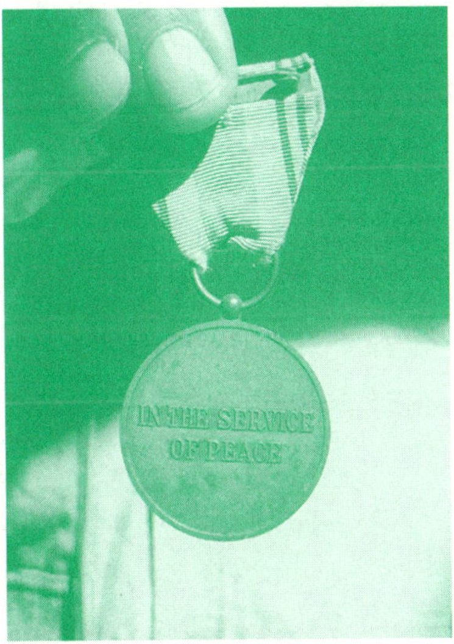

In 1956, Dušan, called Duško by family and friends, was a 19 year old man from Lazarevac, a small village in the Republic of Serbia, in Yugoslavia.

As part of his conscription, he was drafted to the Yugoslav People's Army (YPA) contingent of the United Nations Emergency Forces (UNEF), a UN peacekeeping force established following the 1956 Suez War. He leaves Yugoslavia for Cairo, and ends up in Rafah, a small city in Gaza on the border with UAR-Egypt. Behind him he leaves a young wife, a newly born daughter, and vast plots of farming land.

Once in Cairo, Duško crosses the Sinai, passes through Arish and settles down in the UNEF camp in Rafah. The forces were drafted from many different countries around the world including Brazil, India, Indonesia among others to ensure the end of any future confrontation between the Egyptian and Israeli armies following yet another attempt of colonial expansion in the so called Middle East[1]. The different contingents each had their own sleeping quarters and kept to their own traditions, but they spent most of their time in common tasks. They trained together, kept watch over the camp, cooked and cleaned together and so on.

In his free time, Duško played as a goalie for the UNEF team against the local, Palestinian team. He took pictures on the sandy Rafah beaches. He watched films organized weekly by the UNEF administration.

"The Suez War, also called the Tripartite Aggression was an attempt to regain Western control over the Suez Canal after Gamal Abdel Nasser's nationalisation of the canal. Egypt was attacked by British, French and Israeli forces."

PROPOSAL BY MILICA TOMIĆ

Born in SFRY, lives in Belgrade
Družina A: The Non-Aligned Movement
and its relation to art and society

A group of actors leaves the Contemporary Theatre in Belgrade in 1961. They engage with the public by performing in factories, industrial centres, mines and student halls in order to "together with students and workers, search for the common aesthetic and social denominator"(Družina A).

Early September that same year, just as the first Conference of the Non-Aligned Movement ensues, Družina A investigates the complex relationship of art, society and state, as well as the need, the desire for subjectivation. How to imagine a society defined by anti-colonial struggle outside the frameworks of the state and the institution?

DRUŽINA A:

The year of 1966 was, theatrically, a weak year throughout the world. The only significant theatrical event that year was the staging of [Jean] Genet's *The Screens* (*Les Paravents*), thematize the Algerian War.

OUR CITY'S SMALLEST THEATER

What did direct contact with audience reveal?
An opportunity for local authors
Enthusiasm and belief
High school students, working youth, workers' collectives:
they are Družina A's audience
This is not a recipe, but it is an attempt.

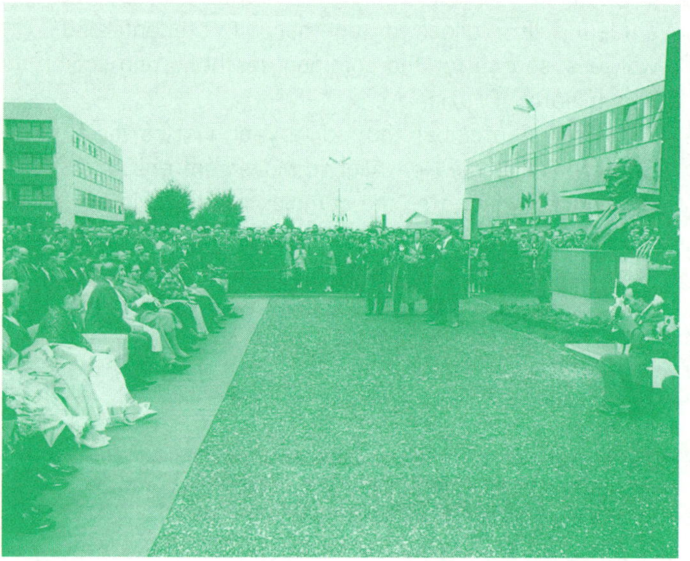

Some of the heads of the delegations of the countries of the Non-Aligned Movement at the opening of the Grand Fair in Zagreb, in the aftermath of the Conference.

AUDIENCE—THE FIRST SURPRISE

> "Working in this way is not a new idea," says Rade Marković. "It was born to many artists within theater. We merely had enough of a desire and courage to be the first to see it through. This is how group "A" sprouted. Our audience is a selected one: students, working youth, workers in big worker collectives. This was a great unknown. How will the audience receive the new type of the game, how will they react, what will they say?
>
> And then came a surprise. Spontaneously, without any preparation, conversation began after each performance, lasting two, three, even four times the length of the performance. Questions and questions: why this, how that, because of what, in which way?"

Little by little, group "A" members realized that the audience had been underestimated. They established that the audience is capable of much deeper and more complex consideration than it was possible to conceive of. Another significant discovery was made. Contemporary spectator demands plays by local authors, linked to his time and his personal problematic. In a word, he wishes for a drama in which he can find himself, the solution for, or an allusion to his own problem and, finally, perhaps an outlet for the feelings hidden deep inside him.

Members of Dramska družina "A" tell us about the endless conversations, about the questions. They are uncovering a world, utterly unknown, a world with its desires, strivings and hopes.

AUDIENCE—THE FIRST SURPRISE

As it turns out, the play is no longer directed by a single director, one person, but the whole auditorium. The auditorium reacts and draws out of the play that which is the most important, most specific to them.

Students place the gravitas on their student life, on all the preoccupations that it brings. And they "direct" the play in accordance with this. By applauding, approving or objecting. In this way, a second rate problem that had hitherto gone unnoticed, has been brought into the foreground. For the spectators live with that which happens in front of them and around them. Workers did not react to the specialization problem. But they gained something completely different from the play. Something dear to them, peculiar for them...

This has not been achieved on the conventional stage. The audience was given a work, rehearsed and ready, but not a work of a creator/author—a work for the audience, which the audience receives according to its affinity.

A RECIPE, OR...

Naturally, we should not deceive ourselves and start believing that Družina "A" has found the ideal, omnipotent way out of the condition of contemporary theater. Rather, this is about searching and experimenting. For no one, not even the members of Družina "A" can state with certainty that tomorrow, in a month, or a year they will still be walking the path they set. This path turns each one of them into an actor as well as a director, technician, make-up artist and administrator.

Tomorrow, or some day, this drama group will change the way they work, partly also because spectators will demand, ask for this. Perhaps the audience, already actively participating in the play, will be the one to find a new, previously unknown path. The last fall of the curtain does not put up an insurmountable barrier between the spectators and the actors. On the contrary, the curtain transforms into a bond between four actors and a thousand spectators, a bond that changed the group's conceptions, and is changing them still.

Duga Magazine,
September, 1961

PROPOSAL BY O'TAM PULTO

Born in Ethopia, lives in Addis Ababa
A Belgrade Version of Love

The Tao of the Dusty Foot Philosopher—Born out of A Thousand Versions of Love is my book on a journey of self-discovery and fulfilment inspired by African Philosophy, ancient Chinese stories and all the world's religions. It is a version, among a thousand versions, of that ancient love of which people of all lands and ages have spoken and sung about in their own, unique ways. I hope to create a thousand versions of this book in collaboration with artists of all cultures to fund a local (Ethiopian) children's book project called *On the Wings of Books*. This, then, is my proposal for creating a Belgrade version. *A Thousand Versions of Love* aspires to reach all the people around the world with a message of love; to create a network of ordinary people engaged in a project to improve the quality of basic education in Africa and preserve indigenous knowledge; to motivate people to see other cultures as sources of inspiration in realizing the potentials latent in one's own culture and soul, thereby promoting unity in diversity.

The Belgrade version of *A Thousand Versions of Love,* the second version in this project, will be illustrated by selected pictures of ordinary people from the photo archive on the Non-Aligned Movement (NAM) at the Museum of Yugoslav History. The NAM was an example of expression of love in the collective history of the human race. Ordinary people like you and me were parts of that movement. As unique individuals in this deeply interconnected global community, you and me can be parts of the making of as yet a new history and write newer versions of love for our children. Yes, we can make a difference!

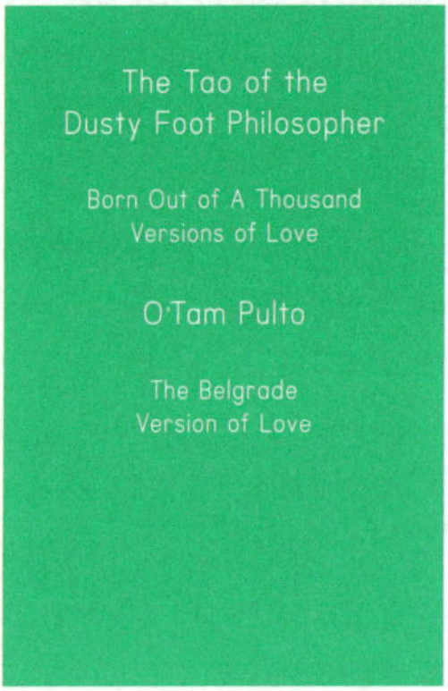

A NAM Version of the Book

The Tao of the Dusty Foot Philosopher:
Born Out of A Thousand Versions of Love

Sinkneh Eshetu (Penname: O'Tam Pulto)
A Proposal Submitted to the Travelling Communiqué
on March 29, 2014

Background: What the Book is About

The Dao (Tao) of the Dusty Foot Philosopher: Born Out of A Thousand Versions of Love (The Tao book for short), is a (my) book on "African Philosophy." Or, I would rather say, an expression of my conception of love. Love has many manifestations; its versions, too numerous to count and recount. Suffice to know that in essence it is the same love. One love. In myriads of lands and ages, among myriads of cultures and generations, in myriads of songs and stories, in myriads of wisdoms and faiths, a single love is expressed. Even in every anger and war, one could see its distorted face. For me, cultural differences are expressions of different versions of love. That is the creativity/beauty in the day-to-day lives of ordinary people that I try to explore in this book and my other works.

I can say that the Tao book is my personal attempt at articulating an African version of love—a poetic (not academic) reflection on the "silent" way of life (worldview/philosophy) shared among the people of Africa, presented as a guide to a personal journey or search for self-discovery and fulfillment (in a way, search for liberation at personal level), applicable for any person of any culture. It also draws attention to an alternative approach for intercultural communication, where meeting cultures discover beauty in each other to realize potentials latent in each other, against the homogenizing forces of globalization.

PROPOSAL BY BRANIMIR STOJANOVIĆ

Born in Yugoslavia, lives in Belgrade
Black on White: How to Continue Without Oneself

Oskar Davičo, a poet and political activist, deduced his poetic communism through a demand for the undoing of the category of ownership within language. Categories of I, the words self, selfhood, authorship are, as the site of the reproduction of ownership, submitted to a radical poetic critique and undoing through the category of the SAME. Thirty years later, in *Crno na belo* [Black onto White] (1962), his travelog through Western Africa, Oskar Davičo re-examines socialist anticolonialism and its potential as the site of undoing the category of ownership through dialog and discussion among the various socialist projects of the sixties.

Performance lecture: June 12, 8 p.m. at Museum of African Art, Belgrade, Andre Nikolića 14, 11000 Belgrade

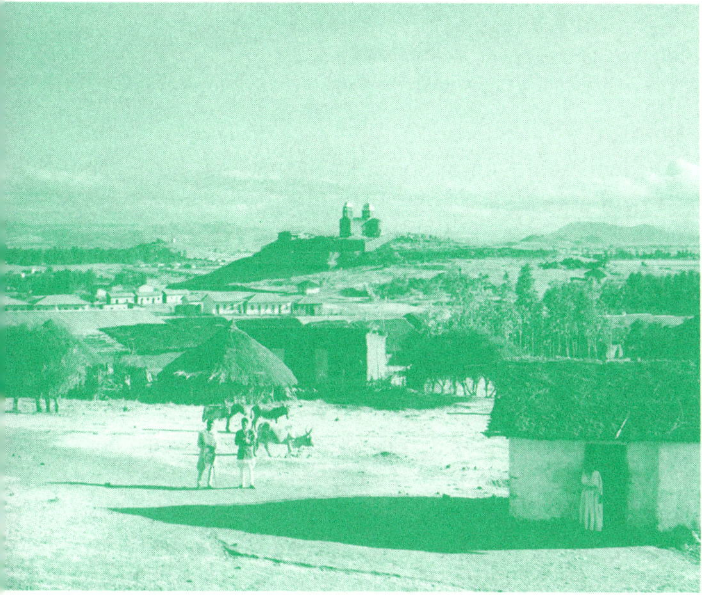

Živela Republika Donjeck!
Živela Republika Donjeck!
Živela Republika Donjeck!
Long Live the Republic of Donjetsk!

PROPOSAL BY HEBA FARID

Born in Egypt, lives in Cairo
Testimonies, Protests, and Photojournalism

A documentation of sporadic events that have shaped Egypt's political and social landscape over the last 60 years: images of the citizen-making process through political mobilization, and active civic engagement. The reading is one focused on the voice—the acts, sites, and circumstances of expression and engagement. There is no coherency here in terms of specific groups, causes, or dates, just a common thread that links the participation of citizens in political life. This work has been re-adapted for the *Travelling Communiqué* from the original three-part work created for the touring exhibition Cairo. *Open City*, curated by Florian Ebner and Constanze Wicke, installed at the Museum für Photographie in Braunschweig e.V. (2012), the Folkwang Museum in Essen (2013), and the Museum für Kunst Gewerbe (MKG) in Hamburg (2013). (April 2014)

Interpretation of the images:
Heba Farid
Menna Khalil
Amgad Naguib
From the Collection of:
Amgad Naguib, Cairo

From: Heba Farid
Date: December 1, 2013 13:00:18 MEZ
To: Armin Linke
Cc: Mende Doreen, Milica Tomić, Mirjana Dragosavljević
Subject: Re: Images from the Non-Aligned Movement

Dear Armin and team,

Thank you for sending me the materials.

I have read the text and looked at the selected archive images.

I would like to respond by highlighting a few points.

Regarding locating archival material in Egypt—
State archives—it is possible to find archives that would have materials (photographs and documents) related to the 1964 NAM conference and visits by various heads of state and their delegations and activities. However, the first obstacle we would encounter is how to obtain the right to use the photographs and/or documents. There are no state agencies or museums holding archives that are open for use. There are no policies regulating this. Therefore, it would be impossible to approach any state institution with this request.

Private archives—it is possible to find archives that would have materials that would be of value—remnants from newspaper archives that have found their way onto the market, private recollections of people that may have attended these events, players on the political scene, or wives of..., etc. Locating these archives, and establishing usage rights would take time and require a small amount of funds, depending on the situation (not for free).

Regarding the reading of images from the MHY archive:
At a first glance, I find the usual expected images from a state visit, in the following categories:

1. heads of state discussions
2. formal meetings (in this case the Arab League location)
3. state dinners
4. women's gatherings
5. military capabilities
6. and of course touristic visits—pyramids at Giza, temples, mosques, palaces, horses, camels, dancers, night clubs ...

What I find unexpected in this archive (I am sure you do too) are the photographs of fisherman:

1964_255_0101.jpg
1964_255_0103.jpg
1964_255_0104.jpg
1955_1956_52_0014.jpg
1955_1956_52_0015.jpg

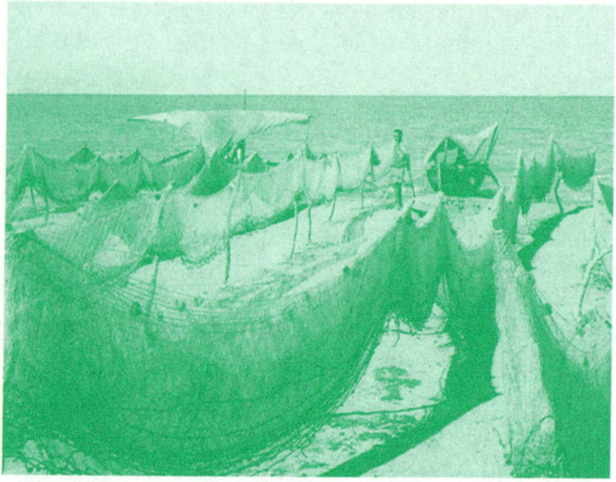

Image 1964_255_0101

Images that are more difficult to read—perhaps produced with an inherent inequality of gaze, perhaps within a larger political intention; images that disturb the agency of the subject and circumstances.

So, with this in mind I would like to show a possible contribution to your to your project: I do not assume that these examples would be considered as part of your project, they are part of a larger work currently on exhibition. I am merely illustrating an example of a recent intervention, in a different context, but that may give clues for further reactions to your project.

The above observations pose a direct question related to the line of investigation of your project—Whom does the NAM address? Who are the protagonists? (and their contemporary applications.) What is the nature of photographic practice in these circumstances?

I find it interesting that such images appear within the larger body, as a break in the narrative, and I am intrigued by the agency of the photographer, by the fact that these images insist on existing. They sharpen a question for me—how are people affected by global-scale rhetoric? How do these ideals impact or change their lives? How does the photographic play into the associated rhetoric?

From the experiences of the last five decades, and since the establishment of NAM, it seems that the core issues of self-determination and self articulation of modernity against hegemony (neo)Colonialism, globalization & neo-liberal economic policies), are still quite relevant today. Through my work in the photographic archives in Egypt, I am finding that this notion is often repeated and amplified. People's desire for recognition of their modernity is still an urgent position.

If the world is still in a state of "(r)evolution," struggling to change social order, conditions, attitudes, and build alternative systems, then there also exists a clear lack of consensus, discord between peoples, all of which lead to protest and conflict. "Peace" is used as a synonym for stability, but more often than not it is a visible result of silence or collusion.

In this intervention, it was my intention to, in the context of protest, expand on the idea of civic engagement in response to recent events, to trace it in documents, remember moments, and document "voice." Although these photojournalistic images may still be focused on ceremony, the camera is refocused on the recipient of such grand ideals as independence, self-determination, etc. They show the public mobilized ... something that has a particular relevance.

Back to the fisherman, and back to a simpler vocabulary, yet still of a camera revealing an inherent fixed inequality in the gaze - again, a notion often repeated and amplified in photographic archives. Whilst related to different circumstances, the image production remains inherently the same. And within the context of the MHY archive, how should they be read?

Below are the captions associated with the three images from *Chapter 2: Testimonies, Protests, and Photojournalism.*

You will find the images in the attachment.

I hope that this answers some of your inquiry. Please do let me know your thoughts.

Regards, Heba Farid

Fig. 1 — National union/public assembly,
July 16, 1960 unknown location, photographers: Abduh Khalil and Taher Hosny; 20 x 30 cm.

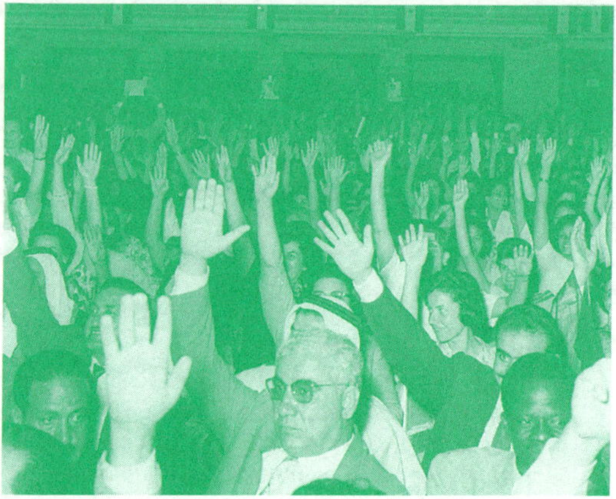

Fig. 1

The final meeting of the national assembly or union - like the former NDP under Mubarak, but with socialist aims, now considered to be fascist.

The creation of the National assembly was to introduce, for the first time, the concept of active participation among citizens in creating a new state. However, in its attempt to rectify the distribution of wealth, Nasser's government confiscated property from many rich landowners, nationalized industries, and applied new rules unfairly.

As now, the army presided over the regulations and implementation of the new laws. People stated that they (the ruling party) had ruined the country, a statement in use similar to today. [Citizens voting on resolutions to be adopted.]

Fig. 2 — Public conference against France's denial of its nuclear bomb testing at the university, July 1, 1960 unknown location, photographers: Abdel Atheem Abdel Fattah; 14 x 18 cm.

Nasser routinely flaunted/boasted the participation of women in his campaign. He promoted social engagement and the inclusion of women in the civic project. He succeeded including women in the police force, and certain military activities, especially ones related to the sciences and social services. [Women stand and lead the protest chants.]

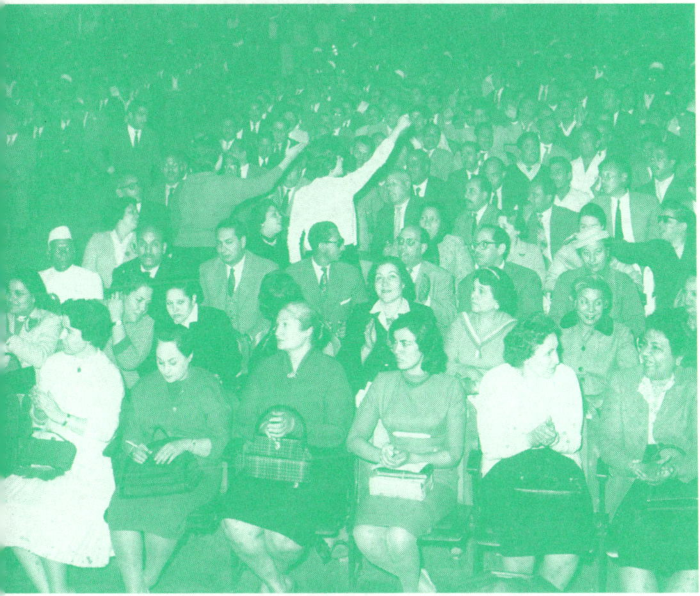

Fig. 2

Fig. 3 — National union/public assembly, May 26, 1962, unknown location, photographer: Abduh Khalil; *Gomhoreya* national newspaper, 20 x 30 cm.

"The specified questions asked regarding representation of the fellahin & worker to be 50% of the assembly, which took a lot of attention from the President, whose response was in favor and enthusiastic, but more than the rest of the members."

During the civic project, redistribution of wealth, civic participation and policies of inclusion, workers and peasants were given voting powers for the first time. Until today, quotas exist for these groups and more developed associations and unions have been responsible for setting into motion events that began in 2005 that eventually led to the 2011 January 25th revolution.

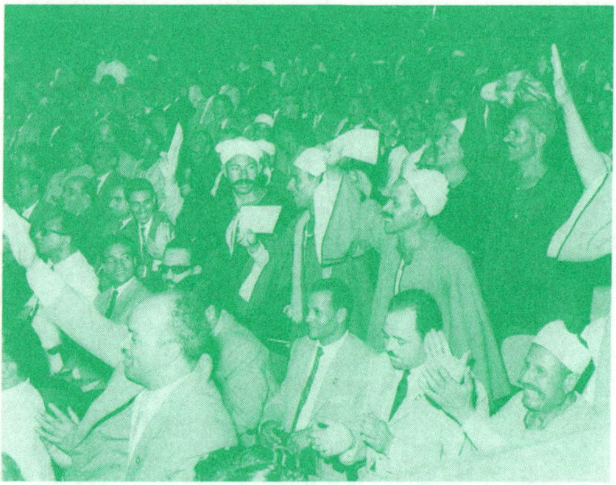

Fig. 3

PROPOSAL BY TAREK ELHAIK & KRISS RAVETTO-BIAGIOLI

Born in Marocco, lives in San Francisco
Born in the U.S., lives in Berkeley, California
Future Remake

Future Remake asks us to think about how the form of mimicry or emulation returns in the form of a copy or appropriation, thereby blurring the lines between homage and duplicity.

Taking cue from *Travelling Communique*'s invitation to reflect on the cartographies and repetitions traced by the travels of a purloined letter, Future Remake is an assemblage that offers itself as an antidote to the contemporary visual, political, curatorial, and media culture that ails from an overinvestment in an increasingly aestheticizing, yet fundamentally humanist drive towards iconicity and impoverished repetitions. Through looped moving-images extracted from the work of Glauber Rocha, Želimir Žilnik, Dušan Makavejev, Sergei Eisenstein, Ruben Gamez, to name only a few, Future Remake opens a space of radical visual critique and clinique, between iconicity and aniconicity, between affect, icon and their symbolic programming.

As an antidote against the iterative assemblages of contemporary culture, these film artists "denounce the neorealist (as well as Marxist) nostalgia or romantic desire for a heroic and moral proletariat or peasantry, and the neodecadent nostalgia for aestheticism. It is important to examine their cinematic strategy: its endless dissimulation, which draws us into its disruption of authorial gestures, yet at the same time forces us to recognize that this enframing will be unable to escape from the rhetorical deceit it denounces" (Ravetto, 2000).

These looped clips, and iconic images are assembled and performed through a permutational logic that installs the inter-medial chaotic intensity of "incurable-images" (Elhaik, 2014), such as those found in Glauber Rocha's Claro (1975). The very repetition and juxtaposition of moving images explodes the iconicity that attempts to pacify them.

Images of decaying modernizing infrastructure, iconic nationalist landmarks and ruins that can no longer be mourned, indigenous monumentalization that have turned into hardened ideological frameworks, and mad theatrical performance, orgiastic performances at border checkpoints, are repeatedly juxtaposed.

FUTURE REMAKE

Le Don (3:33m)
(Raúl Ruiz) 2007; The Gift (Marcel Mauss)
Affect • Icône • Firstness Economy • Circulation • Sacred The Letter • The Given • The Concept

QUE VIVA MÉXICO! Sergei Eisenstein (1932 –); Symbolic Punctum	⟵ SYMBOL / ICON ⟶	MAGUEYES Rubén Gamez (1962); Allegory–Animation
BOLIVAR: THAT WHICH DOES NOT SUFFER DOES NOT LIVE Carlos Castro (2010); Imperceptible	⟵ INDEX^2 X EMBLEM ⟶	INNOCENCE UNPROTECTED Dušan Makavejev (1968); Carnivalesque
OCTOBER Sergei Eisenstein (1928); REMAKE	⟵ MONTAGE = MONUMENT ⟶	BATTLE OF ALGIERS Gillo Pontecorvo (1966); Performing Documents
ACTUALITÉS Alva Brothers (1907); Native Agents	⟵ GAZE ⟶ + GIFT = ETHNOS	ULYSSES' GAZE Theo Angelopoulos (1995); The Lost Gaze
La Rabbia P.P. Pasolini (1963); Political Cosmos	⟵ (LAMENT) • COMPLEXION ⟶	TAKE THIS HAMMER Richard O. Moore (1963); Cosmo-Politics
ULYSSES' GAZE Theo Angelópoulos (1995); Spectre	⟵ DEATH-IMPERFECT ⟶ CINEMA	LA HORA DE LOS HORNOS Fernando Solanas Octavio Getino (1966–1968); Remains

REPETITION DOUBLING

DOUBLE FEATURE

ATOM EGOYAN (2008, 4min)
IMAGE / EXHAUSTION / INORGANIC RESTORATION / RESURRECTION / REDEMPTION

QUEMADA! Gillo Pontecorvo (1969)	← THEFT →	OUTSKIRTS/OKRAINA Pyotr Lutsik (1998)
TITO AMONG THE SERBS FOR THE SECOND TIME Želimir Želnik (1994)	← FARCE →	EL DIA QUE ME QUIERAS Leandro Katz (1997)
OUTSKIRTS/OKRAINA Pyotr Lutsik (1998)	← IRONY →	THE LAND Youssef Chahine (1968)
CLARO Glauber Rocha (1975)	← CHAOS →	INLAND Tariq Teguia (2010)
LA FÓRMULA SECRETA Rubén Gámez (1965)	← APPARITION →	ULYSSES' GAZE Theo Angelopoulos (1995)
VOZ ALTA Rafael Lozano-Hemmer (2008)	← TECHNÉ →	NOTRE MUSIQUE JL Godard (2004)

PROPOSAL BY DOREEN MENDE

Born in East Germany
lives between Berlin and London
Triple Juncture

Two photographs, both reporting on the beginning of the first Conference of the Non-Aligned Movement in Belgrade, in 1961. One translates a moment of excess into an image frame: shortly before 10 a.m., on September 1, 1961, about twenty-five photographers take pictures of the arrival and gathering of all twenty-five Non-Aligned nations's delegations around the oval table. Hundreds of photographic records made for press agencies, archives, newspapers and magazines produce not only an excess of the seen, but also an excess of the unheard, of the missed encounter, the undocumented.

The other image translates a moment of pausing into an image frame: shortly thereafter, at 10 a.m. on the same day, the first Conference of the Non-Aligned Heads of State opens with a minute of silence commemorating the deaths of those who dedicated their lives to the anti-colonial struggle, for the "liberty and independence of their people." The Conference began not by celebrating the new nation-state, as might have been expected, but by commemorating the struggle to bring the nation into existence. If we claim, with *Travelling Communiqué*, to "prolong" the formation of the NAM as a third space of emancipation that sought to unsettle the bipolar world order through a wide variety of anti-colonial thinking, then this prolongation, this mode of travelling, inevitably demands conditions for exhibiting processes by other means:

How can we not only think, but also enact and live the exhibiting processes through the undocumented and through the call for independence?

My proposal departs from image 3.

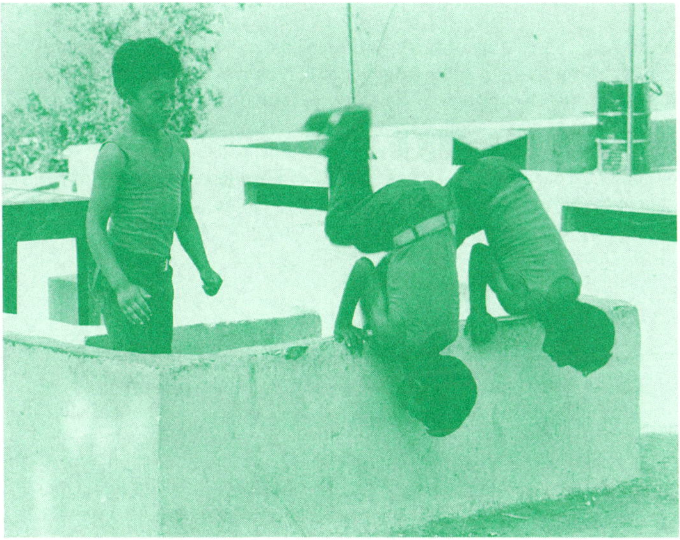

Image 3 (previous page)
My proposal departs from a single image taken by a press photographer from East Berlin, Horst Sturm, in the Sabra refugee camp in Beirut, shortly before the devastating massacre of Palestinians refugees in September 1982. The image is the juncture of the conditions created by an educational collaboration between the Palestinian and East German press agencies, i.e., framed by macro-political structures, and yet also the product of micro-political potency of solidarity. In this context, production of images can be understood as continuation of the Palestinian liberation struggle by photographic means.

During the first Conference of the Non-Aligned Movement in Belgrade in 1961, the German-German division was discussed "what may be called an international frontier" (Jawarharlal Nehru) whilst the Occupation of Palestine was addressed repeatedly. Looking at this image, here, implicates us in the prolonged conflicting wills in the Middle East, in which taking a binary position perpetuates strong forces of European enlightement: representation and individualism. In this frame, an exhibition can only be a symptom as it insists on being interpreted, a symptom of the limits of European modernity.

Image 1 (next page)
Scanned page from *La Conférence des chefs d'État ou de gouvernement des Pays Non-Alignés Belgrade 1–6 September 1961*, published by JUGOSLAVIJA in 1961 in English, French, and Spanish. The book contains protocols per day, conference documents, general debates, the letter sent as a "collective message" from the Conference, declarations, received telegrams, memoranda and messages from various parties, movements, organizations, groups and personalities; and photographs from the Photo Service within Tito's Cabinet.

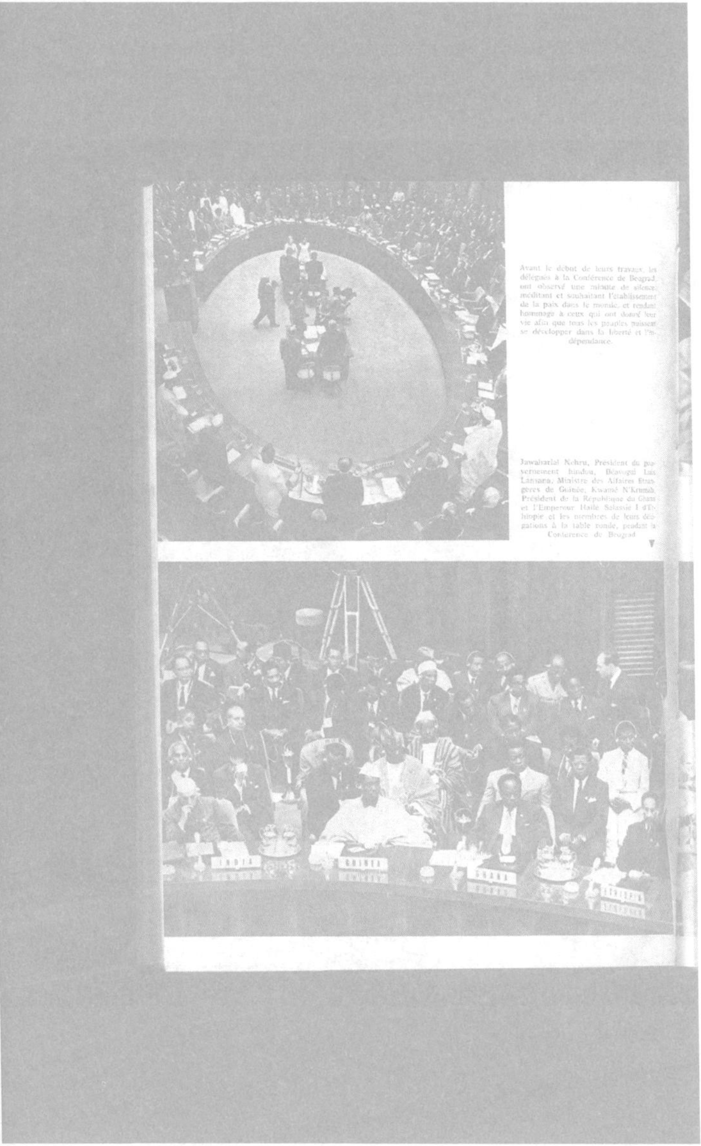

Avant le début de leurs travaux, les délégués à la Conférence de Beograd ont observé une minute de silence, méditant et souhaitant l'établissement de la paix dans le monde, et rendant hommage à ceux qui ont donné leur vie afin que tous les peuples puissent se développer dans la liberté et l'indépendance.

Jawaharlal Nehru, Président du gouvernement hindou, Béavogui Lansana, Ministre des Affaires Etrangères de Guinée, Kwamé N'Krumah, Président de la République du Ghana et l'Empereur Haïlé Sélassié I d'Ethiopie et les membres de leurs délégations à la table ronde, pendant la Conférence de Beograd

Image 2 (bellow)
MYH K-179/30, hall for plenary sessions on the opening day of the Conference of the Non-Aligned Movement, Belgrade, September 1, 1961. © Museum of Yugoslav History, Belgrade.

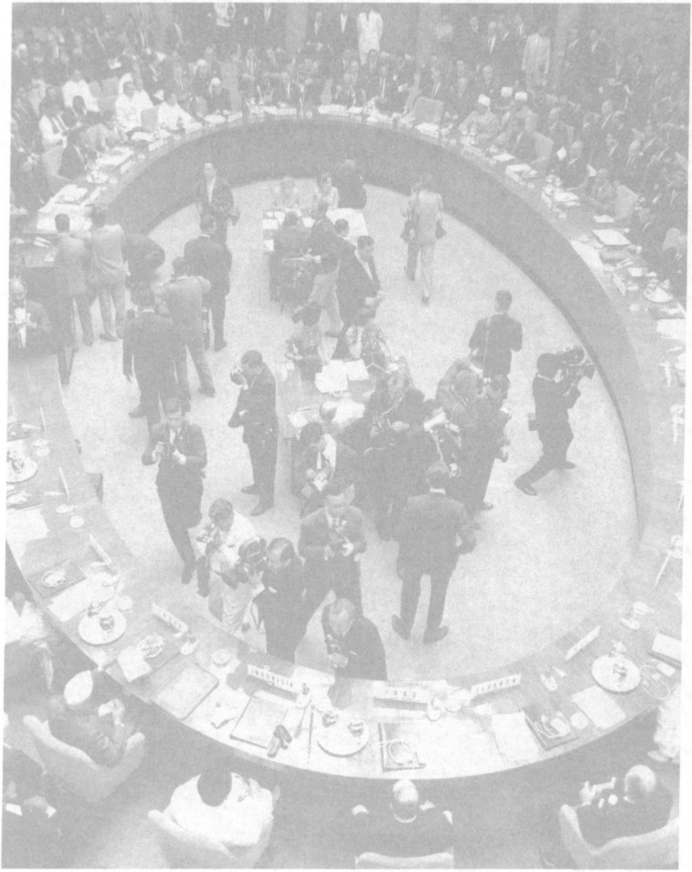

PROPOSAL BY SAMIA HENNI

Born in Algiers, lives in Zurich
Algeria 1961
The Paradigm of Counterinsurgency

In 1961, during the first conference of the Non-Aligned Countries in Belgrade, the Argentinian army, lead by the French, was hosting in Buenos Aires the first inter-American military course on counter-revolutionary warfare. Fourteen American countries, including the United States of America, gathered and studied French Modern Warfare: military counterrevolutionary actions and operations undertaken in Algeria since the outbreak of the Algerian Revolution in 1954.

Algeria had witnessed one of the longest and most violent anticolonial wars in Africa, supported by a number of anticolonial socialist and communist countries.

At the same time, Algeria was subjected to French military counterrevolutionary tactics and strategies, extensively disseminated among several countries of the Western Bloc.

Algeria 1961 endeavours to retrospectively picture one face of the genealogy of what is officially known today as COIN (COunterINsurgency) through which military, political, economic, psychological and civic actions are currently being conducted in order to "restore" the so-called "security of the world." This picture thus portrays the nature of Modern Warfare that occurred to be seamlessly epitomized in the Algerian War of National Liberation (1954-62), and of which the Non-Aligned Movement

Countries had explicitly alerted and forewarned the two opposite blocs, as stated in their letter from September 5, 1961, "Your Excellency has often pointed to the nature of modern war (...) which may well destroy humanity, and has pleaded for the maintenance of world peace."

ALGERIA 1961

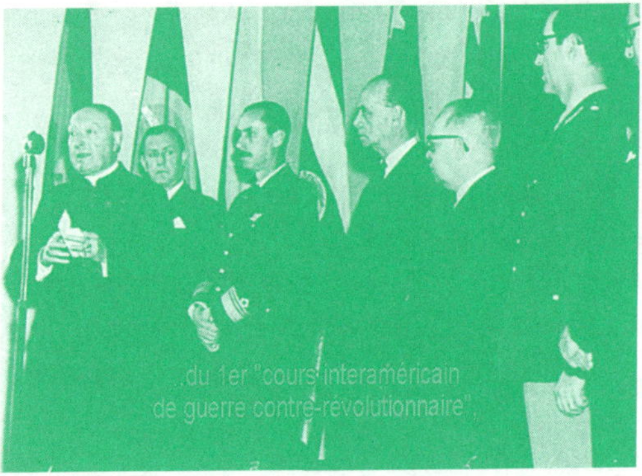

"In 1959, French and Argentinian armies signed an agreement. The French influence reached its peak in 1961, with the organization of the first 'inter-American counterrevolutionary course'."

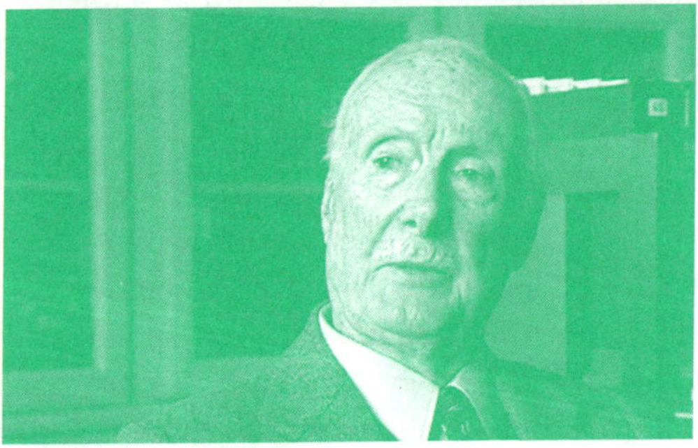

Armin Linke (AL) and Fabian Bechtle (FB)

NOTES TOWARDS A PHOTO ESSAY

with comments by Heike Behrend (HB), Radovan Cukić (RC), Dubravka Sekulić (DS), Sarah Poppel (SP), Philip Ursprung (PU), and Vanessa Vasić-Janeković (VVJ).

(PART 4)

1960_132_077

At the ceremonial Labor Day parade in Belgrade. State: Yugoslavia (Serbia); Location: Belgrade; Keywords: Yugoslav People's Army (YPA) air show, Industry, Panorama, Labor Day, Parade, Sport; Date: May 1, 1960

AL — Is this already a picture of modernism as folklore or of folklore of modernism? Is a parade also a part of folkloristic activity or not?

HB — Folkloristic tradition and folkloristic events are never innocent. They are staged, and they are, of course, political propaganda.

PU — During the industrialization, the religious tradition of carrying the image of a protective saint through the streets was secularized. Tatlin's model for the Third International in Petrograd in November 1920 is the most famous example of an architectural model displayed in a parade. In the early 1960s, nuclear energy is still synonymous with progress and prosperity. But the reactor as such already poses a problem of representation. The scale of the object on the wagon is unclear. Are the two human figures next to the machine in control of or rather controlled by the new technology?

1960_132_077

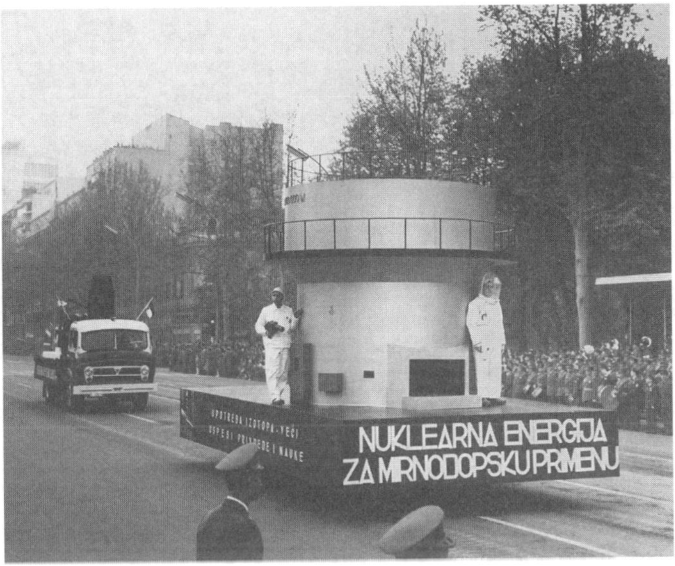

1960_132_079

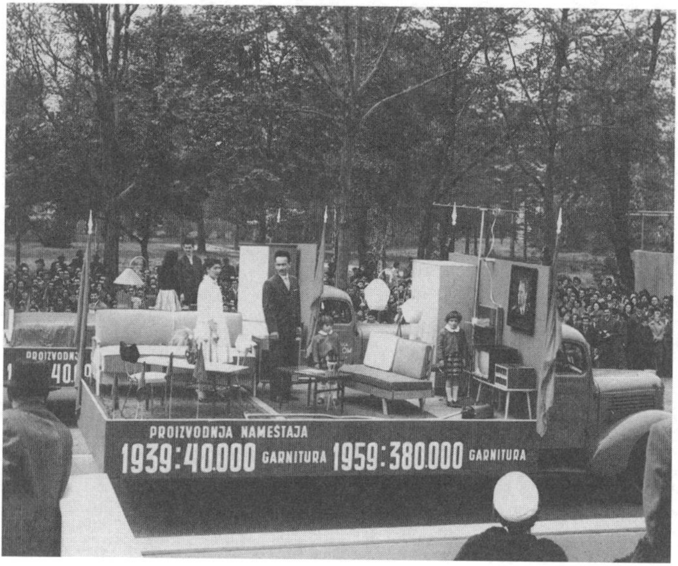
PROIZVODNJA NAMEŠTAJA
1939: 40.000 GARNITURA 1959: 380.000 GARNITURA

1960_132_079

At the ceremonial Labor Day parade in Belgrade. State: Yugoslavia (Serbia); Location: Belgrade; Keywords: YPA air show, Industry, Panorama, Labor Day, Parade, Sport; Date: May 1, 1960

PU — The Yugoslav family of 1960 has nothing to hide. It reproduces itself in a modern environment, which hardly differs from furniture in the United States or the Soviet Union. The so-called "Kitchen Debate" in Moscow in 1959, where Nikita Khrushchev and Richard Nixon joked over the question which country made better household goods, had proved that the Cold War might be an illusion kept alive by the superpowers in order to exploit their citizens. As Michel Foucault pointed out, life itself was the resource that both capitalism and socialism were drawing on.

1961_151_0059

Visit to Ghana: during Jovanka Broz's visit to a children's hospital in Accra. State: Ghana; Location: Accra; Keywords: Health, First Lady; Bilateral Relations: Ghana; Date: March 1, 1961

AL — Is this Ghanaian or Yugoslav flag?

FB — Yugoslav flag was based on Pan-Slavic colors of blue white and red, and the red-yellow-green Ghanaian flag was somehow a reversed version of the Ethiopian flag. In black and white, there is no significant difference between the Pan-African and Pan-Slavic colors.

1961_151_0059

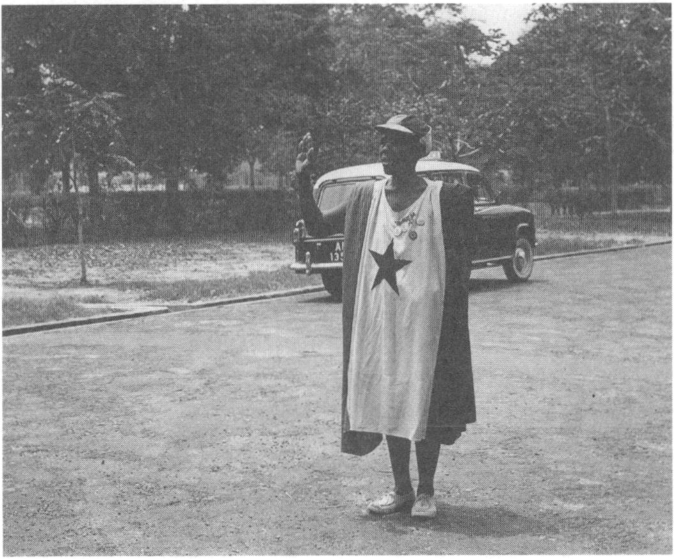

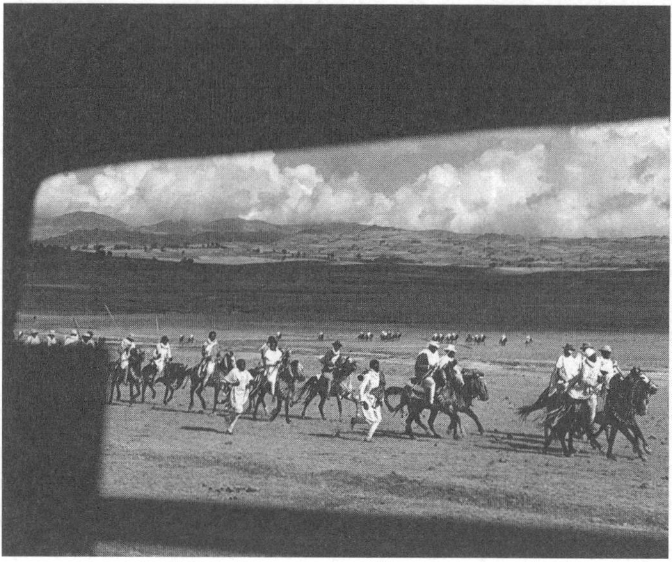

1955_50_0076

On the road to Addis Ababa: camp at Chefa on the way to T'armaber and lunch at T'armaber; on the way to Yercaud. State: Ethiopia; Location: Chefa; Keywords: Landscape, Welcome, Journey, Automobile, Special envoy, Traditional dress, Lunch, Camping; Bilateral Relations: Ethiopia; Date: December 13, 1955

FB & AL — Why are we so seduced by this type of image, despite being fully aware that it is a cliché of romantic landscape we encounter in travel magazines, cinema and epic narrations?

1967_338_087

Visit to Iraq: welcome at the airport and arrival to the residence. Destination: Iraq; Place: Baghdad; Keywords: Residence, Exterior, Journey, Automobile, Parade, Panorama, President of the State, Aeroplane, Non-Aligned Movement, Airport, Ceremonial welcome; Bilateral Relations: Iraq; Date: August 14, 1967

AL — There is an excess of inscription in our gaze, an abstraction of violence presumed to be inherent in this gaze.

VVJ & SP — We come face to face with a delusion of innocence, propped up by reliance on remote control warfare. The long chain of mediatized aerial images of war, from the two World Wars, through Vietnam, and the Gulf Wars could lead us to drone warfare.

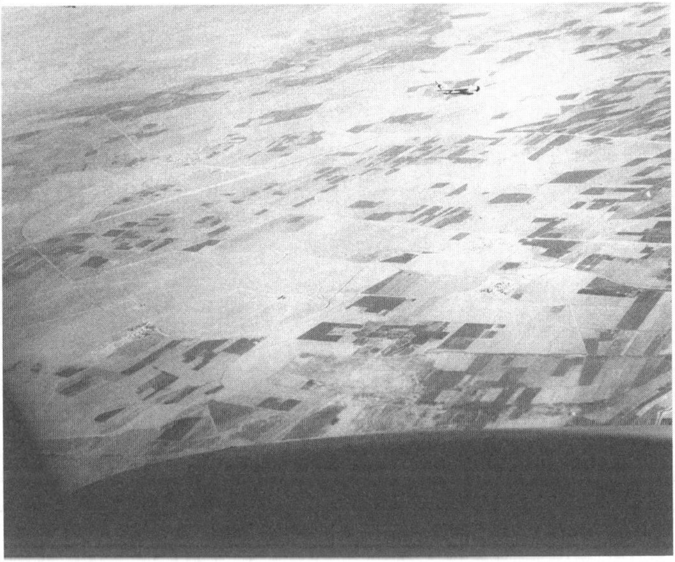

1959_111_0034

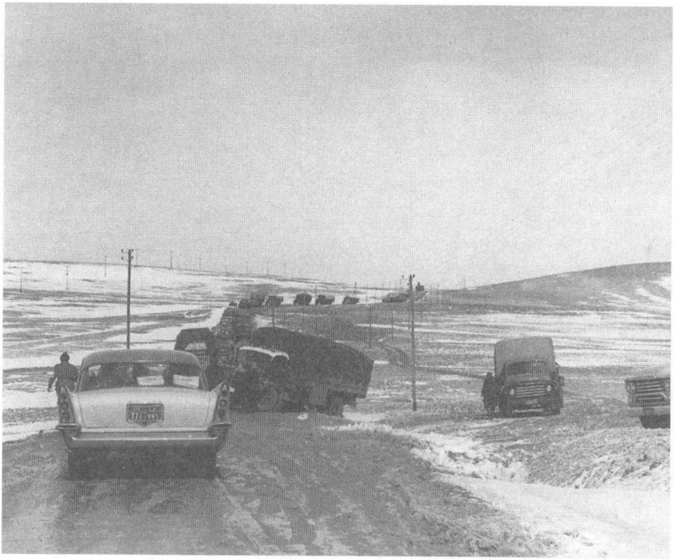

1959_111_0034

Visit to the UAR: on the way to Homs, in Homs and in Hamah. State: UAR (Syria); Location: Homs, Hama; Keywords: Landscape, Welcome, Journey, Panorama, President of the State; Bilateral Relations: UAR; Date: February 25, 1959

VVJ & SP — Military convoy stopped on the road—similar scenes were transmitted almost daily during the first Gulf War, set in the same landscape. The fifties car in this image might disturb our notions of temporality. Instead of clearly pointing to a particular period, it creates both a forward and a backward temporal movement of geopolitical violence.

1956_62_002

Ukrainian landscape. Location: USSR (Ukraine); Keywords: Landscape; Bilateral Relations: USSR; Date: June 21, 1956

1956_62_002

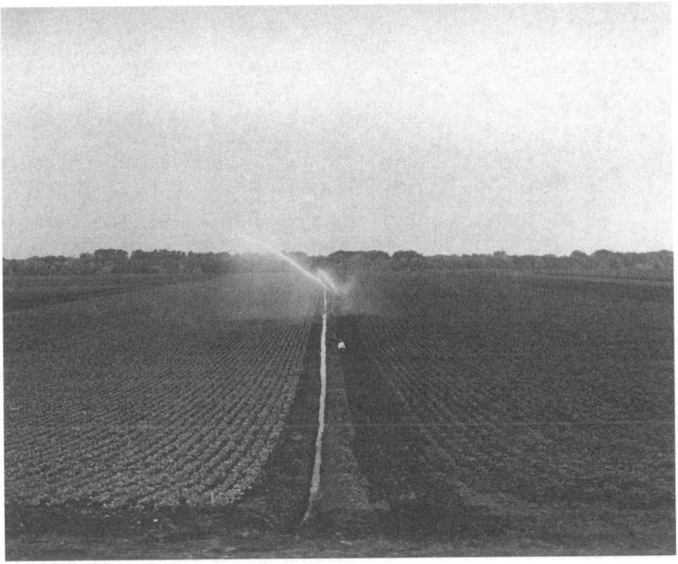

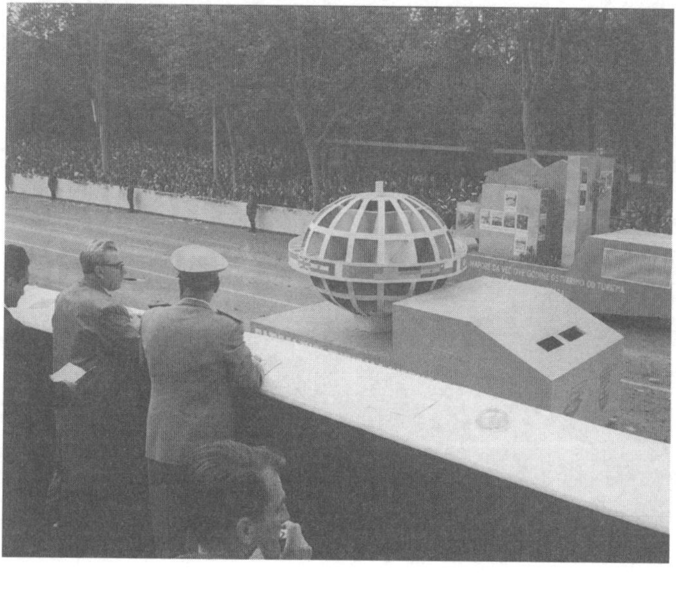

1964_240_033

Labor Day parade. State: Yugoslavia (Serbia); Location: Belgrade; Personalities: Josip Broz Tito, Aleksandar Ranković, Branko Pešić; Keywords: Pioneers, YPA, Panorama, Labor Day, Parade, Sport, Music, Health, Traditional dress, League of Youth of Yugoslavia; Date: May 1, 1964

1970_445_0079

The Third Non-Aligned Conference in Lusaka: before the start of the first session. State: Zambia; Location: Lusaka; Keywords: Exterior, Conference, President of the Government, Monarch, Vice-president of the State, President of the State, Non-Aligned Movement; Bilateral Relations: Zambia; Date: September 8, 1970

DS — At the Preparatory Meeting for the Lusaka Summit, in Lusaka, July 26–27, 1970, "Zambia read out a progress report on the physical arrangements for the Conference... and brought out the following points: (a) That the Conference Hall to be called 'Mulungushi Hall' and a Conference Village to be known as 'Mulungushi village' would be ready by the 25th of August 1970. The Mulungushi Hall will be equipped with simultaneous interpretation equipment and Tele-communication facilities to enable delegates to communicate directly with their various capitals. The Mulungushi Village will accommodate Heads of State/Government and their immediate entourages."

Mulungushi Hall and Village were designed and built by Energoprojekt, a Yugoslav construction company from Belgrade. The project was dubbed "heroic" as the conference hall and sixty-two villas were completed in 107 days.

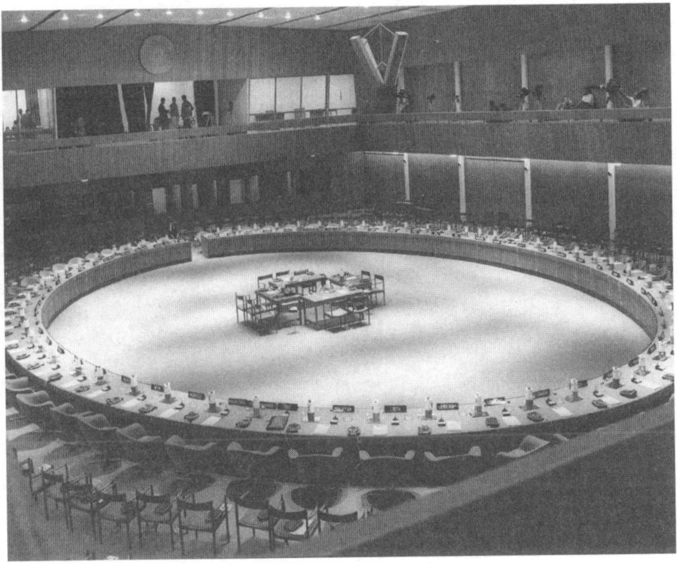

1970_445_0091

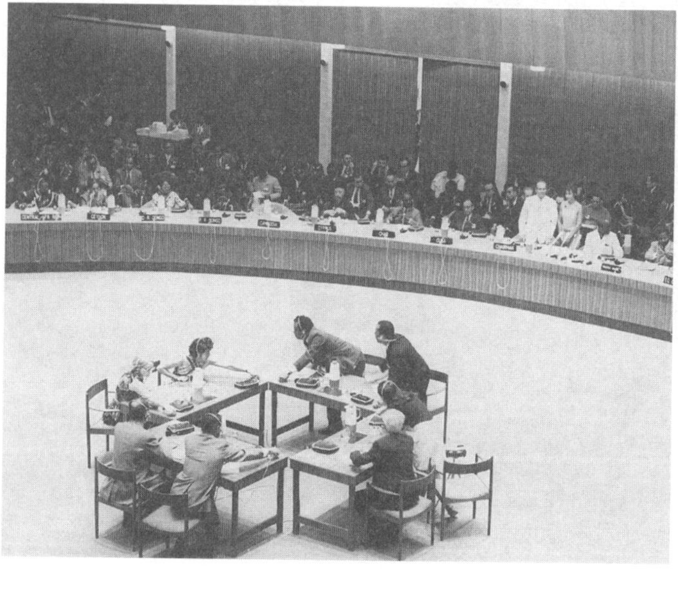

1970_445_0091

The Third Non-Aligned Conference in Lusaka: before the start of the first session. State: Zambia; Location: Lusaka; Keywords: Exterior, Conference, President of the Government, Monarch, Vice-president of the State, President of the State, Non-Aligned Movement; Bilateral Relations: Zambia; Date: September 8, 1970

PU — The assembly hall in Lusaka, built by the Belgrade construction company Energoprojekt speaks the language of international style. One architectural language suffices to represent political, economic and private realms on both sides of the Iron Curtain. The translators are not tucked away in cabins, they are center stage and the speaker has to wait until they are ready. Without them, the image seems to suggest, there is no interaction, no progress, and no power.

1955_50_0099

In Addis Ababa during official visit to Ethiopia. State: Ethiopia; Location: Addis Ababa; Keywords: Residence, Exterior, Parade, Monarch, Traditional dress; Bilateral Relations: Ethiopia;
Date: December 14, 1955

AL — Each step of this sculpture symbolizes a year of Italian fascist occupation. After the liberation, the Ethiopians, instead of destroying the modernist monument, placed the Ethiopian lion on top.

1955_50_0099

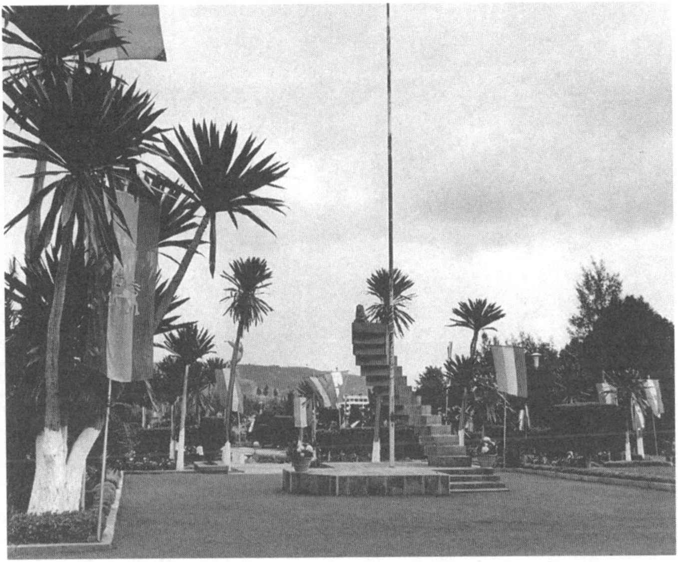

1961_153_0045

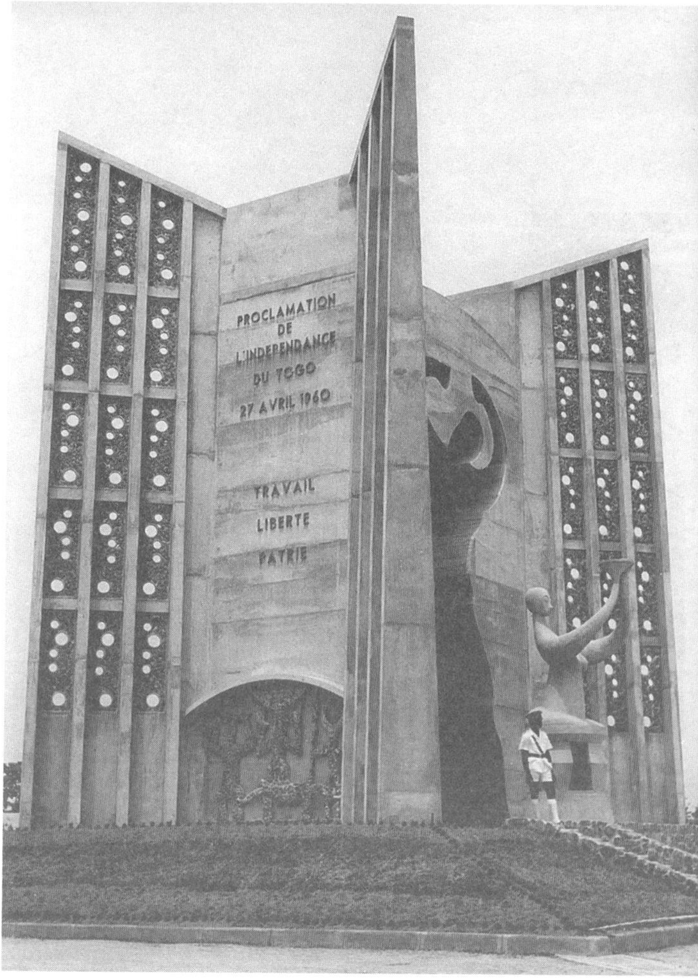

1961_153_0045

Visit to Togo: images from Lomé. State: Togo; Location: Lomé; Keywords: Panorama, Historic-cultural monument; Bilateral Relations: Togo; Date: March 5, 1961

PU — "Work, Freedom, Homeland" is the slogan on the monument to independence. The concrete structure, halfway between sculpture and architecture, seems to embrace the environment like a motherly figure in the foreground. The State as an abstract concept gets a human face and relates to the ground. Such participatory monuments, blending realist and non-figurative forms, were highly popular throughout Yugoslavia from the late fifties to the eighties. No wonder the photographer had sympathy for the structure.

1954_37_0429

Chandigarh: arrival, looking at the scale model of the new town, visiting the Technical High School, children's homes, hospitals and the Supreme Court building. State: India; Location: Chandigarh; Keywords: Automobile, Construction, Panorama, Health, Judiciary, University, Children's home; Bilateral Relations: India; Date: December 26, 1954

AL — Chandigarh under construction—a modernist city planned from scratch by Le Corbusier after India's independence ...

PU — The building is almost completed. The ornamental aspect is striking and not yet hidden behind vegetation. The cyclists in the foreground seem to halt to admire the site.

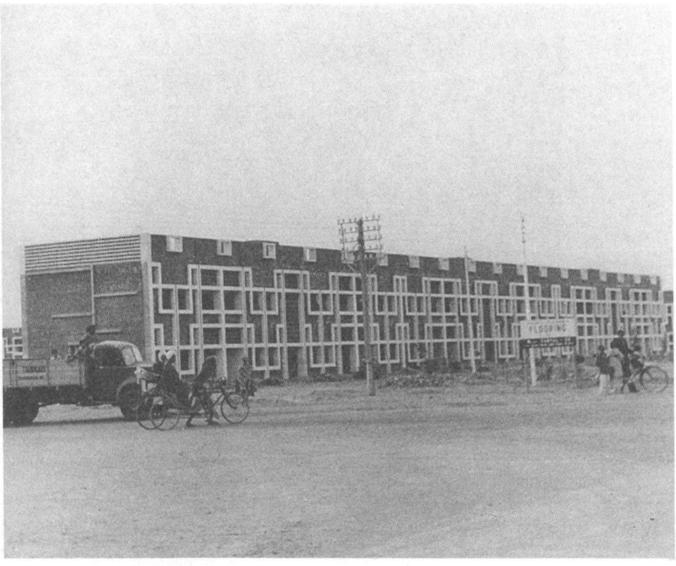

1954_37_0439

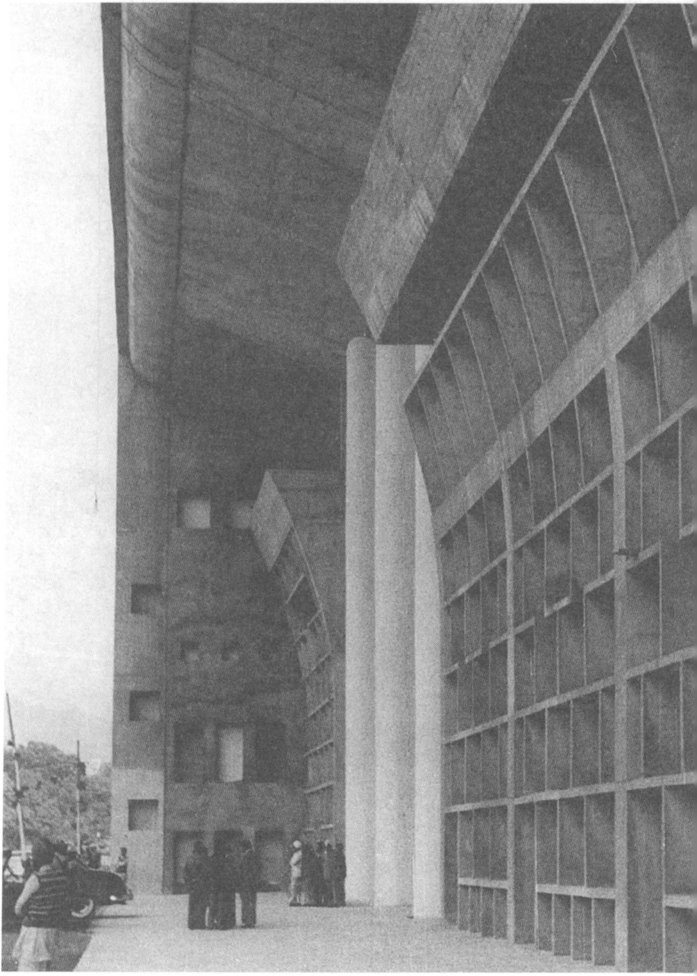

1954_37_0439

Chandigarh: arrival, looking at the scale model of the new town, visiting the Technical High School, children's homes, hospitals and the Supreme Court building. State: India; Location: Chandigarh; Keywords: Automobile, Construction, Panorama, Health, Judiciary, University, Children's home; Bilateral Relations: India; Date: December 26, 1954

PU — The image shows how the building embraces public space. Outside and inside intertwine, there seems to be no such thing as exclusion. It is exemplary of the post-war belief in the blessings of the welfare state.

1968_353_090

Visit to Pakistan: a walk through Islamabad
State: Pakistan; Location: Islamabad; Keywords: Walk, Panorama, Architecture, Book of impressions, President of the State; Bilateral Relations: Pakistan; Date: January 11, 1968

PU — Nature is tamed, yet the overall design tends to avoid symmetry and spatial hierarchy.

DS — Planned as the new capital of Pakistan in the late 1950s by Konstidos Doxiadis, Islamabad was completed mid-1960s. In 1968, it probably reminded the Yugoslav delegation of New Belgrade, their modernist capital in the making.

Though close to the Non-Aligned Movement, Pakistan became a full member only at the 1979 Havana Summit; its membership in the Southeast Asia Treaty Organization and in the Central Treaty Organization were seen as aligning with the Atlantic Pact and counter to the basic concept of the NAM.

1968_353_090

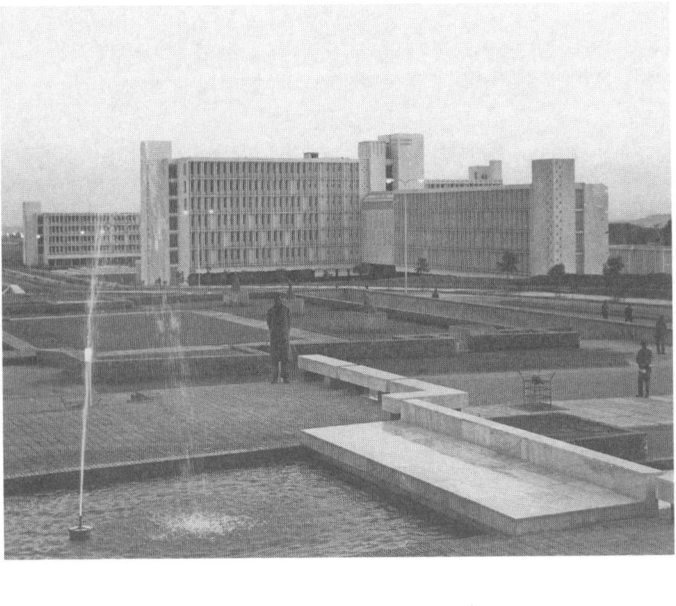

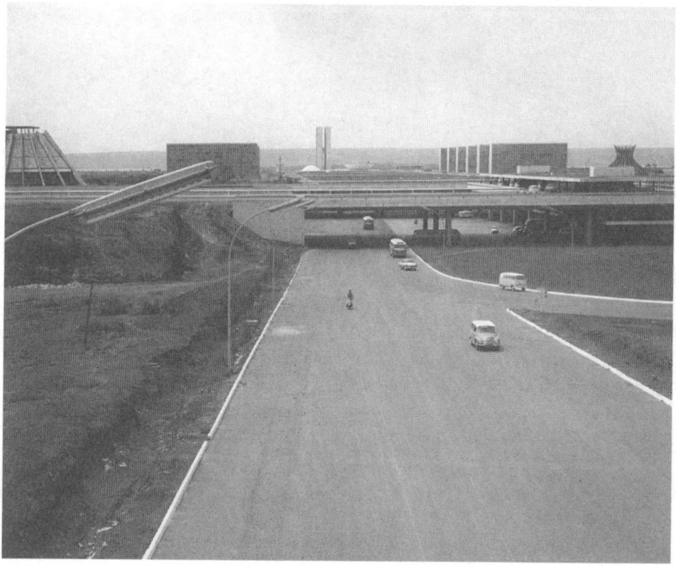

Visit to Brazil: landscapes, details, the "sculpture buildings" of Brasilia. State: Brazil; Location: Brasilia; Keywords Exterior, Landscape, Visual arts, Agriculture, Panorama; Bilateral Relations: Brazil; Date: September 22, 1963

PU — The photographer takes the viewpoint of the urban planner, overlooking his model. The towers of the National Congress Center are fading away in the distance. The roads seem over-dimensioned, something between an urban highway, a runway, and a parking lot. It becomes clear that the city was primarily designed to be perceived from the window of an automobile.

1979_690_143

Visit to Kuwait: Water Towers. State: Kuwait; Location: Kuwait; Keywords: Panorama, Taking photographs, Non-Aligned Movement; Bilateral Relations: Kuwait; Date: February 2, 1979

PU — The Kuwait Towers hold water tanks and a restaurant. Designed by a Danish architect, they were built by Energoprojekt and completed in 1979. No doubt the photographers knew about the Yugoslav origin of the landmark. Today, they invoke the iconic television tower in East Berlin. At the time, it was certainly read as the symbol of triumph of the oil producers of the Gulf area, who were booming during the 1970s recession.

1979_690_143

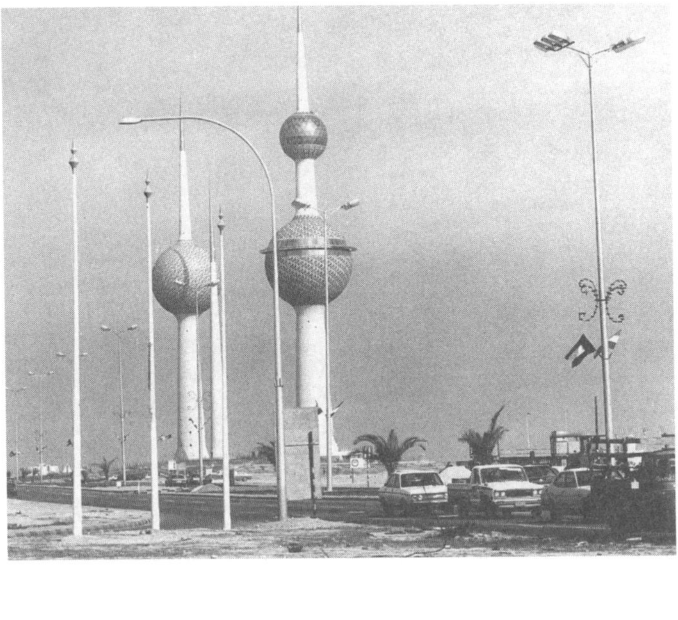

1971_475_0056

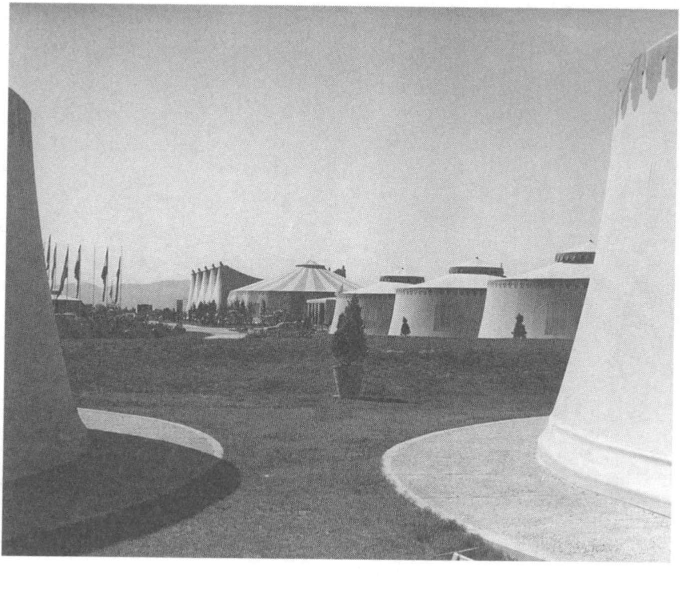

1971_475_0056

Celebrating 2,500 years of the Iranian Empire
State: Iran; Location: Persepolis; Personalities: Jovanka Broz, Lijana Tambača; Keywords: Anniversary, Panorama, First Lady; Bilateral Relations: Iran; Date: October 15, 1971

1959_111_0038

Visit to the UAR: on the way to Homs, in Homs and in Hamah. State: UAR (Syria); Location: Homs, Hamah; Keywords: Landscape, Welcome, Journey, Panorama, President of the state; Bilateral Relations: UAR; Date: February 25, 1959

DS — For architects from Yugoslavia working in Non-Aligned Countries such as Syria, local architecture was both the source of confusion and inspiration. They were perplexed as to how to carry this knowledge into the modernist cannon. Their attempts at translating the experience of traditional architecture into modernist buildings were often naïve and formal.

1959_111_0038

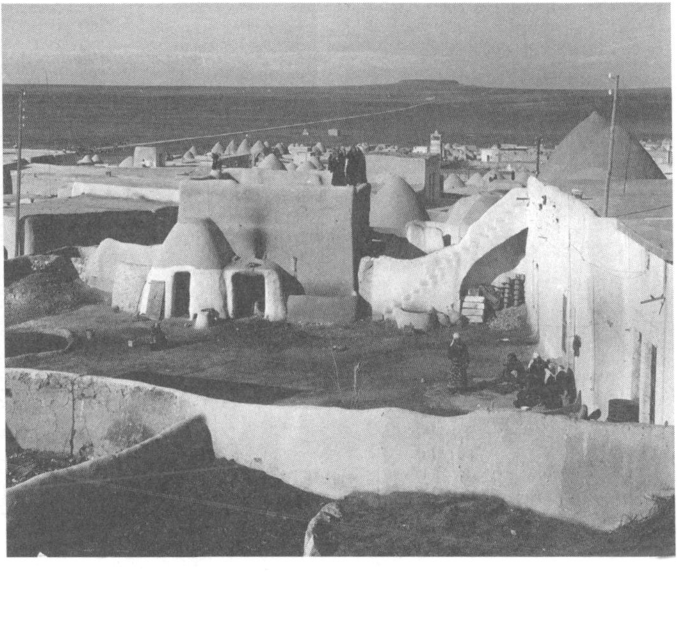

1968_365_083

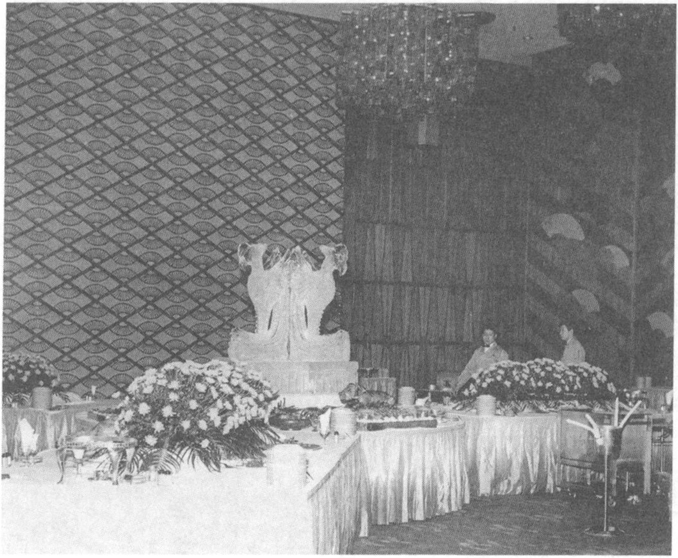

1968_365_083

Visit to Japan: the reception in honour of Emperor Hirohito, in the Hotel New Otani. State: Japan; Location: Tokyo; Keywords: Interior, Ceremonial reception, President of the Government, Monarch, Hotel, Dinner; Bilateral relations: Japan; Date: April 11, 1968

RC — Instead of at the Yugoslav Embassy, Tito held a reception in honor of Emperor Hirohito in the prestigious Hotel New Otani. The Archive of Yugoslavia holds records of how such receptions were held, detailing which delicacies made it onto the Yugoslavian diplomatic menu.

1962_194_102

The opening of the May 25 Museum.
State: Yugoslavia (Serbia); Location: Belgrade; Keywords: Exterior, Panorama, Relay, Museum, Ceremonial opening, Youth Day; Date: May 24, 1962

1962_194_102

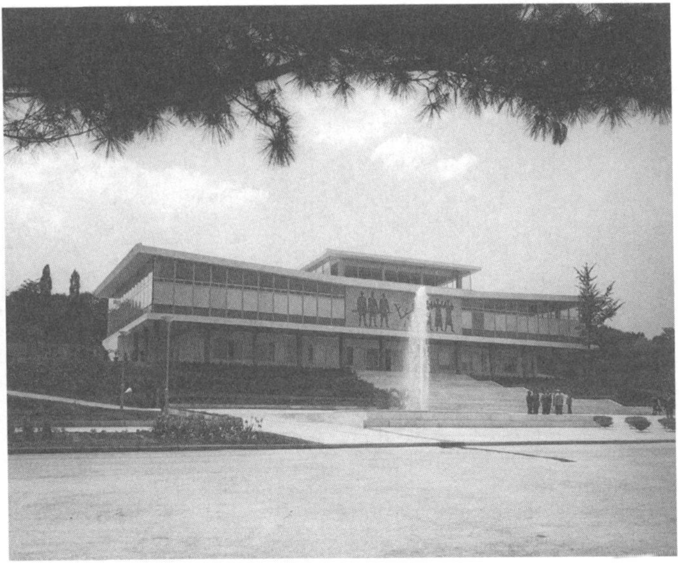

1962_194_111

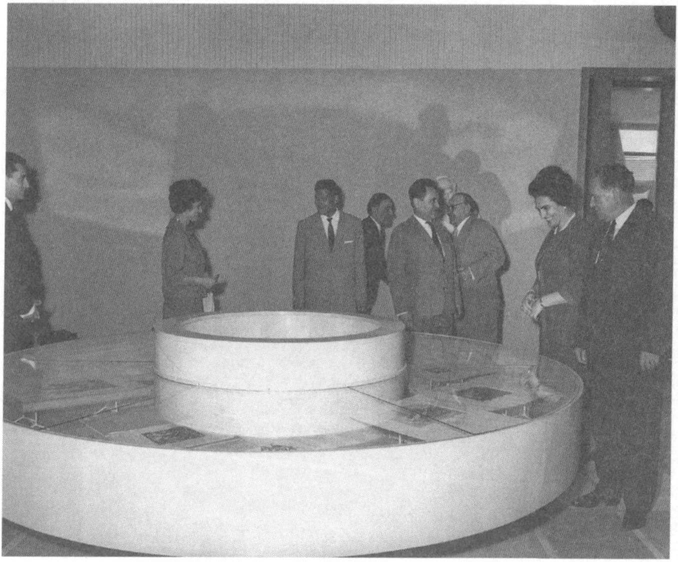

1962_194_111

[Tito] Visiting the May 25 Museum with Jovanka [Broz] and the sculptor [Antun] Augustinčić. State: Yugoslavia (Serbia); Location: Belgrade; Personalities: Jovan Veselinov, Petar Stambolić, Avdo Humo, Mijalko Todorović, Milijan Neoričić, Bogdan Crnobrnja, Veljko Zeković, Luka Božović, Branko Rubinjoni, Dalibor Soldatić, Milojko Drulović; Keywords: Walk, Panorama, Relay, Museum; Date: May 22, 1962

FB — In an interview in 2012, Katarina Živanović, then Director of the MYH, described the museum building as somehow being at the "epicentre of Serbian contemporary history," because of Milošević living in Tito's residence, which is part of the museum complex.

Milošević was there throughout the NATO bombing campaign in 1999; he was holed up in there during the uprising of October 2000, and finally taken from the residence in early 2001, to face trial at the International Criminal Tribunal for the Former Yugoslavia. By 2012 media reports alleged that a part of the former residential complex would become residence for future presidents of Serbia.

As Živanović said, "This geographic point thus attains a very specific energy ... what is also special is that the museum is today also Tito's and Jovanka's grave—a memorial centre!"

1962_194_118

[Tito] Visiting the May 25 Museum with Jovanka [Broz] and the sculptor Augustinčić. State: Yugoslavia (Serbia); Location: Belgrade; Personalities: Jovan Veselinov, Petar Stambolić, Avdo Humo, Mijalko Todorović, Milijan Neoričić, Bogdan Crnobrnja, Veljko Zeković, Luka Božović, Branko Rubinjoni, Dalibor Soldatić, Milojko Drulović; Keywords: Walk, Panorama, Relay, Museum; Date: May 22, 1962

1962_194_118

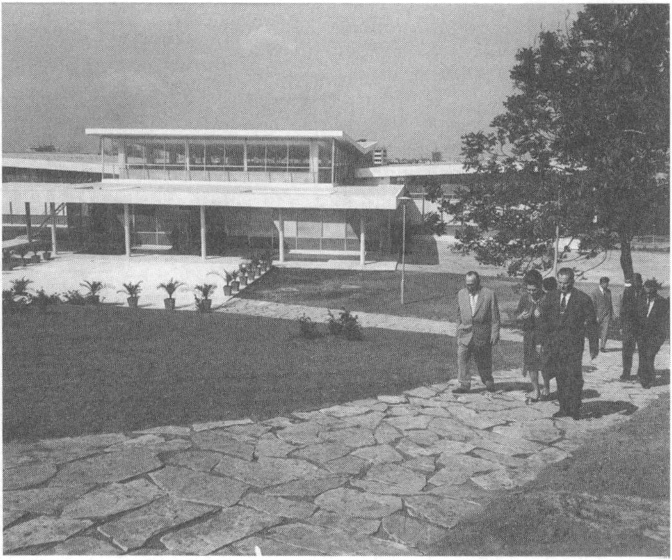

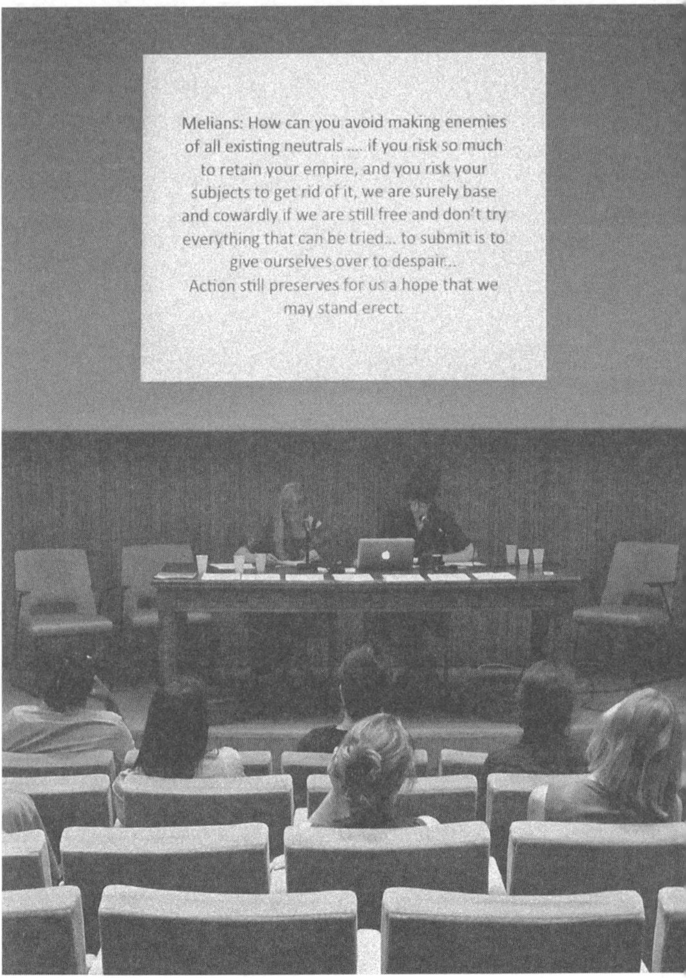

"On Neutrality," lecture-performance by Jelena Vesić and Rachel O'Reilly, Museum of Yugoslav History, Belgrade, 2014

Jelena Vesić and Rachel O'Reilly

ON NEUTRALITY
(Introduction)

Our lecture-performance takes the concept of "neutrality" or "neutralization" as juxtapolitical in terms of its use in political and aesthetical position-taking within different "international relations," especially as a response to discrepancies of power.

In contrast to the moral minimalist concept of neutrality as it is mobilized in liberal governmentalities, historically and today, across art and politics, the project considers the rich variegated recent history of situated, politicized forms of political neutrality concepts, which stemmed from the active positioning of Non-Alignment and "third world countries" gaining independence during the Cold War era and re-claiming neutrality as a politics of de-colonization, independence, peace and non-alignment with the powerful world empires of the time ...

This politicized history of neutrality concepts is juxtaposed with the waves of depoliticizing neutrality, including curatorial neutralizations of politics, which, aided and abetted by the humanitarian rhetoric of contemporary art, persist in attenuating institutional anxiety and agonistic possibilities of production in contexts of re-colonization by multinational corporations.

The lecture performance consists of six chapters:

1. On Genealogies of Political Neutrality
2. *We Are Small and We Have Politics*: On the Logic that Reads as Bafflement
3. Neutrality in Non-Aligned Declarations: *The Wording of the Non-Aligned "Worlding"*
4. Neutralism of the Millennial White Cube
5. EU Turn: On the Empty Chair in Non-Aligned Congress, a Placeholder for the Representative of Yugoslavia Since the Beginning of the 1990s
6. Curatorial or Artistic Neutrality Means to Hide the Conditions of Production Under the Surface of the Visible

This research draws on Jelena Vesić's interests in lecture performance and language based moving images and Rachel O'Reilly's interests in poetry, post-cinema, and expanded politics of installation and governance.

THE JUXTAPOLITICAL FORM OF NEUTRALITY:
Between Non-Aligned Movements and Neoliberal Curatorial Economies
(excerpt from the script)

Neutrality as a political concept has existed as long as there has been warfare. At its simplest, neutrality means not taking part in a war, or more loosely, to remain uncontaminated by great rivalries. But this terminological negativity can get quite complex, juxtapolitical, and highly generative, as it is utilized across both left and right political positions. Different erections of neutrality discourses allegorize the sovereignty of state power in line with individual forms of self-determination, dissociation and detachment from social and economic relations. Further, each erection of the neutral tends to prioritize either politics over economics OR economy over politics, in a dialectical transvaluation of the concept of profit.

Today we encounter "neutrality" nominally connoting European states which actively contribute to the securitization and pacification of the New Economy, through programs of depoliticization and transnational security. These same governmentalities —installed in our everyday forms of professional comportment of neoliberal governance—emphasize the transcendentalism of administrative decisions from the political itself.

What legacies of the Non-Aligned Movement help us to think against this active destructivity of the neutral in the forces of global capital? What kinds of tactics of non-alignment from this present version of the global contemporary are possible?

Neutrality as the moniker of refrain from conflict escalation and *power politics* was meaningfully re-signified in the post Second World War period within the ideology of peace. It was also used relationally in the decolonization processes of newly independent nation states, and the extension of their struggle for equality and international political participation.

In the Wording of the Non-Alignment Worlding, *neutrality* accompanied with the adjective *active* or *politicized* (*active neutrality, politicized neutrality*) was synonymous for non-alignment, for independent politics and (national) sovereignty, for solidarity and friendship, for a politics of "eternal peace," for equality and true democracy, and for the validity of "right" in the figuration of small agents (c.f. might = right).

Because the term is such a placeholder, or empty signifier, the articulations of neutrality by Non-Aligned, as a nominal "good object" predicated on an active, decolonial protagonism in global politics, presents a particularly interesting case of nominal differencing from competing investments in the Neutral.

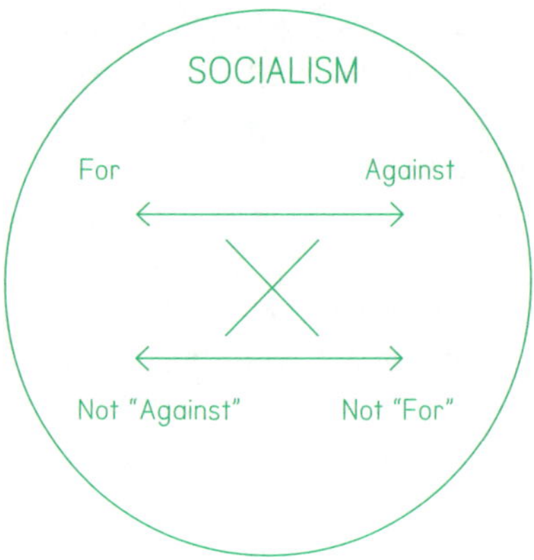

Here, the Neutral is the thought and practice of the non-conflictual, but it is nevertheless bound to assertion, to conflict, in order to make itself heard... By dodging or baffling the paradigmatic, oppositional structure of meaning, it aims at the suspension of the conflictual basis of discourse.

WE ARE SMALL AND WE HAVE POLITICS: ON THE LOGIC THAT READS AS BAFFLEMENT

An early instance of *active neutrality* can be located in the mythologized historical reaction of the people of the island of Melos to the Athenians during the Peloponnesian War. As documented by Thucydides during the war between Athens and Sparta (416–15 BC), neutrality is first argued for by the Melians as a viable (but defeated) oppositional politics of active non-involvement in war.

MELIANS

Your military preparations are too far advanced for us to agree with what you say... we see you are come to be judges in your own cause, and that all we can reasonably expect from this negotiation is war (if we prove to have right on our side and refuse to submit), and in the contrary case, slavery.

ATHENIANS

If you have met with us to reason about presentiments of the future, or for anything other than to consult for your safety, we will give over; otherwise we will go on.

MELIANS

It is natural and excusable, for men in our position, to turn more ways than one both in thought and utterance. However, the question in this conference is, as you say, the safety of our country ...

ATHENIANS

We shall not trouble you with specious pretences, and make a long speech which would not be believed ... in return we hope you don't say that you have done us no wrong AND know as well as we do that "RIGHT" is only in question between equals in power, while the strong do what they can and the weak suffer what they must.

MELIANS

YOU ask us to ignore what is RIGHT, and talk only of interest [BUT] our common protection IS the privilege of being allowed, when in danger, to invoke what is fair and right, and even to profit by arguments not strictly valid if they can be argued well.

ATHENIANS

The end of our empire, if end it should be, does not frighten us:

we come here in the interest of our empire, and the preservation of your country;

MELIANS

HOW could it be as GOOD for us to serve,
as it is for you to rule?

ATHENIANS

Because you would have the advantage of submitting before suffering the worst, and we should gain by not destroying you.

MELIANS

So you would not consent to our being neutral, friends instead of enemies, but allies of neither side.

ATHENIANS

No; for your hostility cannot so much hurt us as your friendship will be an argument to our subjects of our weakness, and your enmity of our power.

MELIANS

Is that your idea of equity, to put those who have nothing to do with you in the same category with peoples that are most of them your own colonists, and conquered rebels?

ATHENIANS

As far as right goes ... if any maintain their independence it is because they are strong ... if we do not molest them it is because we are afraid; so besides extending our empire we should gain in security by your subjection; the fact that you are islanders and weaker than others renders it all the more important that you should not succeed in baffling the masters of the sea.

MELIANS

How can you avoid making enemies of all existing neutrals ... if you risk so much to retain your empire, and you risk your subjects to get rid of it, WE ARE SURELY BASE AND COWARDLY if we are still free and don't try everything that can be tried, ... to submit is to give ourselves over to despair, ... action still preserves for us a hope that we may stand erect.

ATHENIANS

Hope, danger's comforter, may be indulged in by those who have abundant resources...

MELIANS

We are as aware as you are, of the difficulty of contending against your power and fortune. But we trust that the gods may grant us fortune as good as yours, since we are just men fighting against unjust ... Our confidence, therefore, is not so utterly irrational.

What does it mean to propose, to exhibit a proposal, to expose a proposal publicly within the context and politico-formalism of Non-Aligned? Indeed, what does it mean to act as "propositionalist" in any contemporary exhibition regime, within the neoliberal (neocolonial) administration of the aesthetic? Is it that we are framed by the desire for a (non)existent, or impossible politic ... ? Who can be the contemporary receiver of the communiqué addressed by the Non-Aligned political community of the powerless majority, in their decolonizing (class) struggle, within the current global disposition of power?

The question "Who is the addressee of the Communiqué today?" can only be answered by those who actively decide to become an addressee. The politicization of art remains a neutralizing subsitute for political struggle as long as the notion of autonomy comfortably situates itself within the parameters of the known (of contemporary art as institution). Therefore, we introduce (or return to) a third term, "ACTIVE NEUTRALITY" borrowed from the political vocabulary of Non-Aligned Movement ... precisely because the place of the object of politics is left empty, to be filled in the future ... while its subjects are designated as active towards, but also neutrally positioned in relation to the politics of power. Is active neutrality just a reconciliatory synthesis of antithetical logic, of being politically active but acting as politically neutral ... or can it bring us to a new place, where a multitude of negations provides some new space of autonomous activity?

Miroljub Stojanović

ANTICOLONIAL CINEMA

Every social revolution that has come into being since the advent of film, has developed "its own" revolutionary cinema with programmatic basis, aesthetics and ethics. Beginning with Russian revolutionary cinema, this consolidation of cinematic language unfolded firstly on the political and ideological planes, and then through testing for appropriate production possibilities, resulting in a significantly new conception of film and its expressive potential; in thinking the radius of its societal performance anew.

In some places, it was the cinema that prepared the revolution, or at least participated in it. In other places, cinema became the experimental resultant of revolutionary legacies. The cinema of anticolonial struggle or anticolonial cinema has a long tradition of full synchronicity with the efforts of decolonizing aspirations. What interests us in this case, rather than the mutual interfering between film and revolution, is the need to point out why these films are still alive for us today, still valid, topical, inspiring and even, largely unsurpassed.

"Anticolonial cinema" is not the best determinant for legitimizing this aesthetics. In truth, few determinants possess the breadth that might encompass all the aspects and complexities of this kind of cinema. "Militant Cinema," "Third Cinema," "Radical Political Cinema," "Propaganda Films," "Engaged Cinema," etc. are just some of the circular idiomatic creations differentiating this "New Film" from cinema as understood within the classical bourgeois conception: cinema as a petrified model of entertainment and profitability rolling hand in hand as sole measures of its existence.

When Argentine filmmakers Fernando Solanas and Octavio Getino launched, at the end of the sixties, the operative, programmatically charged determinant Third Cinema, within their "Manifesto Towards a Third Cinema!",[1] anticolonial films or authentic films of the revolution had already attained immeasurable significance in various parts of the world.

The Third Cinema manifesto argued for a "cinema of anti-imperialist struggle by the peoples of the Third world and the like-minded within the imperialist countries." The Third Cinema is founded in the deconstruction of the dominant, mainstream cinema and the accompanying mythology, star system and ultra-commercialization; more so, however, it rests on affirming and legitimizing those problem levels of contemporaneity that, in their conflictual proportions, become unavoidable factors in social relations, or rather, on demystifying the true causes of political antagonisms and tensions and finding appropriate cinematic form for this socio-political vivisection. This, then, becomes the imperative creative and moral principle of the Third Cinema.

The maximalization of the cinematic efforts moving in this direction did not begin with Solanas and

1. Available online, at https://ufsinfronteradotcom.files.wordpress.com/2011/05/tercer-cine-getino-solonas-19691.pdf, and put into practice in their 1968 film *La hora de los hornos* (*The Hour of the Furnaces*).

Getino, as they themselves point out. Back in 1965, the great Brazilian director and one of the greatest filmmakers of the Third World ever, Glauber Rocha, anticipated in his legendary polemical manifesto "The Aesthetics of Hunger"[2] the markers framing intensification in the work of Solanas and Getino. It was Rocha who outlined and most concisely explicated the transparent grammar of future cinema.

A chronological overview, though not our intention on this occasion, manifests that anticolonial cinema had its pioneers and anticipating actors. Today, in new constellations of re-evaluating and re-actualizing the significance of their opus, this fact demands our attention. For example, Usmar Ismail has made his exceptional contribution through pronounced anticolonial features in the films *The Long March* and *Six Hours in Yogya*, at the beginning of the fifties, in Indonesia. Little known outside his country, Ismail is one of the fundamentally essential filmmakers of the Third World.

There are also the militant and propaganda films of North Vietnam during the phase of escalating war, prior to the February 1968 Tet offensive; Algerian documentary films from the period of the most brutal French repression; and especially Latin American films made after and during the 1964 coup d'état in Brazil that installed the notorious General Emílio Garrastazu Médici and saw the adoption of fascist, repressive Institutional Act Number Five, in 1968, that brought Brazil to the edge of political chaos by suspending the hard won civic liberties, including creative freedom,

2. Available online, https://www.amherst.edu/media/view/38122/original/ROCHA_Aesth_Hunger.pdf.

and rotated Brazil's democracy into a fascist military clique with unlimited political power. These films are among the most fascinating examples of making, in praxis, the demands put forth by Solanas and Getino. Many more were made that must not be forgotten or allowed to escape our attention. The liberation movements in Africa offered a framework of anticolonial aspirations to a number of fascinating filmmakers of markedly progressive outlook, whose appearance is relevant globally. Med Hondo in Mauritania, Ousmane Sembène in Senegal, Haile Gerima in Ethiopia, Mario Borgneth in Mozambique, Gadalla Gubara in Sudan, the first of the pioneers, and the unsurpassed political charge of Egypt's New Cinema Collective have produced fundamentally significant films of truly anticolonial markings.

A canon of Anticolonial Cinema would include hundreds of works. That such a canon still does not exist on a global plane means only that a possibility for systematization has not come up. We are yet to define parameters enabling some films to either flow in or out of our thematic circle; sorting criteria; subgenre and a-national classifications; or to periodize moments that are not without significance in a purely historiographic order.

We would also be rather unjust towards those progressive filmmakers who gave an authentic contribution to the anticolonial vision, and who are, according to Solanas and Getino, the like-minded of their oppressed brethren, yet living in the imperialist countries. Paradoxically, it is precisely in those countries that the archetype exists and this enchanting dialectic of the negative must not be avoided, for it is simply necessary for understanding and detecting the global phenomenon. The revolutionary cinematic field as mapped by Jean-Luc Godard, even the one reaching back to Nagisa Oshima and his film *Night and Fog in Japan* (*Nihon no Yoru to Kiri*, 1960), remain a sacrosanct legacy as much as a revolutionary cinematic and moral testament. This is what it is, above all, in its surprising topicality today. Today, when the face of imperialism takes new veils, when colonialist aspirations, mimicking globalist aims, manifest more intensely than ever, strengthened by the logistics of domestic oligarchies and transnationalists of various colors, perhaps we need a new cinema simply to parry the ever more aggressive lunges by "corporatism with a human face." Our "interview with history," as in the title of Oriana Fallacci's famous 1976 book, can begin via the necessity of prior experiences and out of almost identical humanist and ethical needs.

There is only one demarcation line within the understanding of progressive tendencies of humanity, stretched out above sectarianism, nationalism, aesthetic preferences, personal charisma and short flights. On the other side of cinema and life, there are only, as Joan Baez put it, diamonds and rust. Rust is the result of a natural process, whilst diamonds are a manifestation of human aspirations, efforts, searching, invention and persistence. Rust is a powerful catalyst and it is the task of us all to render it harmless.

FILM PROGRAM

This Film Program offers neither an evocative, nor retrospective academic view of certain countries's contribution to global film culture. Conceived primarily as a re-actualized model of filmic behavior by wholly anticolonial generations, it demonstrates the multitude of planes on which this model functions, starting with that at which contemporary audiences identify themselves. Simply put, the time of these films has not passed and their reciprocity with the contemporary is truly astonishing.

When Mohamed Lakdar Hamina received Palme D'Or in Cannes, in 1975, for his film *Chronicle of the Years of the Embers*, an irony was reflected in fact that this took place in the country against whose colonial presence in Algeria this film was made.

Today's ironies are altogether subtler and no longer the privilege of imperial strategies alone. This program reflects, above all, the enormous plurality of the aesthetic models of engaged cinema, or militant cinema. Having become a textbook for revolutionaries, this cinema has, more importantly, set new standards of production, form and ethics.

June 13, 2014
Academic Film Center
The Winds of Aures (Algeria, 1966), Mohammed Lakhdar Hamina

June 22, 2014
MYH cinema
Documentary films from North Vietnam

1. A North Vietnamese propaganda documentary film about the war
2. *Vietnam War Documentary: Inside The Viet Cong*
3. *Viet Cong: Know Your Enemy* (a US Training Film)
4. *North Vietnamese Newsreel 40230*

Panelists: Miroljub Miki Stojanović, Film Center Serbia, publicist, Lazar Stojanović, director

July 6, 2014
MYH cinema
Participants: Kodwo Eshun, Doreen Mende, Jelena Vesić and

Miroljub Stojanović
Algerian documentary films

1. *Algerian War for Independence* (1960), material compiled from the CIA archives
2. *Saadi Yacef — Brief History of Algerian-French War*
3. *Algeria — French Auschwitz in Algeria*

Short introduction by Miroljub Stojanović, screening followed by a conversation with the Ambassador of Algeria.

July 9, 2014
MYH cinema
Grin Without a Cat (France, 1977), Chris Marker
Introduction and discussion: Tadej Kurepa and Nenad Glišić

July 11, 2014
MYH cinema
Blood of the Condor (Quechua: *Yawar Mallku*), (Bolivia, 1969), Jorge Sanjinés

August 15, 2014
MYH cinema
Max Havelaar (Indonesia/The Netherlands, 1976), Fons Rademakers
Indonesian cinema: Then and Now, a short talk by Miroljub Stojanović.

August 17, 2014
MYH cinema

1. *Indonesian War of Independence 1945-1949*
2. *November 1828* (Indonesia, 1979), Teguh Karya

Fred Moten

HISTORY DOES NOT REPEAT ITSELF, BUT IT DOES RHYME

> "...the ethical text sustaining our demands for recognition and legal redress should become the object of radical critique."[1]
>
> — Denise Ferreira da Silva

I want to make a plea for insovereignty. More specifically, if surreptitiously, I want to approach a meditation on and in the irreducible blackness of poetry by way of a specific theoretical challenge to the notion/delusion of the sovereignty of the poet who has been figured, depending upon the preference of whoever seeks the state's properly invested embodiment, either as executive, legislator or jurist. The relation of blackness to sovereignty is characterized by flight and fight, and that is where blackness and poetry converge. The problematic of historical rhyming is further evidence that there's a question concerning poetics that lies at the heart of the matter of insovereignty.

I've been reading a lot about the Asia-Africa conference held in Bandung, Indonesia in April of 1955, and for the past year I've been thinking a lot about sovereignty, about modernity as the era of what Angela Mitropoulous calls "the democratization of sovereignty" or what legal scholar Gerry Simpson calls "the diffusion of sovereignty." If anti-colonial

1. Denise Ferreira da Silva, "No-Bodies: Law, Raciality and Violence," in *18 Griffith Law Review*, 212 (2009), p. 234.

mobilization, given and instantiated in an era defined by what came to be called wars of or for national liberation, is a claim upon sovereignty, then I have been trying to consider what it is that my forebears claimed. This has led me to a kind of uncomfortable question, one that could be said to exemplify history rhyming with, if not repeating itself, as Mark Twain once said (and I thank Annett Busch for alerting me to Twain's formulation): Vijay Prashad's book *The Darker Nations* gives a kind of annotated timeline of anti-colonial, anti-imperial struggle in the interest of reviving it, in the interest of reconfiguring the geography of collaboration (which refers not to a place, he says, but a project) called the Third World. But what if the Third World's timeline also includes The Peace of Westphalia and the Berlin conference of 1884–85? (Deeper still, what if the project of the Third World is always already stunted by the concept of world and the structure of timeline]? This would have to do with the illusory coherence in/and spatio-temporal constitution of sovereignty.) This is not just to say that the postcolonial condition is as much a function of colonialism as it is of anti-colonialism. This is to inquire, instead, about the possibilities of a radical discontinuity that remains unclaimed even though it is, at the same time, embedded in the history we do claim. This discontinuity, its deconstitutive force, has to do with how a kind of theoretical irruption and interruption is lived and how we discover clues of/for that living. How do we access and claim the insovereign modes of life that make possible and even instantiate the critique of sovereignty?

Let me proceed by way of two more quotes from a brilliant essay by Denise Ferreira da Silva:

> Self-determination and self-preservation [are] the sovereign's distinguishing attribute and highest duty.[2]

> … raciality assumes that, everywhere and anywhere, across the surface of the planet, that ever-threatening 'other' exists because already named; as such, it is an endless threat because its necessary difference consistently undermines the subject of ethical life's arrogation of self-determination.[3]

I'm interested in the ones da Silva refers to as the NO-BODIES "whose existence spreads beyond the juridical borders of any given state and the ethical borders of every nation." The ones whom the state can put to death in the interest of its self-preservation without any explanation; the ones whom the sovereign can dispose of or dispense with or disperse or disburse, again, in the interest of self-preservation and self-determination. These are the ones who are in passage, not just from this world to the next but from world to earth, world to ground or underground; world to water or underwater. Da Silva charts the trajectory of their externally imposed determination as non-self-determining, as affectable, as there for and under the dominion of a masterful subject whose capacity for reason and reflection

2. Da Silva, p. 212–36, here p. 233.
3. Da Silva, p. 235.

allows him not only to suppress or subordinate his own impulses and appetites but also obligates him to control those who have no such capacity precisely in the way that he is privileged and obligated to control all that shows up for him in the world of things. The thing is, for Kant, the one with no impetus, no internal volition, the one who is affectable. The paradox is that the affectable one must immediately be considered as dangerous in its supposed total lack of armature precisely because the condition of affectability is contagious. The NO-BODIES run amok in overrunning every border. One could look at this excess (in its relation to value, as da Silva would have it, or in its instantiation as the valueless/invaluable, as the ultimate diffusion or the infernal and infertile diaspora of sovereignty, of sovereignty's already given self-endangerment, given in its insistence upon the degraded company it wants, and wants to keep, its brutal desire and absolute need for undercommon insovereignty.[4]

Within this violent proximity, a distinction is operative, as the de/generative condition of self-determination, the sovereign's being and not being there, his material and symbolic bodies: that between persons (internal; individual subjects) and people (external; the nation-state or, as da Silva has it, the ethical-juridical). The self-determination of peoples indexes the creative/preservative power of the state; the self-determination of persons depends upon the restriction of that power. Self-determination is mired in this antagonism, wherein the state preserves peoples by endangering persons. Has the sovereign ever been able to bear this strife? The sovereign's inability to distance itself from mere flesh can be said both to mark and to instantiate a radical incapacity, an already given undoing that tends toward its own redoubling.

Or, put another way: Two figures (undergrounded figures: things) over against which stands the sovereign—two iterations, two figurines, of the NO-BODY: dead flesh, sold flesh. Against these inevitabilities, the incoherence of self-determination trying to preserve itself stands, in free fall. Internal self-determination ends in the disintegration of the sovereign state. External self-determination endangers the sovereign person. Sovereignty moves by way of its own degradation, is enthralled by its own irreducible vulnerability, incompleteness, decay, which it enacts at the intersection of expansion and expression, the constant violation of its own integrity, on impulse, as if it were driven.

What if self-determination inheres not in the Hegelian relation of subject and object but in the Kantian distinction between persons and things? What if the distinction between the subject's mind and the object's body is displaced by that between these—in their systemic interrelation—and (no)thingly flesh Hortense Spillers allows and requires us to think flesh as a theft of body perpetrated within and alongside a general imposition of body—its supposed and impossible coherence and enclosure; the submission

4. For more on the notion of the undercommon(s), as the essential sociality from which a range of brutally regulatory fictions of propriety derive, see Stefano Harney & Fred Moten, *The Undercommons: Fugitive Planning and Black Study* (New York: Minor Compositions, 2013).

of its experiential functionality to transcendental imperatives.[5] At the same time, she also allows and requires us to think flesh as a stealing away from and within that theft; as a fugitive flight, in immanent hapticality, from the imposition of ownership and severalty.[6] Flesh instantiates the ones da Silva calls NO-BODIES as something more than a construction of sovereign power. It opens out onto a broader instrumentality so that the imposition and ascription of affectability, which we must claim, is not what instantiates by both exceeding and falling short of the false universality of the sovereign; it is, rather, the actual universality of the insovereign.

This stealing away from theft in theft is something Senegalese filmmaker Sembene Ousmane brilliantly shows in his rendering of the fate of the captives at the beginning of *Ceddo*[7]—what lives in substitution of one's interest, or even one's place, is aligned with their radical non-alignment, their

5. Hortense J. Spillers, "Mama's Baby, Papa's Maybe: An American Grammar Book," *Diacritics* 17:2 (Summer, 1987), pp. 64–81.
6. In using the term "severalty" I refer to the Dawes Severalty Act of 1887 in which the United States Congress imposed a system of private land ownership on an indigenous population that traditionally held an inhabited land in common. It's not just that severalty and sovereignty imply one another within an ontologic of what Edouard Glissant refers to as "single being;" it's that the imposition of severalty on the indigenous population was understood by U.S. lawmakers to constitute, by way of brutal absorption, a mode of genocide. For Glissant's formulation see Édouard Glissant, "One World in Relation: Édouard Glissant in Conversation with Manthia Diawara," trans. Christopher Winks, *Journal of Contemporary African Art* 28 (Spring 2011), p. 5.

disappearance. The (transfiguration of the) gun they become. Having been moved, the pan-African shi(f)t is already given there as backdrop and precursor and this is given for us, in a slight and all but unmentionable way in these figures—refuse, without refuge, in refusal—whom I'd like to imagine Charles Mudede would claim under the rubric of the inhabitant. What I want to try to approach is, if not a politics without the state, then something like a counter-political or extra-political stateless sociality, given in lives that are normatively considered unnatural, given in the unnaturalizable lives of the sub-subject; the insovereign, the un(self-)determined. This is not meant to romanticize the lives of those who are not the masters of their fate but to think their lives as platforms for the study of the disavowal, as opposed to the reversal, of mastery. What is it to be the servant of fate? This is a question we can ask the stranger or even, in a more pointed formulation, which Sembene gives in *Xala*,[8] the *métèque*, the non-citizen, the one who is subject

7. 120 minutes, 1977, Senegal. The captives are sold for a gun, to a European slave trader (Sembene often spoke of African complicity in slavery). According to Sembene, the Ceddos are people of refusal—in *Ceddo* they resist exploitation, enslavement and colonisation, by their own rulers and their religious and economic allies (Islamic, European, Catholic...). *Ceddo* was banned in Senegal: Sembene attributed this to the fact that the notion of refusal is most strongly expressed in the female character of princess Dior Yacine, who alone restores to Ceddos the right to speak.
8. *Xala* [*The Curse* (of erectile dysfunction)] is Sembene's 1973 novel, a satire on contemporary corruption and exploitation in Senegal, which he adapted into a film in 1975 (*Xala*, 123 minutes, Senegal).

to, but not a subject of the state.[9] In ancient Greece the *metoikos*, the one who is outside of the house, the one who changes houses or households, is usually the freed slave, the former slave. But the history that is intimated in the figures we see in that film declares that there is no such thing as the former slave. The former slave persists as (no) (such) thing. What if this is a field or a relay? Why must I feel like that? Or what if we think of the interplay between Flora M'mbugu Schelling's *These Hands*[10] and Djibril Diop Mambéty's *The Little Girl Who Sold the Sun*[11] as representing an Afro-diasporic formation: having been moved, after the death of Samora Machel, Mozambican women working practically underneath the building trades are stateless in a way that reflects and reflects upon the statelessness of Sili, *la petite vendeuse*, "her" "disabled" "body's" generative and degenerative incompleteness. M'mbugu Schelling works the incompleteness of Mambéty's scarred, amputative trilogy, which moves as if the living embodiment of afro-pessimism, in the "original" sense that indexes the continent as a collection of failed or abortive states/polities/civil societies. These films are dismissed as avatars of hopelessness by some, but what is lost in that dismissal, when hope will have been given in and as the announcement of functional governance under viable states and their apparatuses? See, I want to begin with this

9. For an excellent exploration and explication of this formulation see Brent Hayes Edwards, "Introduction: The Genres of Postcolonialism," *Social Text* 78, 22:1 (Spring 2004), p. 1–15.
10. 45 minutes, 1992, Tanzania.
11. *La Petite Vendeuse de Soleil,* 45 minutes, 1998, Senegal.

proposition: that the lived experience of the citizen is one of statelessness. What would it mean to acknowledge and, then, to embrace this condition?

To consider the political economy of placelessness is only to begin this approach. It's not about making a claim upon global passage as a Smithian right of labor; it's not about passage as an end; it's not about some locally instantiated claim upon the universal right to be and to determine the end(s) of man. It's about the means of passage and the recognition that we are means; it's about the undercommon fugitivity of means, of debt, of the hapticality of our mutual instrumentality. Attunement to difference is not a citizenly obligation but is, rather, happily, what disqualifies one from citizenship. Consider Sili, the insovereign sociality of her flesh, which moves with the interior in(ter)dependence of a drummer, Tony Allen flown in the trap set, and the external in(ter)dependence of a rhythm section, where everyone is held by the ones they carry.

Ultimately, happily, fugitive affectability manifests itself in/as our undercommon opacity, our open secret. Poetry is always and only a matter of collaboration—a geography of collaboration: an earth writing, an earthy, airily undergrounded writing; an earthly, as opposed to worldly, writing. Its necessary opacity, its irreducible and necessary blackness, is a function of collaboration: that held, insistent rub. It's not about solitary expression, the composed delineation of a view of the world, the assertion of worldly (self-)possession: it discomposes and dispossesses that: it's the transmission of the earth and the things of the earth. John Akomfrah speaks of the opacity of his *Transfigured Night* needing support. What emerges is a pedagogical imperative, the responsibility of pan-Africanism, which is yet to have been fulfilled, to produce a pedagogy of blackness, "schooling in the ways of the coming of the demos."[12] Akomfrah says the primal scene of pan-Africanism is the cabin of the plane to Bandung (which Richard Wright describes and narrates in *The Color Curtain*[13]). It's not that this is not true. It's just that it was first true in another place and time that constituted the radical displacement and radical arrhythmia whose iteration Wright describes. The primal scene of pan-Africanism is the hold of the ship; and what was true before that is that the primal scene of pan-Africanism is narrated and described by Sembene at the beginning of *Ceddo*; and that, somehow, both before and after that, in the slow and broken circle of the blackness of time, the primal scene of pan-Africanism is Sili, the little girl the sun sold, NO-BODY, insovereign, dancing her anarepetitive rhyme.

12. John Akomfrah in the conference as part of the exhibition *After Year Zero: Geographies of Collaboration*, October 5, 2013 Haus der Kulturen der Welt, Berlin.
13. Richard Wright, *The Color Curtain: A Report on the Bandung Conference* (Jackson, MS: University Press of Mississippi, 1956).

BIOGRAPHIES

Fabian Bechtle (1980) lives and works in Berlin. He studied Fine Arts in Leipzig and Lyon. In 2012, he received DAAD postgraduate artists scholarship to research the Presidential Photo Archive at the Museum of Yugoslav History (MYH), Belgrade. Bechtle teaches at the Academy of Visual Arts Leipzig. His work has been shown at the Museum of Contemporary Art, Belgrade; NGBK, Berlin; MKC / Dom mladih, Split; Fabbrica del Vapore, Milano; Museum of Yugoslav History, Belgrade.

Radovan Cukić (1982) is a historian with an MA from the University of Belgrade, Department for Yugoslav History. Between 2009 and 2011 he was a history teacher. Since 2011, he has been the Manager of Documentation and Curator of the photo collection at the MYH, Belgrade.

His projects and exhibitions at the museum include: *Visual Archive of Yugoslavia, Figures of Memory, Dissonant Heritage, Serbia through Centuries.* Cukić has, since 2012, been leading the digitization of the MYH photo collection.

Kodwo Eshun is an artist and theorist based in London. He is co-founder of The Otolith Group whose recent works have been presented in solo exhibitions at Serralves, Porto and Bergen Kunsthall and group exhibitions such as *The Anthropocene Project. A Report*, Haus der Kulturen der Welt and *Cut to Swipe*, Museum of Modern Art, New York. In 2010, The Otolith Group was nominated for The Turner Prize. Eshun is the author of *Dan Graham: Rock My Religion* and *More Brilliant than the Sun: Adventures in Sonic Fiction*.

He is co-editor of *World 3, The Militant Image: A Cine-Geography: Third Text*, issue 108, *Harun Farocki: Against What? Against Whom?, A Long Time Between Suns* and *The Ghosts of Songs: The Film Art of the Black Audio Film Collective*. Eshun lectures in Aural and Visual Culture at the Department of Visual Cultures, Goldsmiths, University of London.

Heba Farid is a multidisciplinary artist based in Cairo, with works exhibited and published internationally. Farid is a founding board member of the Contemporary Image Collective (CiC), based in Cairo and the coordinator of the photographic heritage program at the Center for Documentation of Cultural and Natural Heritage (CULTNAT) in Cairo.

Farid curated *Cairo. Open City: The use of images during an ongoing Revolution*, a project encompassing photojournalism and photo albums by the Egyptian military and police. Farid has published articles on, and regularly participates in regional symposia on archiving, photographic heritage and conservation.

Flaka Haliti (1982) lives and works in Munich, Prishtina and Vienna. Having graduated at the Academy of Arts, Prishtina University, Haliti completed her education at Städelschule, Frankfurt.

Her work has been shown in solo and group exhibitions including places and institutions such as MUSAC, ZKM Karlsruhe, Gallery Martin Janda, Weltkulturen Museum, Kosovo National Gallery, BRUSSELS BIENNIAL 1, Stacion-Center for Contemporary Art Prishtina, press to exit project space, HQ Berlin, SPAPORT BIENNIAL Sarajevo, and Haus der Kulturen der Welt. She is a PhD student at the Academy of Fine Arts Vienna. Haliti represented Kosovo at the 56th La Biennale di Venezia.

Elizabeth W. Giorgis was born and lives in Addis Ababa. She received her MA in Museum Studies from New York University and her PhD in History of Art and Visual Studies at Cornell University. Now the director of the Modern Art Museum, Elizabeth curates exhibitions, and teaches at the College of Performing and Visual Art.

Recent publications include special issues of the *North East African Studies Journal* and the *Callaloo journal*; *Gebre Kristos Desta: The Painter Poet*, the first catalogue of contemporary art published in Ethiopia; and *Addis Ababa: The Enigma of the "New" and the "Modern"* accompanying the exhibition of the same title.

Samia Henni was born in Algiers. An architect and researcher, she graduated from the Academy of Architecture, Università della Svizzera Italiana. Samia has also studied at the École Polytechnique d'Architecture et d'Urbanisme, Algiers and the ex-Berlage Institute, Rotterdam.

Her work has been included in various exhibitions, and she has lectured at various institutions. Currently a PhD fellow at the ETH Zurich and a Guest Researcher at Curatorial/Knowledge, Goldsmiths. Her doctoral dissertation explores French military spatial operations (territorial/architectural) and psychological actions (textual/visual) in Algeria during the Algerian War of Independence (1954-62).

Armin Linke (1966) lives in Milan and Berlin. As a photographer and filmmaker he combines a range of contemporary image-processing technologies in order to blur the borders between fiction and reality.

His artistic practice is concerned with different possibilities of dealing with photographic archives and their respective manifestations, as well as with the interrelations and transformative powers between urban, architectural or spatial functions. He was Research Affiliate at MIT Visual Arts Program Cambridge, guest professor at the IUAV Arts and Design University in Venice and was professor at the HfG Karlsruhe.

Mirko Lovrić (1935–2014) was one of the official photographers of Yugoslav President Josip Broz Tito, accompanying him on numerous travels in Yugoslavia and abroad. Student of the Applied Arts School in Zagreb, Lovrić went on to graduate at the Faculty of Philosophy at Belgrade University in 1961.

Mirko Lovrić presented at more than twenty solo shows and at over a hundred important group exhibitions. He is the only Serbian photographer to have had a retrospective at the Museum of Contemporary Art in Belgrade.

Ivan Manojlović (1978) is a curator and art historian, responsible for the technical and cinematography collection at the MYH, Belgrade.

He has authored, co-authored and project managed exhibitions focusing on history, popular culture, culture of remembrance and reinterpretation of cultural heritage of socialist Yugoslavia. Ivan was the organizer and coordinator of all the program activities at the MYH, Belgrade, from 2008 to 2013.

Olga Manojlović-Pintar received her PhD in History from the University of Belgrade. She is Research Associate at the Institute for Recent History of Serbia, Belgrade.

Her research areas include twentieth century history, collective memory and historical consciousness. Recent publications include *History and Rememberance*, "History and Ethics," in *Tokovi istorije*; "Redefining Memories," in *Helsinški odbor* 115/116.

Doreen Mende lives in Berlin and works internationally as a curator, writer and lecturer. Since 2008, Mende has been working in the occupied Palestine/West Bank, Lebanon and in Iran, researching the continuities and discontinuities of the paradoxical principles of solidarity amidst the spectres of socialist internationalism.

Following a research fellowship at the Arab Image Foundation in Beirut, Mende authored *The Itinerant: When Exhibiting Turns Its Back Against Itself* for the *Manifesta Journal*. Mende co-authored *Double Bound Economies. Reading an East German Archive (1967–1990)*, and curated *KP Brehmer. Real Capital-Production* at Raven Row, London. Mende has a PhD in Curatorial/Knowledge from Goldsmiths, and teaches at the Dutch Art Institute.

Fred Moten received his PhD in English from University College Berkeley. A student of Afro-diasporic social and cultural life, poetry, performance studies and critical theory, his books include: *In the Break: The Aesthetics of the Black Radical Tradition, Hughson's Tavern, B. Jenkins, The Undercommons: Fugitive Planning and Black Study* (with his frequent collaborator Stefano Harney) and *The Feel Trio*.

Moten served as a member of the Board of Managing Editors of *American Quarterly* and of the *Editorial Collectives of Social Text and Callaloo*, and of the Editorial Board of *South Atlantic Quarterly*. He is co-founder and co-publisher (with Joseph Donahue) of a small literary press called *Three Count Pour*.

Rachel O'Reilly is an independent writer, artist, critic and researcher, bridging situated cultural practice, media philosophy and political economy. Curatorial projects include *The Leisure Class* at the Gallery of Modern Art and *Australian Cinematheque*, *Videoground for Multi-Media Art Asia Pacific* and the 5th Asia Pacific Triennial.

She holds an MA from the University of Amsterdam, and was a resident of the Jan van Eyck Academie. Current work includes *The Gas Imaginary*, installation and poetry exploring the aesthetic politics of unconventional extraction, and critical writings with Danny Butt on artistic autonomy in settler colonial space. She leads a seminar in "How to Do Things with Theory" at DAI.

Sarah Poppel is an independent art historian based in Berlin. Since 2012, she has been working with the photographer and filmmaker Armin Linke, as well as organizing international art projects and exhibitions.

O'Tam Pulto is an African poet, novelist, and essayist who found himself made in a mosaic of culture and nature in Southern Ethiopia. Writing is to him a means of self-discovery and preservation, of finding and playing his role in society. He ventured into the world of myth to reclaim his paradise lost in the forgotten tales of childhood and found his very self lost in that jangle.

He is now trying to win his way back by fooling around with philosophy, and focusing on children and young people. Having authored eight books, he thinks his major works are yet to come. www.athousandversions.com

Mirjana Slavković (1981) graduated in Ethnology and Anthropology at the University of Belgrade and defended her MA thesis of UNESCO MA program for Cultural policy and Management at the University of Arts and the University Lumière Lyon 2.

Following alternative academic courses in Womens Studies and Peace Studies, Slavković has worked on projects focusing on culture for children and children's rights, as well as for *Feminist Theatre 5 A*, *Beton Hala* Theatre, *BELEF* Festival, Children's Cultural Centre. Since 2010 she has been the PR manager at the MYH, Belgrade.

Branimir Stojanović (1958) lives and works in Belgrade. Stojanović's work, situated between philosophy, psychoanalysis and art, deals with practices of writing and conceptual-political interventions into institutional contexts of philosophy, art and psychoanalysis. Since 1980 he has been publishing articles and essays on philosophy, theoretical psychoanalysis, critique of ideology and art theory.

He is the founder of *Učitelj neznalica i njegovi komiteti* and one of the founders and lecturer at the alternative educational platform *Škola za istoriju i teoriju umetnosti*. He is a founding member of the art/theory collective Grupa Spomenik [Monument Group].

Miroljub Miki Stojanović is a film theorist and critic based in Belgrade. Born in 1958, in Pristina, Stojanović studied World Literature at the Faculty of Philology, Belgrade University. Widely published and translated, he is currently the Editor of Publications at the Film Center of Serbia.

His research is focused on Asian cinemas (the Indian, Japanese and Taiwanese in particular) and cultures, and supported by extensive research journeys in twenty-three Asian countries.

Subversive Film is a cinema research and production initiative that aims to cast new light upon historic works related to Palestine and the region; to engender support for film preservation; and to investigate archival practices and effects.

Other projects developed by Subversive Film to explore this cine-historic field include the digital reissuing of previously-overlooked films, the curating of rare film screening cycles, and the subtitling of rediscovered films. Subversive Film was formed in 2011 and is based in Ramallah and London.

Milica Tomić explores different genres and methods of artistic practice that centers on investigating, unearthing and bringing to public debate issues related to political violence, economy and social amnesia. Tomić heads the Institute of Contemporary Art at the TU Graz and teaches at the Trondheim Academy of Fine Art.

She is founding member of New Yugoslav art/theory group, *Grupa Spomenik*; Tomić has participated in international exhibitions such as the 24th São Paulo Biennial, 49th/ 50th Venice Biennale; 8th International Istanbul Biennial; 15th Sydney Biennale; Prague Biennial; Trondheim Biennale; 10th Sharjah Biennial, Odessa Biennial, *Forensis*, Haus der Kulturen der Welt, Berlin, Germany, The School of Kyiv—The Biennial.

Vanessa Vasić-Janeković works at the intersections of contemporary art, theory, philosophy and activism, researching and articulating registers of value production, at present with the Workers University in Tuzla, Bosnia and Herzegovina.

Françoise Vergès, from Reunion Island and the South by lack of better terms and because she does not want to be associated with a nationality, is currently Chair, "Global South(s)" at the Collège d'études mondiales, Paris.

Françoise grew up in an anticolonial, communist and feminist family. Before her PhD in Political Science at Berkeley, she worked as a journalist and editor in the French feminist movement and was an antiracist and anti-imperialist activist. She has written extensively on living memories of colonial slavery, the economy of predation, Frantz Fanon, Aimé Césaire, postcolonial museography, and the routes of migration and processes of creolization in the Indian Ocean world. She curates exhibitions and works with filmmakers and artists, was a project advisor for Documenta 11 and contributed to the 2012 Paris Triennial.

Jelena Vesić is an independent curator, writer, editor, and lecturer. She was co-editor of *Prelom—Journal of Images and Politics* and co founder of independent organization Prelom Collective. She is active in the field of publishing, research, and exhibition practice that intertwines political theory and contemporary art.

Her latest curatorial projects are based on experiments with the form of lecture-performance, immaterial quality of the exhibits and story telling, and include: *Oktobar XXX: Exposition-Symposium-Performance*; *On Undercurrents of Negotiating Artistic Jobs—Between Love and Money, Between Money and Love*; and *Exhibition on Work and Laziness*. Vesić is also co-editor of *Red Thread* journal (Istanbul).

COLOPHON

This book is part of the Travelling Communiqué, a project that fosters a trans-disciplinary way of working together towards the idea of political friendship.

At work since 2012, Travelling Communiqué has been initiating its own conditions of production within current globalizing forces.

Editorial team:
Travelling Communiqué Project Group (Armin Linke, Kodwo Eshun, Doreen Mende, Milica Tomić) with Sarah Poppel and Vanessa Vasić-Janeković
Graphic design: Žiga Testen with James Oates and Karina Soraya
Lithography: James Oates
Printing and binding:
Alta Nova d.o.o.,
Ugrinovački put 72,
11080 Belgrade

Image copyright:
Museum of Yugoslav History: pp. 8, 11-23, 63, 90-102, 136, 163-170, 189-90, 194-214, 251-95,
Armin Linke: pp. 50, 69, 72, 144
Vladimir Jerić: p. 296

Administration:
Jovanka Vojinović,
ARTIKL Vrtlarska 39/23
11070 Belgrade

Published by
Spector Books
Harkortstrasse 10
04107 Leipzig
www.spectorbooks.com

Distribution
Germany, Austria:
GVA, Gemeinsame Verlagsauslieferung Göttingen GmbH&Co. KG, www.gva-verlage.de
Switzerland:
AVA Verlagsauslieferung AG, www.ava.ch
France, Belgium: Interart Paris, www.interart.fr UK:
Central Books Ltd, www.centralbooks.com
USA, Canada:
RAM Publications+ Distribution Inc., www. rampub.com
Australia, New Zealand:
Perimeter Distribution, perimeterdistribution.com
Other countries:
Motto Distribution, www.mottodistribution.com

(c) 2016;
Spector Books, Leipzig, and the authors

First edition
Printed in Serbia
ISBN 978-3-944669-92-2

Publication supported by

ERSTE Stiftung

GOETHE INSTITUT

Armin Linke (IT/DE),
Doreen Mende (DE) and
Milica Tomić (born in SFRY)
in discussion with
Yero Adugna Eticha (ET),
Kader Attia (DZ/FR),
Fabian Bechtle (DE);
„Conflicting Identities"
at ETH Zürich:
Philip Ursprung (CH),
Marija Marić (BiH),
Seraina Renz (CH),
Dubravka Sekulić
(born in SFRY),
Damjan Kokalevski (MK)
and Haris Piplas (BiH);
Mirjana Dragosavljević
(born in SFRY),
Tarek Elhaik (MA/U.S.) &
Kriss Ravetto-Biagioli (U.S.),
Theo Eshetu (GB/ET),
Kodwo Eshun (GB),
Heba Farid (EG),
Anselm Franke (DE),
Elizabeth W. Giorgis (ET), Fasil
Giorghis (ET),
Jean-Luc Godard (CH) and
Anne-Marie Mièville (FR)
Flaka Haliti (XK),
Roza El Hassan (SYR/HU), Samia
Henni (CH/DZ),
Maja Hodoščček (born in SFRY),
Pramod Kumar (IN),
Milica Lopičić (born in SFRY),
Mirko Lovrić (SRB),
Olga Manojlović Pintar (SRB),
Fred Moten (U.S.);
Museum of Yugoslav History
Research Group:
Radovan Cukić (SRB),
Ivan Manojlović (SRB), and
Mirjana Slavković (SRB), Dorja
Benussi (CRO),
Ivan Benussi (SRB);
the Netsa Art Village Addis
Abbaba with
Helen Zeru Araya (ET),
Tamrat Gezahegn (ET),
Mulugeta Kassa (ET),
Mihret Kebede (ET), and
Tesfahun Kibru;
Garin Nugroho (ID),
The Otolith Group (GB),
O 'Tam Pulto (ET),
Milja Radovanović
(born in SFRY),
Branimir Stojanović (SRB),
Miroljub Miki Stojanović
(born in SFRY);
Subversive Films:
Mohanad Yaqubi & Reem
Shilleh (occupied Palestine);
Žiga Testen (SLO);
Travelling Communiqué at the
Dutch Art Institute, Arnhem:
Jan Adriaans (NL),
Katia Barrett (GB),
Hanan Benammar (DZ/FR),
Anna Dasović (NL),
Coco Duivenvoorde (NL),
Aziza Harmel (TN),
Monique Hendriksen (NL),
Marianna Maruyama (USA/IT),
Celia Eslamieh Shomal (IR),
Aarti Sunder (IN),
Silvia Ulloa (ES),
Larraitz Torres (ES) and
Laila Torres Mendieta (MX);
Dejan Vasić (born in SFRY),
Jelena Vesić (born in SFRY)
and Rachel O' Reilly (AUS),
Vanessa Vasić-Janeković
(born in SFRY),
Francoise Vergès (Réunionnaise),
Jovanka Vojinović
(born in SFRY)
Katarina Živanović
(Director, MYH 2008–2012).

PROPOSAL BY FLAKA HALITI*

Born in Prishtina, lives in Vienna and Munich
Untitled
2014

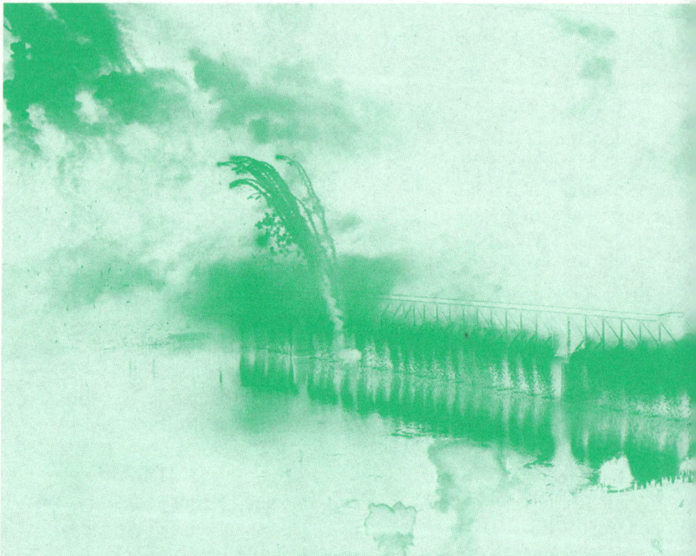

MANIFESTIMI I TË DREJTËS PËR TU MOS U KUPTUAR

Photo Archive from the Conference of Non-Aligned Movement, Belgrade 1961
Place: Museum of Interdependence Yugoslav History
Date: June 2014
Location: Belgrad, Serbia
Keywords: Postcolonial; Experience; Dominate; Contradictions; Produces; Total; Uniformity; Centre; Reduce; Everything; Same; Transparence; Instead; Opacity; Loose; Periphery; Control; Achieving; Contrary; Respect; Decentralisation; Other; Elaborate; Opacity; Enter; Celebrate; Relation; Creating; Right; Not-understandd; Another; Opacity; Language; Equates; Resistance; Equality; Different; Culture; Anti-imperialist; Project; Societies; Counterdiscourse; Subverts; Dominant; Discourse; Totality; Operates; Opposite; Totalitarian; Imply; Freedom; Opacity; Diversity; Equally; Welcome; Opaquenesss.

* See opposite page and spine

ANC African National Congress
DAI Dutch Art Institute
EPRDF Ethiopian People's Revolutionary Democratic Front
EPRP Ethiopian Peoples' Revolutionary Party
ESUNA Ethiopian Student Union in North America
FPRY Federal People's Republic of Yugoslavia
LCY League of Communists of Yugoslavia
MA Masters Degree
MEISONE All Ethiopian Socialist Movement
MYH Museum of Yugoslav History
NAM Non-Aligned Movement
OAU Organisation of African Unity
PLS People's Liberation Struggle
SFRY Socialist Federal Republic of Yugoslavia
TANJUG Telegraphic and News Agency of Yugoslavia
TC Travelling Communiqué
UAR United Arab Republic
UNESCO United Nations Educational, Scientific and Cultural Organization
U.S. United States of America
USUAA University Students Union in Addis Ababa
USSR Union of Soviet Socialist Republics
WWII Second World War
YPA Yugoslav People's Army

* This text and images are displayed in the framework of the proposal. Looking back to Yugoslavia and/or chaptering various sequences in order to construct histoire of the present and the future from the contemporary artistic practice today, I find it important to look at it through the notion of opacity (Glissant, 1997) in relation to the Other, as a strategy of resistance towards the center.

In spite of many emancipatory, especially social achievements, socialist Yugoslavia failed to transcend the "center" and "periphery" logic. In my opinion, Yugoslavia had one "center" voice dominating the other countries that it was made up of. In this case, Kosovo would supposedly be considered the far periphery.

For Glissant, the idea of the "center" is clearly an imperialist one. Instead, he suggests "relation" to the Other in order to decentralize the center; relation that is based in interdependence rather than independence and operates within a totality based on diversity rather than unity (brotherhood and unity). This totality's opposite of totalitarian, because it needs the presence of all its diverse and equal elements. Here the language of the Other as a tool of resistance is introduced as the "right to not be understood," the right to opacity.

Flaka Haliti

1962	1962	1962 Mirko Lovrić appointed the head of Photo Service
1960s Yugoslav support for various liberation movements	1960s	1960s
1956 Tito in France and USSR Tito, Nehru and Nasser in Brijuni	1956	1956
1955 Bandung Conference	1955	1955
1954 Algerian War begins	1954	1954
1953 Tito travels to the UK	1953	1953
1950s FPRY develops new trade links and political friendships	1950s	1950s
1949 Introduction of Yugoslav workers' self-governance and societal ownership	1949	1949
1948 FPRY/USSR split	1948	1948 The archival function of the Photo Service begins
1947	1947	1947 Presidential Photo Service set up
1946 Federal People's Republic of Yugoslavia (FPRY) declared	1946	1946
1945 The United Nations Charter Second World War ends Hiroshima and Nagasaki	1945	1945
1943 –1947 Partisan hysteria	1943 –1947	1943 –1947
1943 Battles of Neretva and Sutjeska Yugoslav resistance declares provisional state	1943	1943
1941 –1945 People's Liberation Struggle	1941 –1945	1941 –1945
1936 –1939 Spanish Civil War		
1935 Italy invades Ethiopia Aimé Césaire travels to Yugoslavia		
1884 –1885 "...what if the Third World's timeline also includes The Peace of Westphalia [1648] and the Berlin conference of 1884-85..."		

THIS TIMELINE IS A TOOL FOR CAPTURING AND NAVIGATING THE MULTIPLE TEMPORALITIES REFLECTED IN THE BOOK.

2014

2014

Travelling Communiqué exhibition at the MYH, with Summer School and Film Programme

DAI students in Addis Ababa,

Second TC group meeting focuses on the archive in discussion with:
- Theo Eshetu
- Elizabeth Giorgis
- Anselm Franke
- Miki Manojlović

TC takes part in the *After Year Zero* exhibition at Haus der Kulturen der Welt in Berlin

2014

2013

2013

DAI MA students form working group

TC becomes part of the Roaming Research Academy at DAI

The team decides to name the project Travelling Communiqué (TC)

Core project team invites artists and theorists to participate in the project:
- Zoran Erić
- Stevan Vuković
- Branimir Stojanović
- Dubravka Sekulić
- Jelena Vesić
- Ana Sladojević
- Maja Hodošček
- Olga Manojlović Pintar
- Mirjana Dragosavljević
- Milica Lopičić

MYH curators form Research Group

2013

The negatives archive at the MYH depot, though mostly used by the MYH, remains open to interested researchers

The Fototeka archive is uploaded to the MYH website

2012

The NAM has 120 members and 17 observer countries

2012

First presentation at the Goethe Institute Belgrade

The team focuses on the NAM and invites contributors, including Kodwo Eshun

2012

A Skype meeting between MYH, Anselm Franke, Heidi Ballet, Elsa de Seyners, Armin Linke, Doreen Mende, Milica Tomić and Helen Zeru

2011

Belgrade hosts 50th NAM Conference

2011

Fabian Bechtle, Armin Linke, Doreen Mende and Milica Tomić form the core project team (to become Travelling Communiqué)

2011

In conversations with artists, Linke and Bechtle in particular, the MYH speeds up digitalization

2010

2010

2010

MYH begins digitizing 30,000 prints in preparation for 50 years of the NAM

2001 –2002	2001 –2002	2001 –2002 Work begins on organising about 132,000 black and white photographs and 250,000 negatives The archive is moved to the MYH
1999 War in Kosovo	1999	1999
1997	1997	1997 The archive is moved into the former royal residence Slobodan Milošević moves into Tito's residence
1996	1996	1996 Foundation of the Museum of Yugoslav History (MYH)
1991 –1995 Wars in Slovenia, Croatia and Bosnia and Herzegovina	1991 –1995	1991 –1995
1989 End of Cold War	1989	1989
1982	1982	1982 Fototeka opens to visitors Tito's residential complex becomes Memorial Centre
1980 Josip Broz Tito dies	1980	1980
1979 Tito's last NAM conference	1979	1979
1978 Tito travels to US	1978	1978
1977 Tito travels to China	1977	1977
1974 Ethiopian revolution and coup d'état by the Derg	1974	1974
1971 Richard Burton as Tito in *The Battle of Sutjeska*	1971	1971
1970 –1971 Jordanian Civil War	1970 –1971	1970 –1971
1968 Palestinian revolution starts Tito travels to Japan	1968	1968
1966 Jean Genet's *The Screens* (*Les Paravents*) staged	1966	1966
1963	1963	1963 Mirko Lovrić writes the Memorandum on improving the work of the Photo Service
1969 Abu Omar/Yasser Arafat in Belgrade as FATAH member	1969	1969